Meteorites

Meteorites

Brian Mason

Curator of Mineralogy

The American Museum of Natural History

New York

John Wiley and Sons, Inc.   New York and London

Library of Congress Catalog Card Number: 62–17466
Printed in the United States of America

Preface

THE stimulus and the opportunity to write this book came as a result of an appointment in 1961 as Visiting Professor in the University of Tokyo, under the auspices of the United States Educational Commission in Japan (Fulbright Commission). I was asked to give a seminar of interest to advanced students and staff in the Institutes of Geology and Chemistry, and chose meteorites as the topic. I must confess that the choice was for my own benefit as well as that of my audience. Having worked on meteorites for some years I was acutely aware of the vast accumulation of published data on these remarkable bodies, and the lack of an adequate synthesis of these data. This lack is equally distressing to research workers in this field and to other scientists wishing to obtain a panorama of the scope and substance of meteorite research. I endeavored to remedy this situation through my seminar, which formed the basis of the present book.

The purpose of this book is to provide a comprehensive account of our present knowledge of meteorites, with special reference to their material nature—their mineralogical and chemical composition and their structure. The emphasis throughout is on the data and their interpretation. Hypotheses and theories are presented but are not exhaustively discussed—the great upsurge in meteorite research along many new lines in recent years has provided a mass of new information yet to be integrated into a consistent and comprehensive theoretical framework.

Tektites are described and discussed in a separate chapter. Although tektites have not been seen to fall and their identification as extra-terrestrial matter is disputed, they retain a position in the overall field of meteoritics unless and until they are proved to be of terrestrial origin.

v

The science of meteorites is a borderline field par excellence. As objects in outer space meteorites are the concern of the astronomers and astrophysicists; their passage through the Earth's atmosphere is a meteorological problem; their impact with the Earth's surface is an intriguing facet of ballistics, and if large enough they produce geological effects of no mean magnitude; their phase composition is a special field of mineralogy and metallurgy; the determination of their elemental composition is an intricate problem of inorganic chemistry (and of organic chemistry, for the complex organic compounds in the carbonaceous chondrites); they contain within them a variety of isotopes produced by cosmic-ray bombardment in outer space which are of significant interest to the nuclear physicists; and the recent observation of obscure "'organized elements" in the carbonaceous chondrites has brought them to the attention of the biologists. Surely no material objects have such manifold significance to so many branches of science. It is appropriate therefore to plead for a general policy of preservation and conservation of meteoritic material. Every meteorite is to some degree unique; and meteorites, unlike terrestrial rocks and minerals, cannot be re-collected when the original material is exhausted. A wise policy of conservation is essential, not only to provide material for current researches, but also to safeguard material for future investigations, the nature and significance of which may be unguessed today.

The literature on meteorites is enormous and widely scattered. A bibliography of this literature from 1490 to 1950 contained some 8600 references from over 1000 periodical publications, and the tempo of research on meteorites has shown an exponential increase since 1950. A large number of papers, many trivial but some of fundamental significance, have been published in obscure journals of limited circulation. I have been fortunate in having access to two excellent libraries, that of The American Museum of Natural History and that of the Geological Institute of the University of Tokyo, both of them rich in original material on meteorites. Although I have attempted to cover the literature as completely as possible, it is unfortunately true that there will certainly be omissions. I would welcome information as to such omissions, and reprints of papers, for future use.

The preparation of this book would never have been undertaken had I not been favored by the curatorship of the meteorite collection of The American Museum of Natural History, with its wealth of material for study. However, even the best of collections is inadequate for a comprehensive study of meteorites, and I would like to acknowledge the availability of comparative material in the collections of the Smithsonian Institution, Harvard University, the Chicago Natural History Museum, the Nininger Meteorite Collection (Arizona State University, Tempe), and the British Museum (Natural History).

My thanks are due to the many persons who have helped me in the preparation of this book. I am especially indebted to E. P. Henderson, who read critically the complete manuscript and who also provided me with much important information from his own files. I have also had the benefit of advice on specific chapters from E. L. Fireman, L. T. Silver, A. A. Smales, C. B. Moore, W. D. Ehmann, and G. Baker. Dr. Michael Fleischer made available to me his comprehensive file of abstracts on the geochemistry of meteorites and tektites. A special word of appreciation is due to H. B. Wiik, my associate in research on meteorites, who has provided me with a great deal of significant chemical data, many of them still unpublished. My own researches on meteorites, the results of which are incorporated in this book, have been supported by grants from the National Science Foundation and the J. Lawrence Smith Fund of the National Academy of Sciences; this support is gratefully acknowledged.

BRIAN MASON

New York City
May 1962

Contents

1

Introduction

Definitions

A meteorite is a solid body which has arrived on the Earth from outer space. Its size can range from microscopic to a mass of many tons. Meteorites smaller than a moderate size, say about 1 cm in diameter, are unlikely to be collected, but they certainly occur. The Holbrook, Arizona, meteorite shower included many hundred individual stones only a few millimeters in diameter. Even smaller meteorites presumably occur, and meteoritic dust is constantly falling on the Earth. Estimates of the amount of extra-terrestrial material falling on the Earth annually range from a few thousand to a few million tons.

A *meteor* is quite distinct from a meteorite; it is the transitory luminous streak in the sky produced by the incandescence of an extra-terrestrial solid body (a *meteoroid*) passing through the Earth's atmosphere. A meteorite is a meteoroid which is large enough and resistant enough to survive this passage; most meteoroids, however, are evidently small particles which are completely destroyed in the upper atmosphere. Meteors occasionally appear as showers which recur at regular intervals; such meteor showers are genetically related to comets. There is no coincidence between the occurrence of meteor showers and the fall of meteorites.

The science of meteorites is known as *meteoritics*.

Composition and Classification

Meteorites consist essentially of a nickel-iron alloy (averaging 90% Fe, 10% Ni), or silicate minerals, mainly olivine [$(Mg,Fe)_2SiO_4$] and orthopyroxene [$(Mg,Fe)SiO_3$], or a mixture of these. They are usually classed as follows:

1. Aerolites or stones (silicate minerals, generally with some nickel-iron). The stones are divided into two subgroups, the chondrites and and the achondrites, according to the presence or absence of chondrules or chondri, which are spheroidal aggregates of olivine and/or pyroxene, usually about 1 mm in diameter.

2. Siderolites or stony-irons (average 50% nickel-iron, 50% silicates).

3. Siderites or irons (nickel-iron with small amounts of accessory minerals).

Natural glasses of non-volcanic origin, known as tektites, have been found in limited regions in several parts of the world. Many authorities believe tektites to be extra-terrestrial in origin, and hence meteorites by the above definition. However, they have never been seen to fall, and their identification as meteorites is therefore not established, and is still a subject of dispute.

Naming of Meteorites

In order to facilitate the comparison, classification, and study of different meteorites it was early found desirable to give each a name. The standard practice today is to name a meteorite from the locality at which it was found, preferably the nearest topographical feature, village, or post office which can readily be identified from a good gazetteer or large-scale map. In the early days of meteorite investigation the name of the discoverer was sometimes applied to the meteorite, or occasionally a name descriptive of its form. As a result many meteorites are known by more than one name, and some have an extensive synonymy; for example the Cape York iron from Greenland has also been known under the following names: Ahnighito (the Eskimo name for it, meaning "tent" in allusion to its shape); Baffin's

Bay; Melville Bay; North Star Bay; Ross's Iron; Savik; Sowallick Mountains. An authoritative guide to the names of meteorites is the Prior-Hey catalog (1953), and their recommended names are used throughout this book.

There are over 1500 well-authenticated meteorites, using the term meteorite for a single occurrence. Each occurrence may, however, comprise many individual pieces (tens of thousands of fragments of the Canyon Diablo meteorite have been picked up around Meteor Crater in Arizona, and it has been estimated that the meteorite fall at Pultusk, Poland, in 1868, comprised 100,000 stones).

Falls and Finds

In discussing meteorites an important distinction is made between falls and finds. A fall is a meteorite which was picked up after it was actually seen to fall; a find is a meteorite which was not seen to fall, but was recognized as such by its diagnostic features—chemical composition, mineralogical composition, and structure. In the Prior-Hey catalog, the following statistics of meteorite finds and falls are given:

	Falls	%	Finds	%	Total	%
Irons	42	6	503	59	545	35
Stony-irons	12	2	55	6	67	4
Stones	628	92	304	35	932	61
Total	682	100	862	100	1544	100

These figures show a remarkable reversal in abundances of the different types between finds and falls. (Irons and stony-irons are common as finds, rare as falls; for the stones the reverse is true.) The reason is not far to seek. The relative abundance of irons and stony-irons as finds is due largely to their being easily recognized as meteorites, or at least as very unusual rocks, and also in part to their resistance to weathering and hence their survival for a comparatively long time on the Earth's surface (meteoritic iron rusts slowly, probably because of its nickel content). A stony meteorite unless seen to fall would easily be overlooked except by an acute observer; stony meteorites are often friable and readily broken down by weathering, and will not survive for as long a time as irons and stony-irons.

Fossil Meteorites

The possible occurrence of meteorites in older geological formations has been a matter of considerable controversy. There seems to be no valid reason to suspect that meteorites have not fallen throughout geological time. Nevertheless, it has been remarked that no "fossil" meteorite has been discovered in the billions of tons of coal, limestone, etc., that have been mined and quarried, nor has one been discovered in the outcrop of a pre-Pleistocene formation. Paneth (1956) indeed claimed that iron and stone meteorites did not fall before the late Quaternary. However, this claim is probably invalid. Meteoritic dust has been identified in deposits of Tertiary age. Henderson and Cooke (1942) described the extremely weathered Sardis (Georgia, U.S.A.) iron, and concluded that it probably fell in the middle Miocene sea and was buried in the Hawthorne formation, with which it was associated when found. Lovering (1959) has reported the discovery of an iron meteorite during the drilling of an oil well in Texas in 1930, at a depth of 1525 feet in rocks probably of Eocene age; the evidence for the identification as an iron meteorite (nickel content, Widmanstatten structure) is good, but unfortunately no material from it has been preserved. The rarity of fossil meteorites is not extraordinary in view of their absolute rarity, and in view of the improbability of their survival in recognizable form in older rocks.

Recognition of Meteorites

A brief discussion of the recognition of meteorites is appropriate here. A museum curator is continually examining a flow of specimens tentatively identified as meteorites by their finders. Regrettably, it is rare indeed that such specimens are genuine meteorites. Material commonly confused with meteorites includes furnace and smelter slag, limonite concretions, and fragments of manufactured iron. Since nickel is universally present in meteoritic iron, a negative test for nickel is sufficient to exclude practically all the latter objects. (This test is made by dissolving a small amount of the metal in nitric acid, making the solution alkaline with ammonium hydroxide, filtering, and adding an alcoholic solution of dimethyl glyoxime to the filtrate; if nickel is present a scarlet precipitate appears.) A positive test for nickel is strongly indicative of a meteorite, but since nickel-iron alloys are made commercially, a positive nickel test is not absolutely conclusive. Consideration must then be given to surface features, and to internal structures. On polishing and etching, most, but not all, iron meteorites show a characteristic lamellar intergrowth known as the Widmanstatten structure, which is not known in artificial alloys. Stony meteorites can usually be readily distinguished from terrestrial rocks by the particles of nickel-iron which they contain; these can be extracted from the crushed meteorite with a magnet and tested for nickel as above. (Awaruite, a terrestrial nickel-iron mineral, is so rare and sparsely distributed in the rocks in which it occurs that it can be left out of consideration.) Weathered stones, in which all the nickel-iron has been converted to oxides, and those rare stones which contain no nickel-iron, can only be certainly identified by expert examination.

Why Study Meteorites?

This may seem to be a rhetorical question, since any natural object is worthy of scientific study, and meteorites, as the only tangible objects we have of the universe beyond our planet, are clearly of unique interest. They have therefore been investigated by astronomers, by physicists, by chemists, and especially by geologists. The reason for the geologists' interest has been well expressed by Shand (1947) in the following passage:

The greatest weakness of petrography, as a method of investigating the composition of the Earth, is that direct observation can only be made upon rocks that have crystallized within a few thousand feet from the surface, say a thousandth part of the Earth's radius. There is good reason, no less on petrological than on geophysical and astronomical grounds, to suppose that the matter that forms the interior of the planet is different in many respects from surface rocks; but direct observation of this matter is naturally impossible. It is here that meteorites come to our assistance. It is quite immaterial what view one holds regarding the origin of meteorites. Astronomy, supported by the spectroscope, has shown that the universe is formed of the same elementary materials throughout; so whether one regards meteorites as shattered stars or shattered planets, nebular knots or condensed comets, as bolts from the sun or bombs from terrestrial volcanoes, the important fact for us is that meteorites bring to our notice a type of rock existing in the solar system but different from anything that occurs in the outer shell of our planet; and this material has just the sort of composition that petrology, geophysics and astronomy combine to indicate as likely to be found in the interior of the Earth.

For the geochemist the study of meteorites is of especial significance, since it is generally believed that the average composition of meteoritic matter probably provides the best information on the relative abundances of the non-volatile elements. Tables of the cosmic abundances of the elements are largely based on the interpretation of meteorite analyses. Such tables are of fundamental importance not only to the geochemists but also to the nuclear physicists and astrophysicists who are concerned with processes of element formation. The examination of radioactive nuclides, both original and produced by cosmic-ray bombardment, is providing a wealth of data bearing on the origin, age, and history of meteorites and of the universe. Finally, the study of the external form and the internal structure of meteorites has given useful information regarding astronautical problems such as the design of "space ships" and the problems of re-entry into the Earth's atmosphere. A meteorite may be described as a natural space probe that was formed somewhere in the solar system sometime during the last five billion years and was recently received from outer space without human aid.

History of Meteorite Research

Falls of stones from the sky, presumably meteorites, are recorded in classical Chinese literature, and also ancient Greek and Latin literature. The oldest meteorite that has been preserved is probably the black stone of the Kaaba in Mecca. The oldest authenticated fall is that of Ensisheim in Alsace, where a stone weighing 127 kg fell on November 16, 1492; pieces from this stone have been widely distributed, but the major part is still in the town hall of Ensisheim. There are a number of well-authenticated falls from the following three centuries, but little material of these has been preserved. Until the beginning of the nineteenth century scientific men were sceptical of stones falling from the sky, and much meteoritic material was probably discarded and lost. This scepticism was finally overcome by the detailed report of the L'Aigle meteorite fall (April 26, 1803) by J. B.

Biot, who showed beyond doubt the reality of the occurrence. From that time onward meteorite falls have been carefully investigated and natural science museums have endeavored to build up collections of these unique objects.

During the first half of the nineteenth century the scientific investigation of meteorites was largely limited to the circumstances of the falls and the chemical analysis of the meteorites themselves. The development of the polarizing microscope around 1860 provided a powerful tool for studying the mineralogical composition and internal structure of the stones and stony-irons. G. Tschermak in Vienna made great advances with microscopic studies and his publication *Die mikroskopische Beschaffenheit der Meteoriten erläutert durch photographische Abbildungen,* published in 1885, is still unequalled by any later work on the subject. Research work on the chemical and mineralogical composition of meteorites continued through the latter part of last century and the early part of this. It was given a new direction by the development of geochemical research from about 1930 onwards, when it was realized that the elemental composition of meteoritic material was probably fairly representative of the universe as a whole. Many analyses of minor and trace elements in meteorites were made by Goldschmidt and his co-workers, and by the Noddacks. Since that time new analytical tools and new methods of research have greatly invigorated research on meteorites and there is probably greater activity now than ever before.

The Literature of Meteorites

Facts, theories, and fantasies regarding meteorites are widely scattered throughout the scientific literature. Papers on meteorites are to be found in journals of astronomy, chemistry, physics, metallurgy, and geology, and in the proceedings of learned societies all over the world. The only journal devoted entirely to meteorites is the Russian periodical *Meteoritika,* published irregularly since 1939. Since 1951 *Geochimica et Cosmochimica Acta* has provided a much-used medium for the publication of meteorite researches. *Mineralogical Abstracts* has had a special section for meteorites since its first issue in 1922, and provides admirable coverage in this field. However, in view of the extremely scattered literature, the few books which pro-

vide a comprehensive account of various aspects of meteorites are of
especial value.   The following may be cited as especially useful:

Krinov, E. L., 1960: *Principles of meteoritics.*   Pergamon Press, New York, 535
   pp.   The English translation of a Russian book dealing comprehensively with
   all aspects of meteorites.
Heide, F., 1957: *Kleine Meteoritenkunde* (second ed.).   Springer, Berlin, 142
   pp.   An excellent account of meteorites, brief, clear, and concise.
Watson, F. G., 1956: *Between the planets* (second ed.).   Harvard Press, Cam-
   bridge, Mass., 188 pp.   An account of the minor bodies in the solar system,
   not only the meteorites but also the asteroids and comets.
Prior, G. T., 1953: *Catalogue of meteorites.*   Second edition by M. H. Hey.
   British Museum, London, 432 pp.   A catalog of all meteorites recorded up to
   1953, with brief descriptions and bibliographic references for each one; an
   essential book for all workers on meteorites.
Nininger, H. H., 1952: *Out of the sky.*   University of Denver Press, 336 pp.
   (Reprinted 1959 as a paperback by Dover Publications, New York.)   A popu-
   lar account of meteorites intended mainly for the lay reader, but useful as an
   introduction to the subject.
Merrill, G. P., 1930: "Composition and structure of meteorites."   *U.S. Natl.
   Museum Bull.*, **149**, 62 pp.   A brief and succinct account, written at the end
   of a lifetime of research on meteorites.
Farrington, O. C., 1915: *Meteorites.*   Published by the author, Chicago, 233 pp.
   At that time a definitive account of meteorites, clear, concise, and comprehensive.
Cohen, E., 1894–1905: *Meteoritenkunde, Parts I–III.*   Schweizerbart'sche Ver-
   lagshandlung, Stuttgart, 340 pp.; 302 pp.; 419 pp.   This publication was
   planned to give a complete account of all work on meteorites up to that time.
   Unfortunately Cohen died before he could complete it.   Nevertheless the parts
   that were completed are excellent, and describe and document the work carried out during the nineteenth century, much of which is still significant.
Wülfing, E. A., 1897: *Die Meteoriten in Sammlungen und ihre Literatur.*
   Laupp'schen Buchhandlung, Tübingen, 461 pp.   A list of all meteorites known
   up to that date, with a complete bibliography for each one, and the location
   of specimens; still an extremely useful reference work.

A valuable guide to the literature is *A bibliography on meteorites*
edited by Harrison Brown (University of Chicago Press, 1953, 686 pp.).
This is a chronological (1491–1950) bibliography of 8650 main entries,
many of which have additional references to abstracts and reviews, the
whole representing a selection of some 25,000 items.   Under each
year the entries are arranged alphabetically by author's name, and
there is an author index; thus in order to find a specific item it is
necessary to know either the year of publication or the author's name.

2

Phenomena of Fall

Orbits of Meteorites

The unpredictability of meteorite falls has meant that information on their orbits has depended largely on chance observations of untrained observers. This information, as compiled by different experts, has led to diametrically opposed conclusions. One group of experts has argued that meteorites, or at least a large number of them, travel in hyperbolic orbits and thus come from beyond the solar system—the evidence has been cogently presented by LaPaz (1958). An equally authoritative group of experts claims that no provable hyperbolic orbit has yet been observed, and that meteorites travel in elliptical orbits within the solar system—the evidence for this has been thoroughly presented by Krinov (1960). The only adequately observed orbit is that of the Pribram chondrite, which fell on the night of April 7, 1959, and was simultaneously photographed from two different points. These observations resulted in the calculated orbit shown in Fig. 1, which shows that this meteorite was traveling in an elliptical orbit which brought it from the asteroidal belt. This provides strong support for the belief that the meteorites and the asteroids have a common origin, and that meteorites belong to the solar system.

Of the abundance, size, and shape of meteorites when they are in outer space we have no precise knowledge. Asteroids range in size from the largest, Ceres, with a radius of 390 km, down to the

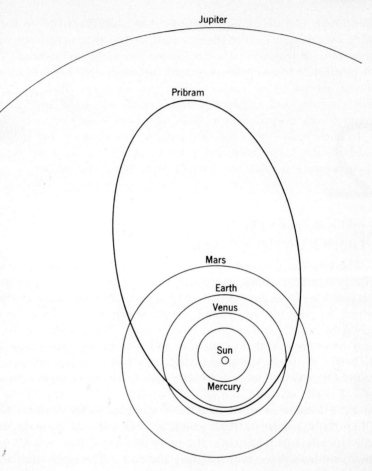

Fig. 1. Orbit of the Pribram meteorite (fell April 7, 1959), as calculated by Ceplecha (1961).

limits of detection by modern telescopes (about 1 km diameter) and presumably progressively smaller. To judge from the way in which their luminosity varies, asteroids are irregular in form. The temperature of a meteorite when it is in outer space will depend upon the balance between absorption and reradiation of solar heat. In the immediate neighborhood of the Earth the internal temperature of a meteorite will probably be considerably below 0° C.

To what extent the range of composition of the meteorites which have been collected and examined is a complete representation of meteoroids is a debatable question. One may speculate on the possible existence of meteorites of a composition that would not survive their fall. It is conceivable that meteorites made up essentially of ice or possibly of frozen gases may exist, although none has ever been collected; meteorites of "contra-terrene material," i.e., made up of positive electrons and negative protons, which would be annihilated on contact with normal matter, have also been suggested.

In outer space meteorites are non-luminous objects and thus effectively undetectable; once they enter the Earth's atmosphere, however, their presence is made manifest by light and sound effects.

Light and Sound Effects

The fall of a meteorite is usually accompanied by light and sound effects which are most impressive to those fortunate enough to witness such a rare event. A meteorite appears as a fiery mass and passes across the sky leaving behind a trail which appears as a luminous streak by night and a cloud of dust by day. The intensity of the light may be as great as that of the sun, and at night may make large areas as bright as day. The illuminated path may be very extensive; the path of the Bath Furnace meteorite, which fell on the night of November 15, 1902, was observed from Louisiana to its point of fall in Kentucky, a distance of about 1000 km; it was also visible from Columbus, Ohio, 200 km north of Bath Furnace. The color of the light is usually described as white, but also as greenish, reddish, or yellow, and may vary from place to place along the path. The smoke trail accompanying the meteorite may be quite dense and persist for a considerable time after its fall; the smoke trail of the Sikhote-Alin meteorite lasted for some hours and was sufficiently dense to totally obscure the sun or reduce it to a dull red ball. Observations on a number of meteorites indicate that they become luminous at about 150 km above the Earth's surface, which is evidently where interaction with the atmosphere is sufficient to raise their outer surface to incandescence.

The sound accompanying the fall of a meteorite has been variously described as resembling cannon fire, thunder, or the passage of an express train. The sound effects will usually follow the first appearance of the luminous meteorite by two or three minutes. Frequently the end of the luminous path is marked by explosion-like effects, at which point the meteorite may actually break up into many fragments.

Velocity Effects

The velocity with which a meteorite enters the Earth's atmosphere will depend upon its inherent velocity and its direction of motion with respect to the motion of the Earth. Meteorites in outer space move in elliptical orbits around the sun with velocities which are less than 42 km/sec. The Earth's velocity around the sun is 30 km/sec. Those meteorites overtaking the Earth have the Earth's velocity subtracted, and thus enter the atmosphere at 12 km/sec or less, whereas those meeting the Earth have the Earth's velocity added, and may enter the atmosphere with a velocity as high as 70 km/sec. Small and moderate-sized meteorites are rapidly decelerated by the atmosphere, so that their cosmic velocities are completely extinguished at a considerable height above the Earth's surface—the region of delay (Krinov, 1961). Below this point, the velocity of such meteorites is due entirely to gravitational attraction, and they hit the ground at comparatively low velocities, about 0.1–0.2 km/sec. Large meteorites, on the other hand, are only partially decelerated by the atmosphere, and thus retain a considerable proportion of their cosmic velocity when they strike the ground. The relationship between mass and velocity is illustrated in Fig. 2, for hypothetical meteorites of different weights entering the atmosphere at a velocity of 40 km/sec. Masses up to 1 ton will lose all their cosmic velocity before striking the ground; masses of 10 tons or more will retain a considerable amount of their cosmic velocity to the end of their flight.

The surface of a meteorite is raised to incandescence high in the atmosphere, and is subjected to ablation by the impact of the molecules of air. The dust cloud defining the path of a meteorite represents material removed from the meteorite itself. It is clear therefore that a meteorite must suffer a diminution of mass during its passage through the atmosphere. It has been estimated that the dust cloud accompanying the Sikhote-Alin meteorite contained 200 tons of material, whereas the weight of meteorite fragments collected was 70 tons.

The highest temperature on a falling meteorite occurs on its front surface, which is also subjected to great pressure. This pressure will promote the breakup of a single meteorite body, resulting in the formation of meteorite showers, after which dozens, hundreds, or even thousands of individual specimens may be collected. Meteorite

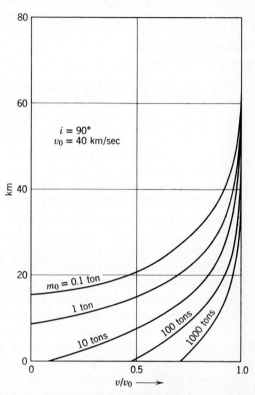

Fig. 2. Diminution of velocity of meteorites of different mass during passage through the Earth's atmosphere, assuming an initial velocity of 40 km/sec and vertical infall (Heide, 1957).

showers are generally spread over an elliptical area called a dispersion ellipse, which may cover many square kilometers. The individual specimens from meteorite showers usually show a characteristic distribution within the dispersion ellipse. The larger pieces travel farthest and are found at the head or far end of the ellipse relative to the direction of travel, the smallest pieces are found in the opposite part, while specimens of intermediate size fall in the middle (Fig. 3).

In this connection it is worth remarking that meteorites are usually only moderately warm on impact, and that there are no authentic records of their having caused fires. This lack of heat is contrary to popular superstition, the common opinion being that meteorites are intensely hot when they reach the ground. Certainly the surface is heated to incandescence in the upper atmosphere. However, the meteorite passes rapidly through this region and below the point where it has completely lost its cosmic velocity the surface will be cooled rather than heated. Since the interior is at the low temperature of outer space, the momentary surface heating has practically no effect on the meteorite as a whole. The accounts of a meteorite being very hot when it fell can be safely assumed to be false, the narrator's preconceived opinion probably influencing his testimony. Some meteorites have been recorded as quite cold when picked up shortly after being seen to fall. The Colby (Wisconsin) stone fell on a hot July afternoon in 1917, and the man who dug it from the

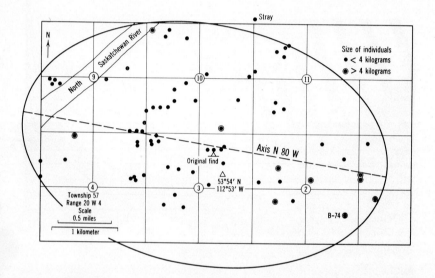

Fig. 3. Distribution ellipse of the Bruderheim, Canada, meteorite shower. The shower moved from west to east, the larger individuals being carried farther by their greater momentum. The squares in the diagram represent a quarter square mile each (Folinsbee and Bayrock, 1961).

ground a few minutes after it fell stated that it was so cold that frost immediately formed on its surface when it was exposed to the air.

Impact Effects

The effects produced when a meteorite strikes the ground will depend on its mass, its mechanical strength, its velocity, and the nature of the ground at the impact point. As we have seen, the velocity and the mass of the meteorite are related—the impact velocities of meteorites of mass 1 ton or less are determined essentially by gravitational attraction, whereas more massive meteorites reach the Earth's surface with some part of their cosmic velocity still retained. For small and medium-sized meteorites (say up to 1 ton) a hole or pit is formed at the point of impact in soft ground, and the diameter of the hole is comparable with the diameter of the meteorite. The depth of the hole will depend upon the softness of the ground: an 8 kg stone which fell in a rice field at Bandong, Java, on December 10, 1871, pene-

Fig. 4. Impact pit of the Norton County meteorite; the meteorite is seen at the bottom of the pit, which is 3 meters deep and about 1 meter in diameter (courtesy University of Nebraska).

trated to a depth of 1 meter; the 10 kg stone which fell near St. Michel, Finland, on July 12, 1910, penetrated 0.5 meter of moraine. Even larger meteorites may make comparatively small holes; a 1000 kg stone (the largest stone yet recorded) which fell in a cornfield in Norton County, Kansas, on February 18, 1948, made a hole 3 meters deep (Fig. 4). When a meteorite falls on a hard surface, both the meteorite itself and the ground may be broken up. It is interesting to note that a number of stones of the Hessle fall in Sweden on January 1, 1869, fell on the surface of a frozen lake but did not break the ice.

It has been estimated that the impact velocities of meteorites producing typical impact pits in soft ground are of the order of 100–200 meters/sec. At higher impact velocities, up to about 4 km/sec, as Stanyukovich (1950) has shown, a meteorite striking soft ground tends to break up, and the meteorite fragments and the ground fly in all directions, producing a crater whose size considerably exceeds that of the meteorite; the greater the impact speed, the larger the crater. The only observed case of the formation of such impact craters is for the Sikhote-Alin shower of iron meteorites; in the dispersion ellipse of this shower 122 such craters were found, of which 17 were from 10 to 26.5 meters in diameter (Fig. 5). On the inside slopes of all these craters, meteorite fragments were discovered mixed with broken rock and soft ground. When the terminal velocity of a meteorite exceeds 4 km/sec (which is only possible for masses of 10 tons or more) the impact effects are, however, quite different: a powerful blast spreads outward from the point of impact and what may be called an explosion crater is formed. This is readily understood from a brief consideration of the energy content of such a meteorite. The kinetic energy $E = \frac{1}{2}mv^2$ increases proportionally to the mass of the meteorite and to the square of the velocity. A meteorite weighing 100 tons and striking the Earth at 10 km/sec would have a kinetic energy of 5×10^{19} ergs, far greater than the same mass of any conventional explosive. The energy of such a meteorite will be consumed in the formation of the

Fig. 5.   Impact crater of one of the Sikhote-Alin meteorites (courtesy Dr. E. L. Krinov).

crater, the production of shock waves, the heating of the surface rocks, and the heating of the meteorite itself. If only 10% of the total energy is consumed in the heating of the meteorite, the meteorite will be completely vaporized. This result is consistent with our knowledge of meteorites. No meteorite of 100 tons or more has been found. It is also not probable that such meteorites, if they occurred, would be overlooked. On the other hand, the dimensions of the largest meteorite craters are so great that one must assume they were formed by meteorites much larger than 1000 tons. It is fruitless to expect to find such giant meteorites, since they will not survive other than as minor fragments that escaped complete vaporization.

Meteorite Craters

From the preceding discussion it is clear that meteorite craters are of two types, which may be characterized respectively as impact craters and explosion craters. These differ completely in size, in general characteristics, and in mode of origin. The first described and most spectacular meteorite crater is Meteor Crater in Arizona (Fig. 6), 1300 meters in diameter and 175 meters deep from rim to floor. Despite the unique geological features distinguishing it from a volcanic crater or a sinkhole, and the distribution of thousands of fragments of meteoritic iron around it (Fig. 7), its identification as a meteorite crater has been disputed from time to time. However, the discovery (Chao et al., 1960) of the high-pressure form of SiO_2, coesite (not previously known as a mineral), in the crushed sandstone at the bottom of the crater, is excellent evidence of violent impact and hence further strengthens the identification. Another high-pressure form of SiO_2, stishovite, has also been found at Meteor Crater (Chao et al., 1962b).

No meteorite sufficiently large to give a crater of the explosion type has been observed to fall. The Tunguska "meteorite" fell in Siberia on June 30, 1908, producing tremendous destruction in the forest around the point of explosion, but no meteorite fragments and no true meteorite crater or craters have been identified; it is believed to have been the core of a comet (Fesenkov, 1961). Table 1 lists the meteorite craters for which the origin is well established by the presence of meteoritic matter associated with them.

Krinov (1961) has pointed out that the explosion craters of Kaali-

Fig. 6. Aerial photograph of Meteor Crater, Arizona; Canyon Diablo is the stream valley in the background (courtesy The American Museum of Natural History).

jarv and Henbury are accompanied by smaller craters which he identifies very plausibly as impact craters. The maximum diameter of an impact crater he puts at "several dozen meters" whereas he doubts that an explosion crater will be less than 100 meters in diameter. Distinguishing features of impact craters and explosion craters, besides size, are the presence of numerous meteorite fragments within impact craters and their absence from the interior of explosion craters, and the presence of a clearly defined swell along the rim of an explosion crater where the surface layers of rock have been lifted and tilted radially outwards by the explosion. He observes that the Haviland crater is of the impact type, being only 17 meters in diameter and containing innumerable meteorite fragments within it.

In recent years interest in meteorite craters has increased greatly, and many geological features, some of obscure origin and great age, have been ascribed to meteorite impact. The evidence for a meteoritic origin is often tenuous at best, although the presence of coesite is reliable evidence of high pressure, presumably produced by impact.

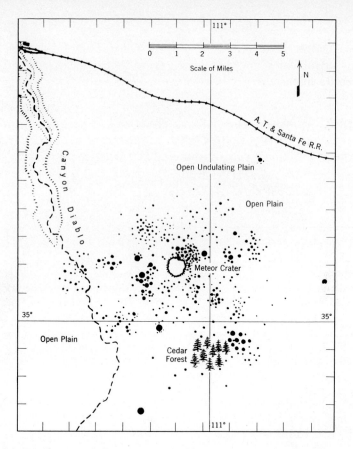

Fig. 7. Distribution of the Canyon Diablo meteorites around Meteor Crater, Arizona (courtesy The American Museum of Natural History).

TABLE 1. METEORITE CRATERS WITH ASSOCIATED METEORITIC MATERIAL

Name	Maximum Diameter (in meters)	Reference
Boxhole, Central Australia	160	Madigan (1937)
Campo del Cielo, Argentina	56	Spencer (1933a)
Dalgaranga, Western Australia	70	Nininger and Huss (1960)
Haviland, Kansas, U.S.A.	17	Nininger (1952)
Henbury, Central Australia	200	Alderman (1932)
Kaalijarv, Estonia, U.S.S.R.	90	Krinov (1961)
Meteor Crater, Arizona, U.S.A.	1200	Nininger (1952)
Odessa, Texas, U.S.A.	150	Nininger (1952)
Sikhote-Alin, Siberia	28	Krinov (1960)
Wolf Creek, Western Australia	840	Guppy and Matheson (1950)

These features are listed in Table 2. Dietz (1961) has coined the term "astroblemes" for the ancient scars left in the Earth's crust by meteorite impact.

TABLE 2. FEATURES IDENTIFIED AS METEORITE CRATERS OR METEORITE IMPACTS, BUT WITHOUT RECOGNIZABLE METEORITE MATERIAL (COESITE HAS BEEN IDENTIFIED FROM THOSE MARKED WITH AN ASTERISK)

Name	Maximum Diameter (in meters)	Reference
Al Umchaimin, Iraq	3200	Merriam and Holwerda (1957)
Amak, Aleutian Islands	60	LaPaz (1947)
Amguid, Sahara		Karpoff (1953)
Aouelloul, Western Sahara	250	Monod and Pourquié (1951)
Bagdad, Iraq	200	Richter (1954)
Brent, Ontario, Canada	3700	Beals (1958)
Carolina "bays," Carolina, U.S.A.	2000	Nininger (1952)
Chubb, Ungava, Canada	3400	Meen (1952)
Crooked Creek, Missouri		Dietz (1961)
Deep Bay, Saskatchewan, Canada	13,700	Beals (1958)
Dzioua, Sahara		Karpoff (1953)
Duckwater, Nevada, U.S.A.	70	Rinehart and Elvey (1951)
Flynn Creek, Tennessee, U.S.A.	3000	Dietz (1961)
Gulf of St. Lawrence, Canada		Cohen (1961)
Hagensfjord, Greenland		Ellitsgaard-Rasmussen (1954)
*Holleford, Ontario, Canada	2400	Beals (1958)
*Kentland Dome, Indiana	1000	Cohen et al. (1961)
Köfels, Austria	4000	Suess (1937)
*Lake Bosumtwi, Ghana	10,000	Littler et al. (1961)
Merewether, Labrador, Canada	150	Meen (1957)
Montagne Noire, France		Geze and Cailleux (1950)
Mount Doreen, Central Australia	610	Sangster (1957)
Murgab, Tadjikstan, U.S.S.R.	80	Bacharev (1956)
*Nordlinger Ries, Germany	25,000	Shoemaker and Chao (1961)
Pretoria Saltpan, South Africa	1000	Rohleder (1933)
*Serpent Mound, Ohio	6400	Cohen et al. (1961)
Sierra Madera, Texas, U.S.A.	2000	Eggleton and Shoemaker (1961)
Steinheim, Germany	2500	Rohleder (1933)
Talemzane, Algeria	1800	Karpoff (1953)
Tenoumer, Western Sahara	1800	Smith and Hey (1952)
Vredefort, South Africa	40,000	Dietz (1961)
Wells Creek, Tennessee, U.S.A.	4800	Dietz (1961)

Geographical Distribution of Meteorites

Meteorites have been found on all the continents, even Antarctica. About 1700 distinct meteorites have been recorded, and their distribution is given in Table 3. Study of Table 3 shows that within a specific region the recognition and recovery of meteorites depends to a large extent on the population density and the cultural level. Meteorites are more likely to be found on alluvial plains than on rocky mountains, and the alluvial plains are usually the regions of dense population. Over 100 meteorites have been found in India and Pakistan, almost all on the plains of the Indus and Ganges Rivers. Some 30 meteorites have been recorded from Japan, a large number for a comparatively small area, but one which reflects the dense population and the high standard of education. There is a remarkable anomaly in the recovery of only 6 meteorites from the whole of China, a region certainly comparable to India and Pakistan in respect to area and population density.

There is a notable contrast in the relative numbers of iron and stone meteorites from different continents. From North America 330 irons and 363 stones are recorded, from South America 59 irons and 37 stones, from Australia 61 irons and 40 stones, from Europe 42 irons and 300 stones, from Asia 47 irons and 200 stones, from Africa 35 irons and 65 stones. The explanation of this contrast is presumably that the art of iron working has been known since prehistoric times in Europe, Asia, and Africa and most iron meteorites have been converted into weapons and tools. In the other continents iron working was almost or completely unknown and so the iron meteorites have survived until the present.

Frequency of Falls

Numerous attempts have been made to deduce the frequency of meteorite falls. Brown (1961) has estimated it on the basis of the number of observed falls over the last century in Japan, India, and Western Europe, all areas with a high density of population where a meteorite fall is not likely to go unrecorded. He arrives at an estimate of one fall per million square kilometers per year, corresponding

TABLE 3. GEOGRAPHICAL DISTRIBUTION OF METEORITES

Country	Chon-drites	Achon-drites	Stony-Irons	Irons	Total
Canada	11	—	2	13	26
U.S.A.	325	15	24	270	634
Mexico and Central America	11	1	2	47	61
North America	347	16	28	330	721
Brazil	9	2	—	9	20
Argentina	18	3	3	8	32
Chile	4	—	5	37	46
Other South America	1	—	1	5	7
South America	32	5	9	59	105
Great Britain and Ireland	19	—	—	1	20
France, Belgium, Holland	55	6	—	1	62
Denmark, Norway, Sweden, Finland	27	1	2	5	35
Germany	24	2	3	7	36
Switzerland, Austria, Hungary, Czechoslovakia, Poland	31	2	1	14	48
U.S.S.R., European	63	7	2	7	79
Romania, Yugoslavia, Bulgaria, Greece	18	—	—	3	21
Italy	21	—	—	1	22
Spain and Portugal	22	2	2	3	29
Europe	280	20	10	42	352
South and Southwest Africa	18	1	2	19	40
Other Africa S. of Equator	12	1	—	2	15
Africa N. of Equator	27	6	1	14	48
Africa	57	8	3	35	103
U.S.S.R., Asiatic	23	2	2	23	50
Japan	23	—	1	6	30
China	6	—	—	—	6
India and Pakistan	104	9	3	6	122
Other Asia	31	2	1	12	46
Asia	187	13	7	47	254
Australia	38	2	8	61	109
Others	13	—	1	4	18
World totals	954	64	66	578	1662

to a total rate of fall on the Earth of about 500 meteorites per year. Since over 70% of the Earth's surface is covered by water, some 350 of these will fall in the sea and be unrecoverable. From these figures it is easy to see that the prospect of actually seeing a meteorite fall is very slight, and the danger of being struck by one is vanishingly small. Indeed the only authentic record of a person being struck by a meteorite is the case of Mrs. E. H. Hodges of Sylacauga, Alabama. On November 30, 1954, Mrs. Hodges was resting on a sofa after lunch when a stone meteorite weighing about 4 kg broke through the roof of her house, ricocheted off a radio, and struck her on her upper thigh, causing a minor bruise. There are a number of records of buildings and animals being struck by meteorites, and these are listed by LaPaz (1958).

When we compare the estimated frequency of meteorite falls with the actual recovery of the meteorites themselves, we find that per- centage recovery is very low. For the period 1800–1960 about 670 falls have been collected, an average of only about 4 per year. When we study the recovery of falls by successive decades (Fig. 8), we note a rather steady increase in numbers—this presumably reflects an in- creased chance of recovery, as a result of increasing population and a growing interest in meteorites. However, the decades 1940–1949 and 1950–1960 show a marked drop from the high peak for 1930– 1939. In view of the low percentage recovery, it would be venture- some to claim that this represents a real decline in the frequency of meteorite falls over the twenty years from 1940 to 1960, especially

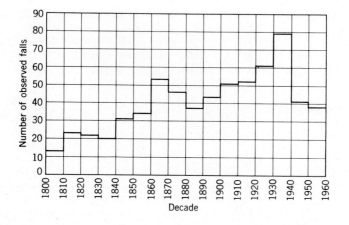

Fig. 8.   Recovery of observed meteorite falls by decades, 1800–1960.

since during the years after 1940 the world was disrupted by war, and the statistics for 1950–1960 are probably incomplete. Nevertheless, it will be interesting to see whether the observed falls continue on the present low level.

Time of Falls

There are marked seasonal and diurnal variations in the fall of meteorites. The monthly variation (Fig. 9) has a broad maximum

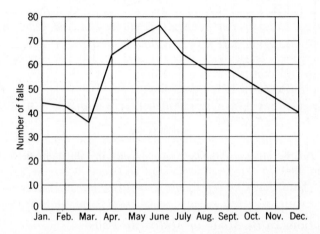

Fig. 9.   Monthly variation in the incidence of meteorite falls, 1800–1960.

extending from April to July and a minimum extending from October to March.   There are two possible explanations for this variation: (*a*) most of the observations originate in the Northern Hemisphere, and the summer is more favorable than the winter for observing and re-covering meteorites; (*b*) during the April-July period the Earth may pass through a region which is comparatively densely populated with meteorites.

The curve for the hour of fall (Fig. 10) has a pronounced peak be-tween 3 P.M. and 4 P.M. and drops to a minimum between 3 A.M. and 4 A.M.   The minimum is clearly conditioned by the few observers likely to be about in the early morning hours.   The afternoon peak, however, probably reflects other factors than simply the presence of large numbers of observers. All meteorites reaching the Earth between noon and midnight must be moving in the same direction as the earth in its orbit. In effect they reach the Earth by overtaking it, or being overtaken by it. This suggests that the majority of meteorites probably move around the Sun in the same direction as the Earth.

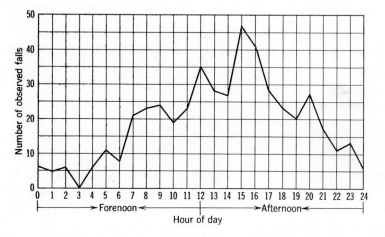

Fig. 10. Hourly variation in the incidence of meteorite falls, 1790–1940 (Leonard and Slanin, 1941).

Observations to Be Made of Meteorite Falls

Although few of us may be privileged to witness a meteorite fall, it may be worthwhile to enumerate the observations that should as far as possible be made of such a unique event. The following points may be listed:

1. At what time (date, hour, minute) was the meteorite first seen?
2. How long did the light effects persist from their first appearance to their extinction?
3. How intense and how large was the luminosity, compared for example with the stars or the moon? What was its form and color?
4. Did the meteorite leave a luminous trail or a smoke trail? If so, what was its form and color, and how long did it persist?
5. What was the position of the meteorite's course through the sky? This is important in fixing the meteorite's orbit, and the course should

be related to identified stars or planets, or to fixed objects on the Earth; the position of observation must be recorded.

6. How much time elapsed between the first appearance of the meteorite and any sound effects? What was the nature of the sound effects, and how long did they persist?

7. How long after the fall was the meteorite or meteorites found? Were they hot or cold? What was the position of the meteorite or meteorites (marked on a large-scale map if possible)? What were the weights of the individual meteorites?

8. What was the nature of the ground on which the meteorite or meteorites fell, and how deep did they penetrate? If the impact pit was not vertical, what was its angle of inclination?

[Photographs illustrating any of the above aspects of a meteorite fall are especially valuable scientifically: as far as possible some object showing the scale (a person, a ruler, a pencil, etc.) should be included in the picture.]

At this point it may be appropriate to enter an urgent plea to all who find a meteorite to treat it with the respect it deserves as a unique and irreplaceable object. Too often meteorites have been broken up or defaced and their scientific (and monetary) value greatly diminished by hammering or even heating in a forge or attack with an oxyacetylene torch. A suspected meteorite should be reported to the nearest large natural history museum; if it is small it should be sent there for an expert opinion, if large, a small piece should be broken off for this purpose.

3

The Morphology of Meteorites

Size

Meteorites range in size from the smallest dust particles up to many tons. The largest single meteorite so far found is the Hoba iron in Southwest Africa (Fig. 11). It measures 2.95 by 2.84 meters on the flat upper surface, and its thickness ranges from 0.5 to 1.2 meters; the weight is calculated to be about 60 tons. The original weight must have been considerably greater, since the meteorite is surrounded by a laminated mass of limonite (so-called "iron shale") up to half a meter thick formed by weathering; Gordon (1931) estimates the weight at the time of fall to have been about 100 tons. As discussed in the preceding chapter, the dynamics of meteorite falls indicate that meteorites much larger than this are unlikely to survive impact with the Earth except as fragments.

No trace of a crater surrounds the Hoba meteorite, which lies in a superficial calcareous tufa apparently deposited about it since it fell. The meteorite probably fell in pre-Pleistocene time and any results of the impact have presumably long since been removed by erosion.

The next largest meteorite is one of the Cape York irons from West Greenland, which was brought to New York by Peary in 1897 and is now in The American Museum of Natural History (Fig. 12). It is an irregular object, the principal dimensions being: length, 3.3 meters; height, 2.0 meters; width, 1.5 meters; the weight is 31 metric

Fig. 11.   The Hoba meteorite, Southwest Africa (Spencer, 1932).

Fig. 12.   Three of the Cape York irons: Ahnighito, 31 tons; Woman, 3 tons; and Dog, 408 kg (courtesy The American Museum of Natural History).

tons. The Eskimos called it "Ahnighito," meaning the tent, in allusion to its shape and size. This meteorite was lying partly buried in moraine, and the ground showed no impact features; this suggests that the meteorite may have fallen on a thick ice cover during the Pleistocene glaciation. Three other large irons, weighing respectively 3½ tons, 3 tons, and 400 kg, were found in the same area and evidently belong to the same fall; the 3½ ton mass is in the Mineralogical Museum in Copenhagen, the other two in The American Museum of Natural History.

Several other iron meteorites weighing between 10 and 30 tons are known. The Bacubirito meteorite, which still lies where it was found in the state of Sinaloa, Mexico, is an irregular mass 4 meters by 1.8 meters by 1.6 meters and is estimated to weigh 27 tons. The Mbosi meteorite in Tanganyika measures 4 meters by 1.2 meters by 1.2 meters, and weighs between 25 and 27 tons. A large iron meteorite weighing about 20 tons is recorded from Armanty in Outer Mongolia. The Willamette iron, found in an Oregon forest in 1902, weighs 14 tons, and is a rather perfect cone-shaped meteorite with remarkable deep pits on the base (Figs. 13, 14); it is in The American Museum

Fig. 13.   Base of the Willamette meteorite, showing large cavities (courtesy The American Museum of Natural History).

Fig. 14. Side view of the Willamette meteorite, showing conical form and presence of shallow cavities (courtesy The American Museum of Natural History).

of Natural History. The larger Chupaderos iron, from Chihuahua, Mexico, also weighs about 14 tons and was accompanied by another mass weighing some 6½ tons; these are now in the School of Mines in Mexico City. A mass of meteoritic iron weighing about 13 tons is reported to occur in the Campo del Cielo district of Argentina; numerous smaller irons (the Otumpa irons) have been collected from this locality. Another iron similar to Willamette in form but somewhat smaller (about 11 tons) is the Morito meteorite from Chihuahua, Mexico, now in the School of Mines in Mexico City.

A number of irons weighing between 1 and 10 tons are known; these include Chupaderos, Mexico (2d specimen), 6.8 tons; Bendego, Brazil, 5.4 tons; Otumpa, Argentina, 4.2 tons and 1.5 tons; Cranbourne, Australia, 3½ tons and 1½ tons; Adargas, Mexico, 3.3 tons; Cape York, Greenland (2d and 3d specimens), 3½ and 3 tons; Santa Catharina, Brazil, 2.2 and 1.5 tons; Chico Mountains, U.S.A., 2 tons; Sikhote-Alin, U.S.S.R., 1.7 tons; Casas Grandes, Mexico, 1.5 tons; Navajo, U.S.A., 1.5 tons; Magura, Czechoslovakia, 1.5 tons; Quinn Canyon, U.S.A., 1.4 tons; Santa Apolonia, Mexico, 1.3 tons; Kouga Mountains,

South Africa, 1.2 tons; Goose Lake, U.S.A., 1.2 tons; Murnpeowie, South Australia, 1.1 tons; and Zacatecas, Mexico, 1 ton.

In contrast to the irons, the largest individual stone meteorite weighs a little over a ton; it is the Norton County enstatite achondrite, which fell in Nebraska on February 18, 1948. Other large stones are Long Island, U.S.A., 564 kg (2 pieces, evidently broken on landing); Paragould, U.S.A., 372 kg; Bjurbole, Finland, 330 kg (broken into fragments on landing); Hugoton, U.S.A., 325 kg; Clovis, U.S.A., 283 kg; Knyahinya, U.S.S.R., 239 kg.

No very large stony-irons are known. The Port Orford (Oregon, U.S.A.) pallasite was reported to weigh at least 10 tons by its original discoverer, but has never been relocated. The Bitburg, Germany, pallasite weighed about 1½ tons, and the Huckitta pallasite from South Australia 1.4 tons. The largest single mesosiderite is one of the Estherville, U.S.A., meteorites, which weighed 200 kg.

At the other extreme in size we have the smallest particles that can be recognized as individual meteorites. Krinov (1959) has illustrated meteorites from the Sikhote-Alin fall less than 1 mm in diameter and weighing as little as 0.3 mg. Nininger (1952) collected numerous small stones of the Holbrook fall, which ranged down to about 2 mm in diameter and weighed as little as 18 mg. Minute meteorites such as these are probably present in most, if not all, meteorite showers, but are seldom preserved because of the difficulty in recognizing and collecting them.

Krinov applies the term micrometeorite to such individual meteorites of microscopic size. The term micrometeorite has been used in a different sense, for extra-terrestrial particles which pass through the Earth's atmosphere practically unaltered because of their small size (Whipple, 1950). Krinov prefers to call such material extra-terrestrial or cosmic dust. In addition to the extra-terrestrial dust, the surface of the Earth receives an increment of material which is ablated from the surfaces of meteorites during their passage through the atmosphere. Buddhue (1950) has provided a useful account of investigations on meteoritic dust made up to that time. Since then, however, much has been published on this subject.

The difficulty in collecting and identifying meteoritic and cosmic dust lies in the enormous contamination by terrestrial (both natural and industrial) dust at most places on Earth. Meteoritic and cosmic dust can best be collected from places as far removed from terrestrial contamination as possible. These places include deep-sea deposits (and their fossil equivalents—Hunter and Parkin (1961) have identified cosmic dust in two samples of Tertiary rock from the Oceanic formation on Barbados), polar ice-caps (Thiel and Schmidt, 1961), and the upper atmosphere. The occurrence of cosmogenic particles in deep-sea sediments has been discussed in detail by Goldberg (1961). He notes that Murray in 1876 first called attention to the occurrence of highly magnetic spherical particles in deep-sea sediments; Murray showed that they seldom exceeded 0.2 mm in diameter, and that they generally had a nucleus of metallic iron and a shell of magnetite. Murray suggested that these spherules were meteoritic in origin, a suggestion that has been confirmed by chemical analyses, which show that these spherules resemble iron meteorites closely in their content of nickel, copper, and cobalt. These spherules have been collected from the deep-sea bottom by the use of magnetic rakes (Bruun, Langer, and Pauly, 1955); besides the metallic spherules, other magnetic particles have been collected, including some reniform slag-like particles consisting of a silicate groundmass with magnetic crystals, some irregular pieces of metal, and spherules containing no metal, which resemble chondrules from stony meteorites (Fig. 15). Pettersson and Fredriksson (1958) have made quantitative measurements of the magnetic spherules in deep-sea cores, and estimate that the rate of accretion of such material is of the order of 2500–5000 tons annually for the whole Earth.

Hunter and Parkin (1960) have extended the observations on the metallic spherules and have extensively investigated the nature of the silicate chondrules. The size distributions obtained both for the nickel-iron spherules and for the olivine-pyroxene chondrules found on the deep-ocean floor are in remarkable disagreement with the tentative size distribution of cosmic dust obtained by impact counting from satellites. An exponential increase in number of particles with decreasing size below 0.01–0.02 mm is indicated by the satellite observations, whereas the cosmic particles from the ocean floor show a drastic decrease in frequency below 0.025 mm, and a comparatively large number of big (0.09–0.3 mm) silicate chondrules. This indicates that the cosmic material found on the ocean floor represents debris of meteorites rather than original cosmic dust.

The infall of cosmic dust from the upper atmosphere has been estimated by Pettersson (1960), who filtered the dust from measured volumes of air at an altitude of 11,000 feet on Mauna Loa, Hawaii. The material collected on the filters contained appreciable amounts of nickel, averaging 0.014 mg per 1000 cubic meters of air. Assuming the average nickel content of cosmic dust to be 2.5%, it follows that the

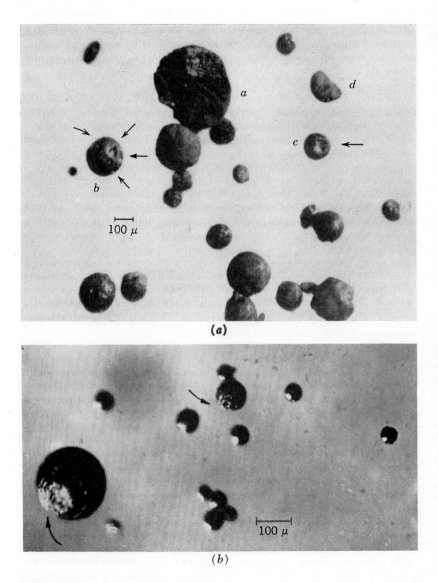

Fig. 15. Meteorite dust from deep-sea sediments: (a) stony spherules resembling chondrules; (b) iron spherules (Hunter and Parkin, 1960).

cosmic dust content of 1000 cubic meters of air is 0.6 mg. This leads
to the conclusion that the annual rate of accretion of cosmic dust is
of the order of 5 million tons. Hodge and Wildt (1958) have made
similar collections of atmospheric dust, and have identified opaque
spherules which they believe to be the products of meteorite ablation.
They estimate an accretion of about 500,000 tons for the Earth annually. This figure may not be in conflict with Pettersson's estimate,
which includes cosmic dust as well as material ablated from meteorites.

Shape

Inspection of a large collection of meteorites gives the impression
of an almost endless variety of shapes. Nevertheless, there is a general tendency, especially among the stones, to roughly equi-dimen-
sional forms. Irons tend to be more irregular, and may have sharp
protuberances or deep cavities; one of the Tucson irons is ring-shaped
(Fig. 16).

The forces which may have modified the original form of a meteorite are many: erosion and collisions in outer space, ablation and frag-

Fig. 16. The Tucson ring iron; the maximum diameter of the hole is 70 cm
(courtesy The American Museum of Natural History).

mentation during the passage through the Earth's atmosphere, impact with the Earth's surface, and weathering.

The possibility of the modification of the form of a meteorite by collision with like objects in outer space is generally admitted, even if the occurrence of such collisions is not susceptible to proof. In view of the much greater mechanical strength of the irons as compared to the stones, the latter presumably suffer much greater fragmentation from such collisions. The fact that all large meteorites are irons probably reflects their mechanical strength, rather than a mode of origin that systematically produced large irons and smaller stones.

The erosion of the surface of a meteorite in outer space may be due to the effect of interplanetary gas, dust, protons, or other particles. The degree of such erosion will presumably be greater for stones than for irons. Calculations of the amount of such erosion are possible from a consideration of the cosmic-ray exposure ages (Whipple and Fireman, 1959; Fireman and DeFelice, 1960; Fisher, 1961). Whipple and Fireman arrived at a maximum surface erosion of the Sikhote-Alin meteorite of 1.5×10^{-7} cm/year; for the Grant meteorite Fisher estimates a maximum erosion rate of 1.1×10^{-8} cm/year. Both these meteorites are irons. For a large iron meteorite the percentage loss will evidently be small even for periods as long as 10^{9} years, but it will be significant for small irons and probably for all stones.

The modification of the shape of a meteorite during its passage through the atmosphere is probably the most important factor in determining its final form. The high temperature developed on the surface by the friction of the atmosphere results in the removal of large amounts of material by actual melting, and the mechanical stresses set up in the body of the meteorite lead to fragmentation. Ablation will tend to smooth the surface of an irregular meteorite (although locally pits and cavities may be developed), whereas fragmentation will tend to produce angular forms.

The effect of fragmentation is spectacularly shown on the Boguslavka iron, which fell in Siberia as two masses, of 199 kg and 57 kg respectively, about half a kilometer apart. As shown by Fig. 17, these two masses fit together perfectly along two cleavage surfaces at right angles to each other. Boguslavka is a hexahedrite, and consists of a single crystal of kamacite (alpha-iron), which has a good cubic cleavage. This meteorite presumably entered the atmosphere as a single body and split along the cleavage planes at a late stage in its

Fig. 17.   The Boguslavka iron, a hexahedrite which parted along cubic cleavage faces during its fall (courtesy Dr. E. L. Krinov).

passage, since practically no material has been lost by ablation since the breakup.

The hexahedrites are especially prone to show rectangular fracture surfaces, as a result of their crystal structure. The octahedrites tend to break along octahedral surfaces, but less readily than the hexahedrites. Stony meteorites, which consist of small grains of different minerals usually in random orientation, can be expected to break irregularly, but nevertheless they frequently show comparatively flat fracture surfaces which intersect to give polyhedral forms (Fig. 18).

The modification of the shape of a meteorite by ablation will be conditioned by the orientation of the meteorite during its passage through the atmosphere. If the meteorite maintains a constant orien-

Fig. 18. A collection of stones from the Forest City shower, illustrating various forms; the stone at the top left is hemispherical, and the fusion crust clearly shows the orientation of the stone during its fall (courtesy The American Museum of Natural History).

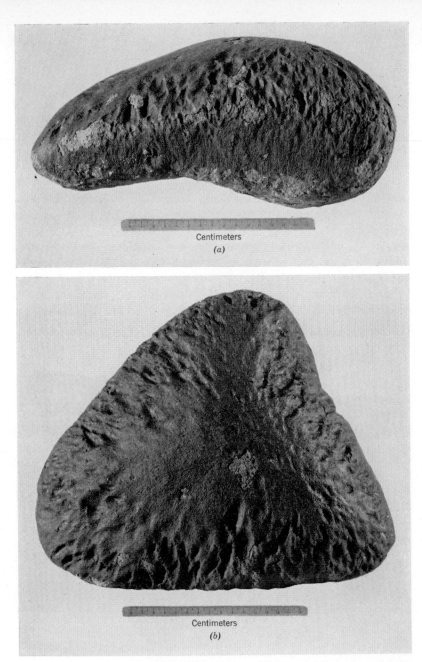

Centimeters
(a)

Centimeters
(b)

Fig. 19. Top (a) and side (b) views of the Miller, Arkansas, stone, showing the dome-shaped form and the ablation furrows around the periphery; the dimensions of the upper surface are 32 x 30 x 30 cm, the maximum thickness at right angles to this surface is 12 cm (courtesy The American Museum of Natural History).

tation, ablation will be concentrated on the corners, and the final form will be conical or dome-shaped—such meteorites are classed as oriented (Figs. 19, 20). The front surface during flight (sometimes called *brustseite* from the German term) is markedly different from the rear side (Fig. 21). Whether or not a meteorite will be oriented depends upon its shape when it enters the atmosphere. The stable position for a solid object moving through a gas is with a maximum surface exposed in the direction of flight. Thus a meteorite with a discoidal form will always travel face forward; a cone will travel with the point forward; a hemisphere will have its convex face forward. A spherical or roughly spherical body will have no clearly defined stable orientation; such a body will be slow to orient itself in flight, and may simply tumble through the atmosphere without any particular orientation until it strikes the ground.

Estimates of the intensity of ablation during passage through the atmosphere show that a meteorite suffers a great loss of mass by this

Fig. 20. The Long Island stone, showing the sharply conical form and the furrowed surface; the diameter of the base is about 70 cm (courtesy the Chicago Natural History Museum).

(a)

Fig. 21. Front (a) and rear (b) surfaces of the Cabin Creek iron (about one-quarter natural size), showing the difference in the size of the "thumbprints" on these two surfaces (courtesy E. P. Henderson).

process. Hence its form on landing is largely determined by the ablation, unless its shape has been modified by fracture at a late stage in its flight. In recent years estimates of ablation loss have been made from a consideration of the range of cosmic rays in meteorites and the distribution of He^3 produced by these rays. Martin (1953) estimated mass-losses by ablation of spherical meteorites as a function of their velocities and found that those with minimum velocities (about 11 km/sec) should lose about 54% of their pre-atmospheric mass by ablation, while those with velocities greater than about 30 km/sec should be virtually completely destroyed in the atmosphere. Fireman (1958) determined the distribution of He^3 in the Carbo iron (Fig. 22) and

(b)

concluded that 5 cm of metal must have covered the present surface where He^3 values are highest, and a much thicker layer where He^3 is lower. A similar study on the Grant iron (Fireman, 1959) indicated that about 45% of the extra-terrestrial mass of this meteorite must have been removed to account for its present shape. However, both these meteorites are finds and some of the material may have been removed by weathering. Lovering, Parry, and Jaeger (1960) have calculated mass-losses of two iron meteorites based on the rate of ablation calculated from the thermal gradients in their alteration rims. For a small meteorite (Wedderburn) they calculate a 60% loss of its pre-atmospheric mass, for a considerably larger meteorite (Tawallah Valley), a 27% mass-loss. From these figures it is clear that ablation must have a major role in the shaping of meteorites.

Impact normally has little effect on the shape of small and moderate-sized meteorites, which land with the velocity of free fall. Stones

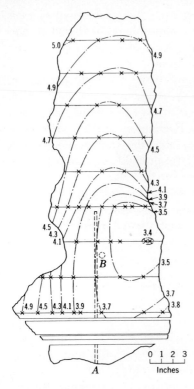

Fig. 22. Contours of constant He^3 content in the Carbo meteorite in units of 10^{-6} cm^3/g; the points measured are indicated by crosses (Fireman, 1958).

falling on hard ground may chip, or be broken into several fragments. Large meteorites which retain some of their cosmic velocity will literally explode on impact. It is conceivable that this explosion may be sufficiently powerful to vaporize and destroy the meteorite completely. However, around Meteor Crater in Arizona and the Henbury craters in Australia thousands of highly distorted fragments of meteoritic iron have been collected; the shapes of these fragments are evidently largely determined by the disintegration on impact.

The weathering of meteorites has been extensively discussed by Buddhue (1957). Weathering may modify the shape of meteorites either by smoothing out irregularities or by accentuating them, or in an inhomogeneous meteorite it may attack some phases much more readily than others and hence produce surface irregularities. A possible case in point is the Willamette meteorite (Figs. 13, 14). On one surface, evidently the rear surface as it traveled through the atmosphere, are large rounded cavities, some of them as much as a meter in largest dimension. It has been suggested that these cavities were present when the meteorite entered the atmosphere, or that they represent molds after troilite nodules that were melted out and removed by ablation during passage through the atmosphere, or that they were produced by weathering during the period that the meteorite lay on the ground. Since the deep cavities occur only on the rear face, which was the surface exposed to the weather, the last hypothesis may seem the most likely, and was accepted by Farrington (1915). However, Henderson and Perry (1958) point out that the shallow depressions on the conical surface of this meteorite are probably remnants of cavities similar in size and shape to those on the rear surface—ablation having removed a great deal of material from the sides but little from the rear surface. They conclude that the rear surface may have some topographic similarity to the surface that existed there before the meteorite entered the Earth's atmosphere.

Surface Features

The surface of many freshly fallen meteorites is comparatively smooth and featureless. Some meteorites, however, show furrows, shallow depressions, and sometimes deep cavities. The commonest surface irregularities are the shallow depressions resembling the imprints of fingers on soft clay, and hence known as thumbmarks (or as regmaglypts or piezoglypts). They are especially characteristic of iron meteorites (as, for example, the Cabin Creek meteorite, Fig. 21, which shows the way in which they are usually best developed on the front surface of the meteorite). These thumbprints are evidently developed by localized ablation during flight.

The deep cavities that sometimes occur on iron meteorites are not so readily explained. In some meteorites these cavities are bowl-shaped, but some cavities are two to four times as deep as they are wide, and resemble drill holes. These cavities have one almost universal characteristic: the width of the opening at the surface is less than the diameter measured down in the hole. The usual explanation of these cavities is that they formed by the burning-out of nodular inclusions of troilite and/or graphite during the passage of the meteorite through the atmosphere. However, Henderson and Perry (1958), who have carefully studied these cavities in the Goose Lake meteorite, believe that they existed before the meteorite entered the atmosphere, and suggest they may be primary features which persisted throughout the pre-terrestrial and terrestrial history of this meteorite.

Fusion Crust

A freshly fallen meteorite is covered with a fusion crust, except on fracture surfaces produced on or shortly before impact. The nature of the fusion crust varies somewhat, according to the composition of the meteorite. On most meteorites it is black, but on the enstatite achondrites it is colorless or pale yellow, because of the almost complete absence of iron in these meteorites. The fusion crust on iron meteorites is very thin, only a fraction of a millimeter, and consists of magnetite. The fusion crust on stone meteorites is thicker, and consists of a black glass which includes fragments of the less fusible minerals, such as olivine. On chondrites and the calcium-poor achondrites the crust is usually dull, but on the calcium-rich achondrites, which are more fusible than other stony meteorites, the crust is shiny and lustrous, and also thicker than on other types. Sometimes the crust shows a network of fine cracks, similar to the "crazing" which appears in the glaze of pottery. Krinov (1960) has made detailed studies of the nature of the fusion crust of meteorites, and presents the following classification:

Class I. Crust of Frontal Surfaces

Type 1. Close-textured. The crust is perfectly smooth, as though it had been pressed, with practically no indications of structure. Observed mainly upon iron meteorites and covers surfaces, which generally exhibit considerable marks of atmospheric action, regardless of whether the surface has regmaglyptic relief.

Type 2. Nodular. Upon a smooth, close-textured crust, fine angular nodules are visible scattered over the surface of the meteorite. Upon stony meteorites, on which this type of crust is mainly found, the nodules represent fused inclusions of nickeliferous iron.

Class II. Crust of Lateral Surfaces

Type 1. Striated. Upon a smooth, close-textured crust thin striae are visible that seem to be flowing across the surface of the meteorite.

Very often the striae are directed toward the rear part of a meteorite, thus clearly indicating the direction of its motion. Upon iron meteorites the striae quite often end in drops, which are sometimes of spherical form. There are also observed curves or even seemingly broken striae which abruptly change direction. Now and then an intricate pattern of the striated crust can be seen. In rarer cases several systems of striae are observed, superimposed one on top of the other and intersecting at various angles. In such cases the striae of the bottom system appear to be wide and flat, while those of the upper system are thin.

Particularly sharply defined striated crustal structure is observed near the sharp edges of lateral surfaces, adjacent to the rear surfaces of iron meteorites. Upon stony meteorites more or less distinct striae are usually observed along the edges of lateral surfaces. Striae are easily distinguishable on the rims between regmaglypts.

Type 2. Ribbed. Represents an intermediate type between the nodular and striated crust and is found only upon stony meteorites. The ribs appear like underdeveloped striae.

Type 3. Net. The crust is formed of short striae running together, lending it the appearance of a fine-mesh net. Individual cells of the mesh appear like stitches. Is observed mainly upon more friable stony meteorites, usually near the edges of lateral surfaces or near protuberances.

Type 4. Porous. At magnification of 15–30× tiny pores can be seen clearly upon the crust. Sometimes the crust appears to be sintered. This effect is observed upon iron as well as upon stony meteorites in the vicinity of the edges of the lateral surfaces, which make no sharp borders with the rear surfaces. It is also observed within various depressions on the surfaces.

Class III. Crust of Rear Surfaces

Type 1. Warty. This type of crust is particularly prevalent and sharply defined upon iron meteorites, and on large meteorites it is clearly visible with the naked eye. Under a magnifying glass, a close texture can be seen made up of individual warts, covering the surface of the meteorite. Each node represents a group of finer nodules which are partly fused together. Quite often among the nodes single globules can be seen of perfect spherical form.

Warty structure upon stony meteorites is as a rule considerably less distinct and is encountered only rarely. It is observed primarily within depressions or along the edges of rear surfaces.

Type 2. Scoriaceous. This type of crust is found primarily among the stony meteorites, for which it seems to be characteristic. Upon iron meteorites the scoriaceous crust is observed only on single portions and in the vicinity of sharp edges or near protuberances. The scoriaceous crust has the appearance of clinkered slag.

4

The Classification of Meteorites

MANY attempts have been made to achieve a workable and satisfactory classification of meteorites. Difficulties have arisen because of lack of agreement on the criteria for classification and how they should be applied. Criteria which have been used include chemical composition, mineralogical composition, internal structure, and color. The possible permutations and combinations of these criteria are many, and meteorite classifications have been simple or complex, depending upon the inclination of the classifier.

The simple differentiation of iron from stone meteorites was made already by Klaproth in 1807, and this fundamental distinction has been observed by all later classifiers, although with variations. Maskelyne in 1863 introduced the group of stony-irons for those meteorites with approximately equal amounts of nickel-iron and silicate minerals, and this group has been retained in most later classifications. In the latter half of last century two different classifications were developed in Europe, one by Meunier in France and the other by Rose in Germany. Meunier's classification was based on the principle of adopting certain meteorites as types; in its final form (1909) Meunier's classification comprised 67 types. This classification never achieved wide acceptance, and is essentially moribund today, although some of Meunier's type names still appear in the literature. Rose's classification was based mainly on mineralogical composition and structure. It was enlarged and modified by Tschermak and Brezina, so that it is now generally known as the Rose-Tschermak-Brezina system. The classification in its final form, as given by Brezina in 1904, is as follows:

Stones—Silicates Prevailing

A. Achondrites.—Stones poor in nickel-iron, essentially without round chondrules.
1. *Chladnite*, Chl. Chiefly bronzite.
2. *Veined Chladnite*, Chla. Bronzite with black or metallic veins.
3. *Angrite*, A. Chiefly augite.
4. *Chassignite*, Cha. Chiefly olivine.
5. *Bustite*, Bu. Bronzite with augite.
6. *Amphoterite*, Am. Bronzite with olivine.
7. *Rodite*, Ro. Bronzite with olivine, breccia-like.
8. *Eukrite*, Eu. Augite with anorthite.
9. *Shergottite*, She. Augite with maskelynite.
10. *Howardite*, Ho. Bronzite, olivine, augite and anorthite.
11. *Breccia-like Howardite*, Hob. Bronzite, olivine, augite and anorthite, breccia-like.
12. *Leucituranolite*,* L. Leucite, anorthite, augite and glass.

B. Chondrites.—Bronzite, olivine and nickel-iron, with round or round and polyhedric chondrules.
13. *Howarditic Chondrite*, Cho. Polyhedric secretions prevailing, round chondrules scarce. Crust partly bright.
14. *Veined Howarditic Chondrite*, Choa. Polyhedric secretions prevailing, round chondrules scarce. Black or metallic veins.
15. *White Chondrite*, Cw. White, rather friable mass with scarce, mostly white chondrules.
16. *Veined White Chondrite*, Cwa. White, rather friable mass with scarce, mostly white chondrules; black or metallic veins.
17. *Breccia-like White Chondrite*, Cwb. White, rather friable mass with scarce, mostly white chondrules; breccia-like.
18. *Intermediate Chondrite*, Ci. Firm, polishable mass with white and gray chondrules breaking with matrix.
19. *Veined Intermediate Chondrite*, Cia. Firm, polishable mass with white and gray chondrules breaking with the matrix; black or metallic veins.
20. *Breccia-like Intermediate Chondrite*, Cib. Firm, polishable mass, white and gray chondrules breaking with matrix; breccia-like.
21. *Gray Chondrite*, Cg. Firm, gray mass, chondrules of various kinds breaking with matrix.
22. *Veined Gray Chondrite*, Cga. Firm, gray mass, chondrules of various kinds breaking with matrix; black or metallic veins.
23. *Breccia-like Gray Chondrite*, Cgb. Firm, gray mass, chondrules of various kinds breaking with matrix; breccia-like.

---

* The single stone on which this class was based has since been discredited as a meteorite.

24. *Orvinite*, Co.   Black infiltrated mass, fluidal texture; surface uneven, crust interrupted.
25. *Tadjerite*, Ct.   Black, half-glassy, crust-like mass without crust on surface.
26. *Black Chondrite*, Cs.   Dark or black mass, chondrules of various kinds breaking with matrix.
27. *Veined Black Chondrite*, Csa.   Dark or black mass, chondrules of various kinds breaking with matrix; black or metallic veins.
28. *Ureilite*, U.   Black mass, chondritic or granular; iron in veins or incoherent.
29. *Coaly Chondrite*, K.   Dull black, friable chondrite with free carbon, low specific gravity, metallic iron nearly or wholly wanting.
30. *Globular Coaly Chondrite*, Kc.   Dull gray or black, friable mass with free carbon; chondrules not breaking with matrix; metallic nickel-iron.
31. *Veined Globular Coaly Chondrite*, Kca.   Dull black firm mass with free carbon; chondrules not breaking with matrix; metallic veins.
32. *Globular Chondrite*, Cc.   Friable mass with hard (radiated) chondrules not breaking with matrix.
33. *Veined Globular Chondrite*, Cca.   Friable mass with hard (radiated) chondrules not breaking with matrix; black or metallic veins.
34. *Breccia-like Globular Chondrite*, Ccb.   Friable, breccia-like mass with hard (radiated) chondrules not breaking with matrix.
35. *Ornansite*, Cco.   Friable mass of chondrules.
36. *Ngawite*, Ccn.   Friable breccia-like mass of chondrules.
37. *Crystalline Globular Chondrite*, Cck.   Hardly friable, crystalline mass with hard (radiated) chondrules, partly breaking with matrix, partly not.
38. *Veined Crystalline Globular Chondite*, Ccka.   Hardly friable, crystalline, veined mass with hard (radiated) chondrules partly breaking with matrix, partly not.
39. *Breccia-like Crystalline Globular Chondrite*, Cckb.   Hardly friable, crystalline, breccia-like mass with hard (radiated) chondrules partly breaking with matrix, partly not.
40. *Crystalline Chondrite*, Ck.   Hard crystalline mass with hard (radiated) chondrules breaking with matrix.
41. *Veined Crystalline Chondrite*, Cka.   Hard crystalline veined mass with hard (radiated) chondrules breaking with matrix.
42. *Breccia-like Crystalline Chondrite*, Ckb.   Hard, crystalline breccia-like mass with hard (radiated) chondrules breaking with matrix.

C. Enstatite-Anorthite-Chondrite.—Enstatite, anorthite and nickel-iron with round chondrules.

43. *Crystalline Enstatite-Anorthite Chondrite*, Cek.   Hard, crystalline mass with hard (radiated) chondrules.

D. Siderolite.—Transitions of stones to irons.   Nickel-iron in the mass cohering, on sections separated.

44. *Mesosiderite*, M.   Crystalline olivine and bronzite.
45. *Grahamite*, Mg.   Crystalline olivine, bronzite and plagioclase.
46. *Lodranite*, Lo.   Granular-crystalline olivine and bronzite.

Iron-Meteorites—Metallic Constituents Prevailing or Alone

E. Lithosiderite.—Transition from stones to irons; nickel-iron cohering in mass and on sections.

    47. *Siderophyre*, Si. Grains of bronzite with accessory asmanite in the trias (trias is an obsolete term for nickel-iron in the forms kamacite, taenite, and plessite).

    48. *Pallasite-Krasnojarsk group*, Pk. Rounded crystals of olivine in the trias.

    49. *Pallasite-Rokicky group*, Pr. Polyhedral crystals of olivine partly broken, and fragments separated by nickel-iron.

    50. *Pallasite-Imilac group*, Pi. Olivine crystals cracked and squeezed.

    51. *Pallasite-Albach group*, Pa. Olivine crystals in fine brecciated trias.

F. Octahedrite.—Kamacite, taenite and plessite (trias), in lamellae and concamerations of the four octahedron faces.

    52. *Finest Octahedrite*, Off. Lamellae up to 0.2 mm. thickness. Fields prevailing on lamellae.

    53. *Fine Octahedrite Victoria group*, Ofv. Lamellae of troilite and schreibersite in fine trias.

    54. *Fine Octahedrite*, Of. Thickness of lamellae 0.2–0.4 mm.

    55. *Mollified Fine Octahedrite*, Ofe. Figures fallen in disorder by mollifying; points instead of troilite lamellae.

    56. *Medium Octahedrite*, Om. Thickness of lamellae 0.5–1 mm.

    57. *Mollified Medium Octahedrite*, Ome. Figures fallen in disorder by mollifying; points instead of taenite lamellae.

    58. *Coarse Octahedrites*, Og. Thickness of lamellae 1.5–2.0 mm.

    59. *Mollified Coarse Octahedrite*, Oge. Figures fallen in disorder by mollifying; points instead of taenite lamellae.

    60. *Coarsest Octahedrite*, Ogg. Thickness of lamellae 2.5 mm. and more.

    61. *Breccia-like Octahedrite, Netschajevo group*, Obn. Medium octahedrite with nuggets of silicate.

    62. *Breccia-like Octahedrite, Kodaikanal group*, Obk. Fine octahedrite brecciated with nuggets of silicate.

    63. *Breccia-like Octahedrite, Copiapo group*, Obc. Coarsest octahedrite brecciated with silicate-nuggets.

    64. *Breccia-like Octahedrite, Zacatecas group*, Obz. Octahedral nuggets, breccia-like with globes of troilite.

    65. *Breccia-like Octahedrite, Ngoureyma group*, Obzg. Molten and tracted iron of the Zacatecas group.

G. Hexahedrite.—Structure and cleavage hexahedral.

    66. *Normal Hexahedrite*, H. Neumann-lines ungrained.

    67. *Grained Hexahedrite*, Ha. Structure and cleavage running through the whole mass consisting of grains with differently orientated sparkling.

    68. *Brecciated Hexahedrite*, Hb. Mass consisting of differently orientated hexahedral grains.

H. Ataxite.—Structure interrupted.

    69. *Cape group*, Dc. Rich in nickel; sharp (hexahedral?) etching bands in dull mass.

70. *Shingle Springs group,* Dsh. Rich in nickel; not sharp parallel spots.
71. *Babbsmill group,* Db. Rich in nickel; lusterless, homogeneous mass.
72. *Linnville group,* Dl. Rich in nickel; meandering-veined or latticed.
73. *Nedagolla group,* Dn. Poor in nickel, grained, no ridges.
74. *Siratic group,* Ds. Poor in nickel; ridges, incisions or enveloped rhabdites.
75. *Primitiva group,* Dp. Poor in nickel; silky streaks and luster.
76. *Muchachos group,* Dm. Poor in nickel, grained, porphyritic with forsterite.

The Rose-Tschermak-Brezina classification has been widely adopted by workers on meteorites, and the names and symbols for the individual groups are commonly used in the literature. However, the classification is unsatisfactory in several respects, especially in its subdivision of the large group of chondrites, for which color and the presence or absence of veins are used to distinguish many of the classes. These characters are of little fundamental importance, and the multiplicity of classes has tended to obscure the essential similarity of many of the chondritic meteorites. In addition, the identification of the minerals is frequently imprecise or erroneous. Brezina applied the name bronzite to any orthorhombic pyroxene, whereas in terms of the conventional subdivision of the orthopyroxene series either enstatite, bronzite, or hypersthene may be present in a specific meteorite. Other investigators have called any orthorhombic pyroxene enstatite. What Brezina calls augite is usually pigeonite, true augite being present in only one meteorite, Angra dos Reis.

These defects in the Rose-Tschermak-Brezina classification were pointed out by Prior, and in 1920 he proposed a revised and simplified version. Prior's classification, with minor modifications suggested by more recent investigations, is as follows:

Chondrites, divided according to their mineralogy (which reflects increasing content of oxidized iron and decreasing free iron) into:
  (*a*) Enstatite chondrites
  (*b*) Olivine-bronzite chondrites
  (*c*) Olivine-hypersthene chondrites
  (*d*) Olivine-pigeonite chondrites
  (*e*) Carbonaceous chondrites
Achondrites, divided into (*a*) calcium-poor achondrites and (*b*) calcium-rich achondrites.
  (*a*) Calcium-poor achondrites, subdivided into:
    1. Enstatite achondrites, or aubrites
    2. Hypersthene achondrites, or diogenites
    3. Olivine achondrites, or chassignites
    4. Olivine-pigeonite achondrites, or ureilites

[Prior distinguished a group of hypersthene-olivine achondrites, the rodites and amphoterites; however, the rodites are not essentially different from the diogenites, and the amphoterites contain chondrules and are included with the chondrites.]

  (b) Calcium-rich achondrites, subdivided into:
   1. Augite achondrites, or angrites
   2. Diopside-olivine achondrites, or nakhlites
   3. Pyroxene-plagioclase achondrites, comprising the eucrites, in which the pyroxene is largely pigeonite, and the howardites, in which it is largely hypersthene; shergottites are eucrites in which the plagioclase is replaced by maskelynite

Stony-Irons, divided according to the nature of the silicate minerals into:
  (a) Olivine stony-irons, or pallasites
  (b) Bronzite-tridymite stony-irons, or siderophyres
  (c) Bronzite-olivine stony-irons, or lodranites
  (d) Pyroxene-plagioclase stony-irons, or mesosiderites

Irons, divided according to structure, which is related to nickel content, into:
  (a) Hexahedrites,* with nickel 4–6%
  (b) Octahedrites, with nickel 6–14%; according to the width of the kamacite bands and generally to increasing percentages of nickel, may be divided into coarsest, coarse, medium, fine, and finest octahedrites
  (c) Nickel-rich ataxites, with nickel generally greater than 12%

Prior's classification is primarily based on mineralogical composition, but, as might be expected, shows a close correlation with chemical composition also.

Some alternative classifications have been proposed, of which those of Leonard (1956) and Yavnel (1958) will be briefly described. Leonard (1956) adopted the major groupings of Prior's classification, but divided these groups into some thirty subclasses, based essentially on the detailed mineralogical composition. In the construction of the thirty subclasses he distinguishes ten varieties of pyroxene, and six of plagioclase, but makes no subdivision of olivine. The principle behind his classification is a valid one, but the classification is unsuccessful and unsatisfactory. The principal reasons for this are: firstly, that for many meteorites the mineralogy is poorly known, so they cannot be pigeonholed in Leonard's classification; and secondly, his classification utilizes arbitrary divisions of the pyroxene and plagioclase minerals, but fails to utilize the equally significant compositional

---

* A group of nickel-poor ataxites, similar in composition to the hexahedrites, is sometimes distinguished, but Perry (1944) has shown that there is no definite demarcation between them, and the nickel-poor ataxites are here included with the hexahedrites.

differences in olivine, as important and widespread a mineral as pyroxene in meteorites.

Yavnel (1958) has discussed the principles of classification of meteorites, and has summarized the different classifications that have been used. He has proposed a classification according to chemical composition, which uses the subdivisions established by Prior, with some modifications. The principal modification is the recognition of five different groups for each of six subclasses (calcium-rich achondrites, calcium-poor achondrites, chondrites, mesosiderites, pallasites, and irons). He postulates that each of these groups was derived from a separate parent body, and to that extent his classification involves a theory of genesis. Since such a theory is speculative, the basis of classification is speculative also.

Of all the classifications proposed for meteorites, that developed by Prior is both most logical and most workable, and is used in this book. It is presented in summary form in Table 4.

TABLE 4. CLASSIFICATION OF THE METEORITES (FIGURES IN PARENTHESES ARE THE NUMBERS IN EACH CLASS)

Group	Class	Principal Minerals
Chondrites	Enstatite (11)	Enstatite, nickel-iron
	Olivine-bronzite ⎫ (~900)	Olivine, bronzite, nickel-iron
	Olivine-hypersthene ⎭	Olivine, hypersthene, nickel-iron
	Olivine-pigeonite (12)	Olivine, pigeonite
	Carbonaceous (17)	Serpentine
Achondrites	Aubrites (9)	Enstatite
	Diogenites (8)	Hypersthene
	Chassignite (1)	Olivine
	Ureilites (3)	Olivine, pigeonite, nickel-iron
	Angrite (1)	Augite
	Nakhlites (2)	Diopside, olivine
	Eucrites and howardites (39)	Pyroxene, plagioclase
Stony-irons	Pallasites (40)	Olivine, nickel-iron
	Siderophyre (1)	Orthopyroxene, nickel-iron
	Lodranite (1)	Orthopyroxene, olivine, nickel-iron
	Mesosiderites (22)	Pyroxene, plagioclase, nickel-iron
Irons	Hexahedrites (55)	Kamacite
	Octahedrites (487)	Kamacite, taenite
	Ni-rich ataxites (36)	Taenite

5

The Minerals of Meteorites

BEFORE proceeding to the detailed description and discussion of the individual groups of meteorites, a description of the minerals which have been recorded from meteorites will be given here. The minerals known from meteorites at this time are listed in Table 5. A series of brief commentaries on these minerals, arranged alphabetically, follows:

Alabandite: This mineral was found in meteorites for the first time by Dawson, Maxwell, and Parsons (1960), in Abee, an enstatite chondrite. It was identified in a single chondrule by its X-ray diffraction pattern, and optically as round gray inclusions in kamacite-taenite areas. However, no chemical analysis was made, and the identity of this mineral with MnS is by no means certain. In view of the extensive miscibility of the sulfides of the bivalent metals, it may be a solid solution of magnesium, manganese, and iron sulfide.

Apatite: The phosphate minerals of meteorites are apatite, merrillite, and in one meteorite the recently described farringtonite. The phosphorus content of meteorites is uniformly low, so these minerals are only present in accessory amounts. In appearance and optical properties merrillite and apatite are very similar, and they are almost impossible to distinguish except by tedious and time-consuming techniques. If the phosphate shown by analyses of stony meteorites is all combined as apatite, then the average P_2O_5 content (0.21%) indicates that they contain about 0.6% apatite; this is, however, an overestimate, since the phosphorus may also be present as merrillite and

TABLE 5. THE MINERALS OF METEORITES
(AN ASTERISK INDICATES THOSE NOT
KNOWN TO OCCUR IN TERRESTRIAL ROCKS)

Mineral	Symbol
Nickel-iron	(Fe,Ni)
Copper	Cu
Gold	Au
Diamond	C
Graphite	C
Sulfur	S
Moissanite	SiC
Cohenite	Fe_3C
*Schreibersite	$(Fe,Ni)_3P$
*Osbornite	TiN
Troilite	FeS
*Oldhamite	CaS
Alabandite	MnS
Pentlandite	$(Fe,Ni)_9S_8$
*Daubreelite	$FeCr_2S_4$
Chalcopyrrhotite	(Cu,Fe)S
Valleriite	$Cu_3Fe_4S_7(?)$
Chalcopyrite	$CuFeS_2$
Pyrite	FeS_2
Sphalerite	ZnS
*Lawrencite	$FeCl_2$
Magnesite	$MgCO_3$
Calcite	$CaCO_3$
Dolomite	$CaMg(CO_3)_2$
Ilmenite	$FeTiO_3$
Magnetite	Fe_3O_4
Chromite	$FeCr_2O_4$
Spinel	$MgAl_2O_4$
Quartz	SiO_2
Tridymite	SiO_2
Cristobalite	SiO_2
Apatite	$Ca_5(PO_4)_3Cl$
*Merrillite	$Na_2Ca_3(PO_4)_2O(?)$
*Farringtonite	$Mg_3(PO_4)_2$
Gypsum	$CaSO_4 \cdot 2H_2O$
Epsomite	$MgSO_4 \cdot 7H_2O$
Bloedite	$Na_2Mg(SO_4)_2 \cdot 4H_2O$
Olivine	$(Mg,Fe)_2SiO_4$
Orthopyroxene	$(Mg,Fe)SiO_3$
Clinopyroxene	$(Ca,Mg,Fe)SiO_3$
Plagioclase	$(Na,Ca)(Al,Si)_4O_8$
Serpentine	$Mg_6Si_4O_{10}(OH)_8$

schreibersite. Shannon and Larsen (1925) have analyzed the apatite from the New Concord chondrite and have shown that it is a chlorapatite; this is presumably true for other meteorite apatites also.

Bloedite: DuFresne and Anders (1962) found a single grain of this mineral in the Ivuna carbonaceous chondrite.

Calcite: This mineral has been recorded only once in meteorites, in the Boriskino carbonaceous chondrite by Kvasha (1948).

Chalcopyrite: Ramdohr (1962) has recorded chalcopyrite as a trace constituent in Karoonda, an olivine-pigeonite chondrite, and in the troilite nodules of some irons.

Chalcopyrrhotite: This mineral, an isometric high-temperature solid solution with the formula $(Cu,Fe)S$, is not uncommon as an accessory constituent in chondrites (Ramdohr, 1962). It is similar in appearance to troilite, and on this account is easily overlooked. Chalcopyrrhotite is possibly a high-temperature polymorph of cubanite, $CuFe_2S_3$.

Chromite: The small amount of Cr_2O_3 (average 0.36%) in stony meteorites is normally present largely as chromite, except in the enstatite chondrites, where the chromium is present as daubreelite. Chromite has also been recorded in some irons and stony-irons (Admire, Coahuila, Marjalahti, Sikhote-Alin). Some analyses of meteoritic chromite show a considerable amount of Al_2O_3 (up to 28%) and MgO (up to 21%).

Clinopyroxene: Clinopyroxene of various kinds has been described from meteorites. The pyroxenic achondrites (aubrites and diogenites) show patches of polysynthetically twinned clinoenstatite or clinohypersthene within the large fragments of orthorhombic pyroxene; the general features suggest that the clinopyroxene has resulted from the mechanical deformation of the orthopyroxene [a mode of formation demonstrated experimentally by Turner, Heard, and Griggs (1960)].

Monoclinic pyroxenes have been described from the calcium-rich achondrites, and from some chondrites and mesosiderites. Such pyroxenes have usually been referred to as augite; however, the few analyses that are available show that the pyroxene is low in CaO, has little Al_2O_3, and is actually a pigeonite. True augite is known from only one meteorite, the achondrite Angra dos Reis. Diopside which is practically iron-free has been recorded from the Bustee and Pena Blanca Spring meteorites (enstatite achondrites); a monoclinic pyroxene intermediate in composition between diopside and hedenbergite makes up a large part of the Nakhla and Lafayette meteorites. Pyroxene near diopside in composition occurs in accessory amounts

in many chondrites, generally intergrown with or mantling orthopyroxene grains.

The clinopyroxenes from meteorites have been extensively described
by Wahl (1907).

Cohenite: This mineral has been recorded as an accessory constituent in the following iron meteorites: Bendego, Canyon Diablo,
Cosby's Creek, Cranbourne, Magura, Pittsburg, Wichita County, and
Youngedin. These are all coarse octahedrites with a nickel content
of not more than 7%; cohenite has apparently not been found in the
higher nickel (medium and fine) octahedrites, nor in the nickel-rich
ataxites. Cohenite evidently forms only when the nickel concentration relative to free iron is low. It has been recorded in Abee (Dawson, Maxwell, and Parsons, 1960) and in other enstatite chondrites
(Ramdohr, 1962), but it has otherwise not been found in the
stony-irons or the stones. However, Perry (1944), who has given a
careful description of the occurrence of cohenite, points out that it is
very difficult to distinguish from schreibersite and it may therefore
be more common than the few records suggest. Henderson (pers.
comm.) states that it occurs in Coolac, Lexington, Mooranoppin,
Mount Ayliff, Mount Stirling, Odessa, Rosario, St. Francois County,
Seligman, Smithville, Yenberrie (coarse octahedrites), and Navajo
(nickel-poor ataxite).

Ringwood (1960*b*) has pointed out that the free energy of cohenite
is such that it is unstable relative to carbon-saturated iron and graphite
at zero pressure at all temperatures below 1153° C. It is a stable
phase at high pressures. From the thermodynamic data Ringwood
concludes that all meteorites containing cohenite must have cooled
under pressures exceeding 25,000 atmospheres. However, since the
thermodynamic data are for the iron-carbon system, caution is indicated in applying these data to meteorites, in which appreciable
amounts of other elements, especially nickel, are present.

Copper: Until recently native copper has been recorded from comparatively few meteorites, mostly chondrites. However, Ramdohr
(1962) has shown that it is present in many meteorites, both stones
and irons, usually as minute grains included in nickel-iron which is
associated with troilite. Since the copper content of meteorites is
low (about 0.01%) the amount of copper present is always very small.

Nininger (1943) has reported the finding, at Eaton, Colorado, of a
meteorite consisting entirely of a copper alloy. The identification of
this specimen as a meteorite has, however, been questioned, and
further investigation is required before this report is acceptable.

However, Paneth (1951) has drawn attention to a seventeenth century report on the fall of copper meteorites.

Cristobalite: This mineral has been identified in the Abee meteorite, an enstatite chondrite, by Dawson, Maxwell, and Parsons (1960). It occurred in association with quartz, and was identified by its X-ray powder pattern, although it was not detected by optical means. It was the alpha or low-temperature form of this mineral. Cohen (1900) described an accessory mineral from the Kendall County iron which he tentatively identified as cristobalite.

Daubreelite: This mineral was discovered by J. Lawrence Smith (1876) in the Coahuila meteorite, and has since been observed in many irons. Perry (1944) remarks that it is commonest in hexahedrites, much less common in other irons, and that it is usually associated with troilite, adjoining or bordering it, or intergrown with it on the (0001) plane. Unlike troilite, daubreelite is said not to be attacked by hydrochloric acid, though dissolved by nitric acid.

Ramdohr (1962) has recorded daubreelite in the enstatite chondrites, which are in a highly reduced state. In other stony meteorites, however, the chromium is present in the oxidized form as chromite.

The conditions for the formation of daubreelite in iron meteorites have been elucidated by Vogel and Herman (1950), using their data on the phase relations in the Fe-Cr-S system.

Diamond: Diamonds were first observed in meteorites by Jerofejeff and Latschinoff (1888), in the Novo Urei achondrite; this occurrence has recently been confirmed by Ringwood (1960a). Sandberger (1889) reported that he had observed a small black diamond in the Carcote chondrite. Weinschenk (1889) found diamonds in the Magura iron. Foote (1891) reported diamonds in the Canyon Diablo iron, and this observation was confirmed by X-ray diffraction by Ksanda and Henderson (1939) and subsequently by other investigators. Urey, Mele, and Mayeda (1957) searched for diamonds in Cape Giradeau, Cold Bokkeveld, Forest City, Holbrook, Indarch, Richardton, Warrenton (all chondrites), and in Goalpara (an achondrite similar to Novo Urei); diamonds were found in Goalpara only. Sarma and Mayeda (1961) examined seventeen meteorites, mainly chondrites, and found no diamond, except possibly in Taiban, a black chondrite. Cubical aggregates of graphite, known as cliftonite, have been recorded from the Magura, Youngedin, Cosby's Creek, Smithville, and Toluca irons; these may be paramorphs after diamond.

The occurrence of diamonds in meteorites has been generally interpreted as indicating crystallization under high gravitational pressures in a meteorite parent body. However, Lipschutz and Anders (1961) have demonstrated that the diamonds in the Canyon Diablo meteorite could have formed upon impact with the Earth, and suggest that all meteoritic diamonds were produced by catastrophic events, either impact with the Earth or during the breakup of the meteorite parent bodies.

Dolomite: DuFresne and Anders (1962) report the occurrence of dolomite as an accessory mineral in the carbonaceous chondrites Orgueil and Ivuna.

Epsomite: Berzelius in 1834 observed that the Alais meteorite, a carbonaceous chondrite, contained some 10% of water-soluble salts, principally magnesium sulfate. Water-soluble salts have been noted in other carbonaceous chondrites. Some authorities have claimed that these salts are not original constituents, but have been formed after the meteorites reached the Earth by the action of atmospheric moisture on sulfur compounds. However, Daubree (1864) showed that the water-soluble material in Orgueil was an original constituent of this meteorite. Every specimen of Orgueil shows a white salt throughout the friable mass of the meteorites; the salt is hydrated magnesium sulfate, $MgSO_4 \cdot 7H_2O$, according to DuFresne and Anders (1961). However, the state of hydration will vary with the humidity, and the state of hydration when the meteorite was in outer space is unknown.

Farringtonite: This is a new mineral, anhydrous magnesium phosphate, which has been described from the Springwater pallasite by DuFresne and Roy (1961). It occurs in small amounts in this meteorite, peripheral to the olivine grains.

Gold: Two small (diameter 0.2 mm) grains of gold were observed in the Wedderburn iron (Edwards, 1953). In view of the very low average gold content of iron meteorites (about 1 ppm) the occurrence of free gold is surprising; nevertheless, Edwards' description seems to exclude the possibility that the gold was accidently introduced. The occurrence of free gold in meteorites has been confirmed by Ramdohr (1962), who has identified it in Atlanta, an enstatite chondrite.

Graphite: This is a common accessory mineral in iron meteorites. It may occur as plates or grains, but is frequently in the form of nodules, which may reach considerable size (Fig. 23)—one nodule in Cosby's Creek was as large as a small pear and weighed 92 grams. The graphite is frequently intimately associated with troilite. Graphite has been recognized by X-ray powder photographs in the achondrites Goalpara (Urey, Mele, and Mayeda, 1957) and Novo Urei

Fig. 23.   Graphite nodule (8 cm across) in the Canyon Diablo iron (courtesy The American Museum of Natural History).

(Ringwood, 1960a).   It is an accessory mineral in some of the enstatite chondrites.

The peculiar group of carbonaceous chondrites contain free carbon in amounts up to 5%.   This carbon has been identified as graphite. However, it is amorphous to X-rays and appears to be a non-crystalline "soot," perhaps a complex organic compound of high molecular weight.   Much of the free carbon in iron and stony-iron meteorites lacks the characteristic properties of graphite and may also be amorphous.

Gypsum: A large euhedral single crystal of gypsum was found in the Mighei carbonaceous chondrite by DuFresne and Anders (1962). They comment that it may be due to contamination; however, gypsum crystallizes from water extracts of the Orgueil carbonaceous chondrite, and it thus seems probable that this mineral is present in at least some of the carbonaceous chondrites.

Ilmenite: This mineral has seldom been recorded from meteorites. However, Ramdohr (1962) has shown that it is common in accessory amounts in chondrites and achondrites. The titanium content in stony meteorites is generally low (average TiO_2 in 94 chondrites is 0.11%), and some of this may be present in silicate minerals, so the amount of ilmenite will always be small.

Lawrencite: The exudation of drops of ferrous chloride solution from freshly cut or broken surfaces of iron meteorites was early noted, but it was not until 1855 that J. Lawrence Smith found the mineral as a soft solid of green-brown color in the Tazewell iron. The solid mineral has also been reported in the Laurens County and Smith's Mountain irons. Henderson (pers. comm.) has observed it in several pallasites and in the Odessa and Sardis irons. Little description of the appearance of the mineral has been given; it is simply stated that it occurred in crevices and became soft on exposure. Ferrous chloride is deliquescent and decomposes in air to give ferric hydroxide (limonite) and hydrochloric acid, which immediately attacks the meteoritic iron, causing "sweating" and rapid disintegration. Some irons, such as Cranbourne, are particularly subject to this disintegration; the specimen of Cranbourne in the British Museum is kept in a closed glass case in an atmosphere of dry nitrogen. Small amounts of lawrencite are probably present in many stone meteorites, since on cutting or breaking they frequently become rust-brown or freckled with rust-colored spots.

Magnesite: Pisani (1864) identified the ferroan variety of magnesite, known as breunnerite, as a minor constituent of the Orgueil meteorite, a carbonaceous chondrite. It occurred in small amounts in minute rhombohedral crystals. Recently the writer extracted a few grains of this mineral from the Orgueil meteorite by means of heavy liquids; it gave the X-ray powder pattern of magnesite, and an omega refractive index of 1.74, indicating a content of about 20 mole per cent of the $FeCO_3$ component.

This mineral has been identified in Boriskino, another carbonaceous chondrite, by Kvasha (1948).

Magnetite: This mineral is an important constituent in many of the carbonaceous chondrites. X-ray powder photographs of the Type I carbonaceous chondrites of Wiik (1956)—Alais, Ivuna, Orgueil, and Tonk—show lines of magnetite only. Magnetite is also present in the olivine-pigeonite chondrites and has been recorded in the calcium-rich achondrites Shergotty and Padvarninkai. In chondrites it is recorded as a constituent of the glassy crust formed during the passage of the meteorite through the atmosphere. Magnetite also forms as a secondary mineral in some meteorites by the oxidation of nickel-iron after the meteorite has fallen.

Recent investigations in this institution have shown that the magnetite phase in the Type I carbonaceous chondrites has a cell edge of about 8.42 A, considerably higher than that of pure Fe_3O_4 and approximately that of $NiFe_2O_4$ (trevorite); it is probable that the nickel in these meteorites is present in this form.

Merrillite: In 1883 Tschermak described the occurrence in the groundmass of chondritic meteorites of a colorless accessory mineral, as optically biaxial grains with weak double refraction; he was unable to identify it but suggested that it might be monticellite. Merrill (1915) showed that this monticellite-like mineral was a phosphate. Wherry (1917) applied the name merrillite to it, but it was first separated and chemically analyzed by Shannon and Larsen (1925). They gave it the formula $NaCa_3(PO_4)_2O$, but the analysis was made on a very small amount of material; no X-ray investigations of the mineral have been reported.

Moissanite: This mineral, naturally occurring carborundum, was found by Moissan (1904) in the residue left after dissolving a 53 kg piece of the Canyon Diablo iron in hydrochloric acid, and treating this residue with hydrofluoric acid and boiling sulfuric acid. The mineral occurred as small hexagonal crystals varying in color from pale green to emerald green; it was unattacked by acid but gave potassium silicate on fusion with KOH and CO_2 on fusion with $PbCrO_4$. In physical and chemical properties the mineral agreed with the previously known and artificially produced carborundum. Merrill (1930) comments, "The fact that meteoric irons are commonly sawn by crushed carborundum raises a doubt as to the actual meteoric source of this material." The writer recently dissolved 1 kg of Canyon Diablo in hydrochloric acid and found no moissanite in the residue. The occurrence of this material as a meteoritic mineral is doubtful and needs confirmation.

Nickel-iron: This is an almost omnipresent constituent of meteorites. The siderites consist almost entirely of nickel-iron; it is a major constituent of the stony-irons; the chondrites average about 13% of metal, the content ranging from less than 1% to 25%. Only the carbonaceous chondrites and some of the achondrites and the olivine-pigeonite chondrites have no free metal or only trace amounts.

The nickel-iron occurs as two distinct minerals, kamacite and taenite. Kamacite, the alpha-iron of the metallurgist, is a nickel-iron alloy with a fairly constant composition of 5.5% Ni; it crystallizes in a body-centered cubic lattice. Taenite, the gamma-iron of the metallurgist, is a nickel-iron alloy of variable composition, ranging from about 27 to about 65% Ni in different meteorites; it crystallizes in a face-centered cubic lattice. Eutectoid intergrowths of kamacite and taenite, known as plessite, are a common constituent in most octahedrites and many chondrites. A thorough account of meteoritic nickel-iron is given by Perry (1944).

Oldhamite: This mineral was described by Maskelyne (1870) in the Bustee meteorite, an enstatite achondrite. It occurred as chestnut-brown rounded spherules up to 6 mm in diameter. It is readily attacked by water with the formation of gypsum. Oldhamite is limited to meteorites which have been subjected to a high degree of reduction. It is probably present in accessory amounts in most, if not all, enstatite chondrites and enstatite achondrites.

Olivine: This mineral is an essential component in most groups of meteorites except the irons: the pallasites are composed of nickel-iron and olivine; it is a major constituent in all the chondrites, except the enstatite chondrites and some of the carbonaceous chondrites; and it is present in some achondrites. In composition it is usually a magnesium-rich variety with between 15 and 30 mole per cent of the Fe_2SiO_4 component; pure forsterite (Mg_2SiO_4) has been recorded from the Shallowater and Pena Blanca Spring meteorites, both enstatite achondrites, and in Pine River and Tucson (irons); a forsterite with 6 mole per cent Fe_2SiO_4 has been recorded in accessory amounts in the Canyon Diablo iron. The only occurrence of an iron-rich olivine in a meteorite is in the Nakhla achondrite; this olivine contains 65 mole per cent of the Fe_2SiO_4 component, according to the analysis of Prior (1912).

Orthopyroxene: This mineral, next to olivine, is the commonest silicate in meteorites. It is a major constituent of most chondrites, and is an important mineral in the mesosiderites and many achondrites. The orthopyroxene is usually distinguished as enstatite, bronzite, or hypersthene according to its iron content; with less than 10 mole per cent of the $FeSiO_3$ component it is enstatite, with 10–20% bronzite, and with more than 20% hypersthene. The sequence is not continuous in meteorite orthopyroxene, however; as Farrington (1915) noted, the enstatite is generally close to $MgSiO_3$ in composition, and pyroxenes between this and bronzite are lacking. Nor does the composition range extend to iron-dominant orthopyroxene; the hypersthene from meteorites seldom exceeds 30 mole per cent $FeSiO_3$.

Osbornite: This mineral was described by Maskelyne (1870) as minute yellow octahedrons in the Bustee meteorite. On account of the very small amount, Maskelyne was unable to determine its composition. Bannister (1941) showed that it is titanium nitride, TiN. It has not been recognized in any other meteorite.

Pentlandite: Ramdohr (1962) has shown that this mineral is not uncommon as an accessory mineral in chondrites. It is most abundant in some of the olivine-pigeonite chondrites where free iron is almost or completely lacking (e.g., Karoonda); in such meteorites almost all the iron is combined in silicates or magnetite, and the nickel, which would otherwise alloy with free iron, now enters a sulfide phase.

Plagioclase: This mineral is a common constituent, in small amounts, of many of the stony meteorites. Michel (1912) has written an extensive account of meteoritic plagioclase. In most chondrites it is present in about 5–10%; the composition is usually oligoclase, but anorthite contents ranging from 5 to 34% have been recorded. Preuss (1951) has shown that plagioclase in the Oldenburg chondrite is the high-temperature variety, and Miyashiro (pers. comm.) has found this to be true for a number of Japanese chondrites. This is an important observation, since it implies that the plagioclase-bearing chondrites crystallized at a fairly high temperature (above 700° C) and were cooled rather rapidly. In feldspar-bearing achondrites the plagioclase is usually bytownite or anorthite, the albite content being about 10%. The plagioclase from Juvinas, a pigeonite-plagioclase achondrite, has been carefully described by Game (1957).

Tschermak (1872b) identified and described a colorless isotropic material in the Shergotty meteorite, which he named maskelynite (Fig. 24). Maskelynite is a glass of plagioclase composition, hence is not a true mineral in terms of the definition of a mineral as a crystalline substance. It has been found in a number of chondrites; sometimes it is associated with plagioclase grains. Generally it appears to have formed by the fusion of pre-existing plagioclase.

Pyrite: Ramdohr (1962) has recorded a single occurrence of pyrite (in myrmekitic intergrowth with pentlandite) in the Karoonda meteorite, an olivine-pigeonite chondrite.

Quartz: This mineral has been identified in the insoluble residues of a number of iron meteorites, originally by Rose in 1861. Doubts have been expressed as to the extra-terrestrial origin of this quartz, some workers believing that the quartz is detrital grains embedded in the surface crust of these meteorites. Quartz was doubtfully identified in the St. Marks stone by Cohen (1906) and confirmed by Mer-

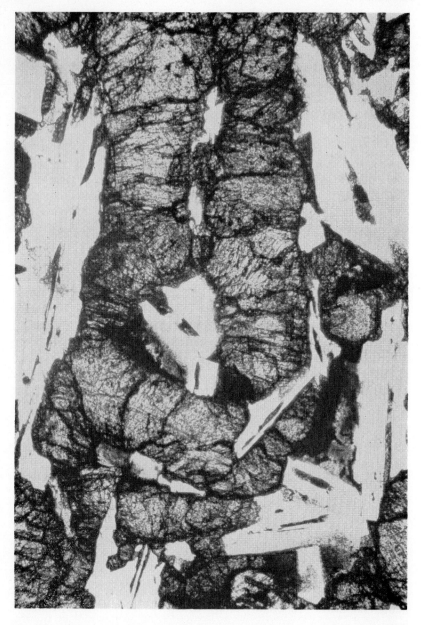

Fig. 24.   Thin section (60×) of the Shergotty meteorite, consisting of pigeonite (gray) and maskelynite (white); the maskelynite has the form of lath-shaped plagioclase crystals (courtesy U.S. National Museum).

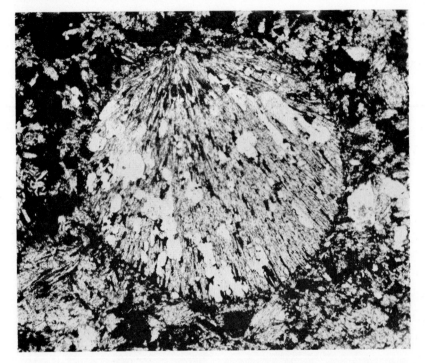

Fig. 25. Thin section of the St. Marks meteorite, showing a chondrule (1 mm diameter) of radiating enstatite (gray) with quartz (white); black is nickel-iron and troilite (courtesy J. Weber).

rill (1924). This quartz is within the body of the meteorite and is certainly part of its extra-terrestrial composition (Fig. 25). Quartz has been identified, always in accessory amounts, in the calcium-rich achondrites Chaves, Jonzac, Peramiho, and Stannern (Berwerth, 1912), and in the enstatite chondrite Abee (Dawson, Maxwell, and Parsons, 1960).

Schreibersite: This mineral was described and named by Haidinger in 1847 as a constituent of the Magura iron, and seems to be universally present as an accessory mineral in iron meteorites (Fig. 26). It also occurs in the stony-irons, and is common in small amounts in many chondrites (Ramdohr, 1962), usually in association with nickel-iron.

Schreibersite commonly occurs in thin plates, often oriented in the kamacite parallel to the Naumann lamellae. This variety is called

Fig. 26. Schreibersite (black lamellae) and troilite (black nodules) in the Bella Roca iron meteorite; the specimen is 30 cm long (courtesy The American Museum of Natural History).

rhabdite and was formerly believed to be a distinct mineral; it is probably formed by exsolution from the kamacite. Schreibersite also occurs as a shell around nodules of troilite. The color is tin-white when fresh, but it tarnishes readily to bronze-yellow. The mineral is brittle, magnetic, and almost insoluble in acids. Numerous analyses of schreibersite and rhabdite have been made, all indicating a formula $(Fe,Ni)_3P$; the Fe/Ni ratio ranges from about 7:1 to 5:3.

Serpentine: As long ago as 1860 Wohler suggested that the silicate material of Cold Bokkeveld, a carbonaceous chondrite, consisted largely of serpentine. This observation was overlooked or disbelieved for many years. Kvasha (1948) identified chlorite or serpentine in the Boriskino carbonaceous chondrite, and later in the Mighei carbonaceous chondrite also. It seems to be characteristic of the Type II carbonaceous chondrites of Wiik (1956), which consist in large part of this mineral.

The identification of this mineral as serpentine rather than chlorite rests on the following grounds: (*a*) X-ray powder photographs do not show the 14 A reflection characteristic of chlorite; (*b*) the bulk composition of the meteorites in which it occurs is very low in Al_2O_3 (about 2%)—if the mineral were chlorite the Al_2O_3 content should be much higher. Unfortunately, the mineral is very fine-grained and intimately mixed with black carbonaceous material, which makes it impossible to determine its optical properties. From the lath-like or

Fig. 27. Electron micrograph (24,000×) of serpentine from the Erakot carbonaceous chondrite; the lath-like or tubular form is characteristic of chrysotile
(courtesy J. D. Bernal).

tubular form shown in electron micrographs (Fig. 27), it is the chryso-tile variety of serpentine.

Sphalerite: In view of the low abundance of zinc in meteorites, sphalerite can only be present in trace amounts. Ramdohr (1962) has recorded it from Pillistfer and Hvittis, both enstatite chondrites.

Spinel: This mineral was recently identified in the Kaba meteorite, a carbonaceous chondrite, by Sztrokay (1960). It has also been found in Vigarano, a carbonaceous chondrite very similar to Kaba. In both these meteorites it is present in very small amounts, and has been identified by its optical properties and its X-ray powder photograph.

Foote (1912) recorded red-brown spinel in the Holbrook chondrite; Merrill (1912) was unable to confirm this, nor were Mason and Wiik (1961b); the latter suggest that this material was chromite.

Sulfur: Sulfur in the amount of 1% or more can be extracted by carbon disulfide, or other solvents, from some carbonaceous chondrites, Alais, Cold Bokkeveld, and Orgueil for example. Although the sulfur has not been recognized as discrete particles in these extremely fine-grained meteorites, there is little reason to doubt that it exists therein in the free state.

Tridymite: This mineral is not uncommon as an accessory in the calcium-rich achondrites; it has been observed in Moore County, Pasamonte, Chaves, and Juvinas. It has also been recorded from the stony-irons Steinbach, Vaca Muerta, and Crab Orchard, and from the enstatite chondrite Indarch. Since tridymite is not stable above about 3000 kg/cm² pressure at any temperature, its presence in these meteorites places a severe restriction on their conditions of crystallization.

Troilite: This mineral is present in accessory amounts in practically all meteorites. It is difficult to estimate the average amount in iron meteorites, since the troilite usually occurs as comparatively large nodules very irregularly distributed; in the chondritic meteorites the mineral occurs as small grains randomly distributed, and the amount is fairly constant, averaging 5–6% by weight. The presence of free iron in most meteorites would appear to ensure that the composition of troilite is stoichiometric FeS, with no deficiency of iron as in terrestrial pyrrhotite; this has been confirmed in some instances by measurement of the lattice dimensions. However, in metal-free meteorites, such as some of the olivine-pigeonite chondrites, carbonaceous chondrites, and achondrites, it is conceivable that the iron sulfide mineral is actually pyrrhotite. Curvello (1958) has given a detailed account of the mode of occurrence of troilite in several irons. Troilite from meteorites has been carefully studied by Nichiporuk and Chodos

(1959), who have shown that it frequently contains inclusions of daubreelite, chromite, kamacite, graphite, and schreibersite; they also record the presence of pyrrhotite as well as troilite.

Valleriite: This mineral, a copper-iron sulfide of uncertain formula, was first recognized in meteorites by Ramdohr (1962), who records it in some chondrites as a decomposition product of chalcopyrrhotite and as an exsolution product of pentlandite.

6

The Chondrites

Introduction

The distinction between the two groups of stony meteorites, the chondrites and the achondrites, is normally a clear-cut one: the presence of chondrules is readily seen in the chondritic meteorites, and their absence in the achondrites is coupled with other differences, textural, mineralogical, and chemical. However, a few stones considered as chondrites, specifically some of the carbonaceous chondrites and enstatite chondrites, actually contain no chondrules, but are so classed because they are chemically and mineralogically similar to the chondrule-bearing stones of the same type. Kvasha (1958) has shown that the amphoterites, which Prior classed as achondrites, contain chondrules and belong to the olivine-hypersthene chondrites.

In terms of abundance, the chondrites are far more significant than the achondrites; Table 3 lists 954 chondrites to 64 achondrites. Indeed, the chondrites are the commonest of all meteorites; in terms of observed falls the chondrites comprise 621 out of a total of 726 of all types, or 85.5%. Outer space is evidently populated by chondritic meteorites almost to the exclusion of other types; in any hypothesis as to the origin of meteorites primary attention must be given to this group, and especially the explanation of the peculiarities of chondrite structure and composition.

Classification

The initial differentiation of the chondrites from other types of stony meteorites was made by Rose (1863). In 1872 Tschermak extended Rose's classification by subdividing the chondrites into groups according to their color and structure, a subdivision later extended by Brezina, until in his final presentation (1904) no less than 31 groups were recognized. This classification, commonly known as the Rose-Tschermak-Brezina classification, was generally adopted and is still widely used.

Prior (1920) criticized this classification as complicated, over-elaborate, and based on the superficial characters of color and the presence or absence of brecciation and veining. He proposed a classification based on chemical and mineralogical composition, and recognized three groups, as follows:

1. Enstatite chondrites: consisting essentially of crystalline nearly pure non-ferriferous enstatite, with nickel-iron in large amount up to 25% and poor in nickel (Fe/Ni about 13), troilite, and some oligoclase.

2. Bronzite chondrites or strictly olivine-bronzite chondrites: consisting essentially of bronzite and olivine in approximately equal amounts, with some oligoclase, nickel-iron, and troilite. The nickel-iron is less poor in nickel than in the enstatite chondrites, and is less in amount, though this is generally over 10%. The ratio of MgO to FeO in the ferromagnesian minerals in the type meteorite (Cronstad) is about 5.

3. Hypersthene chondrites or strictly olivine-hypersthene chondrites: of similar composition and structure to the preceding group, except that the iron is richer in nickel (Fe/Ni varying from about 7 to 3) and generally in less amount, and the ferromagnesian minerals are correspondingly richer in ferrous oxide (MgO/FeO varying from about 4 to $2\frac{1}{2}$).

In the development of his classification Prior established certain chemical and mineralogical regularities within the chondrites. These relationships, generally known as Prior's rules, can be stated as follows:

1. The smaller the amount of nickel-iron in a chondrite, the higher the Ni/Fe ratio in the nickel-iron.

2. The smaller the amount of nickel-iron in a chondrite, the higher the FeO/MgO ratio in the ferromagnesian silicate minerals.

Prior's rules have been questioned by Urey and Craig (1953), but recent work by Ringwood (1961a) has confirmed their general validity.

In spite of the use of mineralogical terms to describe the individual groups, Prior's classification was based on chemical composition. He pointed out that the group to which a chondrite belonged could be established by any one of three criteria:

1. The MgO/FeO ratio in the bulk analysis.
2. The MgO/FeO ratio in the silicate material insoluble in HCl (essentially pyroxene with a little plagioclase).
3. The amount and Fe/Ni ratio of the nickel-iron.

The names enstatite, bronzite, and hypersthene chondrite imply the second criterion, with the divisions at the bronzite boundaries of MgO/FeO 9 and 4 ($FeSiO_3$ 10–20 mole per cent). However, the first criterion has been generally used, since a bulk analysis is more commonly available than a reliable analysis of the pyroxene. The two criteria give on the whole concordant results, since the MgO/FeO ratio in the bulk analysis is usually close to that in the pyroxene; this ratio is normally slightly higher in the pyroxene.

Prior's classification is logical and straightforward, but its application in the form outlined above leads to certain difficulties. It cannot be applied to the numerous chondrites which have not been analyzed. Many analyses of chondrites are incomplete, doubtful, or demonstrably inaccurate, especially the figure for FeO, essential to the classification (FeO in chondrite analyses is a calculated figure, determined from total iron after subtracting Fe as nickel-iron and Fe combined with total S as FeS; all the errors in the latter determinations accumulate in the FeO figure, which is especially serious where the true FeO figure is low). If the chondrite is weathered (and most finds are weathered to some degree) the MgO/FeO figure will be influenced by the oxidation of nickel-iron and troilite and cannot be used for the classification of the meteorite. Mason (1962) has shown that Prior's classification can be more readily and more generally applied by the determination of the composition of the olivine in a chondrite by measurement of its refractive indices. He has also extended Prior's classification by the addition of two groups, the olivine-pigeonite chondrites and the carbonaceous chondrites. Chondrites belonging to these two groups were included by Prior in the olivine-hypersthene chondrites. However, in the olivine-pigeonite chondrites pigeonite is the dominant pyroxene, and the carbonaceous chondrites contain little or no pyroxene. These two groups also show additional mineralogical and chemical differences which clearly differentiate them from the other groups of chondrites. The two groups are small in numbers; 12 olivine-pigeonite and 17 carbonaceous chondrites have been recognized, whereas the olivine-bronzite and olivine-hypersthene chondrites number many hundreds and are by far the commonest of all meteorites.

Chemical Composition

The chemical composition of the chondritic meteorites is illustrated by the data in Table 6, which gives an analysis of one meteorite of each of the five groups. As we shall see during this discussion, within each group there is a comparatively small range of composition, so that an analysis of one meteorite can be considered as fairly representative for all meteorites of that group. This feature was noted as early as 1878 by Nordenskiöld. The uniformity of composition also extends to the different groups, as can be seen when the analyses are recalculated in terms of the so-called "non-volatile" elements, i.e., on a S-, C-, H-, O-free basis, as suggested by Wiik (1956). This is shown in Table 7. The overall similarity is quite remarkable. The close similarity between the elemental composition of the olivine-bronzite chondrite, the olivine-pigeonite chondrite, and the carbonaceous chondrite is especially noteworthy, in view of the marked dissimilarity between the carbonaceous chondrites and the other groups in overall composition and mineralogy. The olivine-hypersthene chondrite is similar to these groups, except for somewhat lower iron and higher silicon; the enstatite chondrite differs in having somewhat higher iron and lower magnesium.

When analyses of the different groups are compared, certain sequential relationships are clearly seen. There is a decline in free iron from the enstatite chondrites to the carbonaceous chondrites, coupled with an increase in combined iron (iron reported as FeO). The percentage of nickel alloyed with the free iron remains fairly constant, so that the metal phase is progressively richer in nickel in going from the enstatite chondrites to the olivine-pigeonite chondrites,

TABLE 6.   ANALYSES OF METEORITES BELONGING TO DIF-
FERENT CHONDRITE GROUPS

	1	2	3	4	5
Fe	23.70	15.15	6.27	4.02	0.00
Ni	1.78	1.88	1.34	1.43	0.00
Co	0.12	0.13	0.046	0.09	0.00
FeS	8.09	6.11	5.89	5.12	3.66(S)
SiO_2	38.47	36.55	39.93	34.82	27.81
TiO_2	0.12	0.14	0.14	0.15	0.08
Al_2O_3	1.78	1.91	1.86	2.18	2.15
MnO	0.02	0.32	0.33	0.20	0.21
FeO	0.23	10.21	15.44	24.34	27.34 [b]
MgO	21.63	23.47	24.71	23.57	19.46
CaO	1.03	2.41	1.70	2.17	1.66
Na_2O	0.64	0.78	0.74	0.69	0.63
K_2O	0.16	0.20	0.13	0.23	0.05
P_2O_5	trace	0.30	0.31	0.20	0.30
H_2O	0.34	0.21	0.27	0.10	12.86
Cr_2O_3	0.23	0.52	0.54	0.58	0.36
NiO	0.11	—	—	0.00	1.53
CoO	—	—	—	0.00	0.07
C	0.32	—	0.03	0.19	2.48
	99.89 [a]	100.29	99.67	100.08	101.01 [b]

1. Enstatite chondrite (Daniel's Kuil; Prior, 1916, p. 14); a:
includes CaS, 0.86; Cr_2S_3, 0.29.
2. Olivine-bronzite chondrite (Oakley; Wiik, 1956, p. 280).
3. Olivine-hypersthene chondrite (Kyushu; Mason and Wiik,
1961a, p. 274).
4. Olivine-pigeonite chondrite (Warrenton; Wiik, 1956, p. 280).
5. Carbonaceous chondrite (Mighei; Wiik, 1956, p. 280); b: Wiik
reported all S as FeS, but it is given here as S, and the corresponding Fe is reported as FeO; Melikoff and Krschischanowsky
(1899) found 3.69% total S in Mighei, divided as follows: FeS,
0.46%; S (free), 3.19%; SO_3 (sulfate), 0.85%; S_2O_2 (thiosulfate),
0.12%. Wiik also reports 0.36% loss on ignition, mainly organic
matter.

as originally established by Prior.   Prior explained this relationship
by the hypothesis that the chondritic meteorites have crystallized
from a magma which has passed through successive stages of progressive oxidation.   In the original magma, from which the enstatite

chondrites crystallized, silicon and magnesium were completely oxidized, whereas the iron was completely unoxidized. With progressive
oxidation there would be an increasing production of ferrous iron,
at the expense of the free iron, which in the resulting meteorites
entered more and more into the composition of the magnesium silicates, while the residual nickel-iron became richer and richer in
nickel, since little or no oxidation of nickel would occur so long as
any iron remained unoxidized. Ringwood (1961a) has pointed out
that this sequence is more plausibly explained by progressive reduction of material of carbonaceous chondrite composition to give the
other chondrite types, a postulate also argued by Mason (1960b),
but opposed by Urey (1961).

Urey and Craig (1953) made an exhaustive study of all analyses
of chondritic meteorites, using objective criteria to judge whether an
analysis was accurate or not. Of about 300 available analyses, 192
were rejected as unreliable and 94 accepted as trustworthy—a sober-
ing reflection on the difficulty of analyzing such complex objects as
stony meteorites! Their criteria for acceptance or rejection of an
analysis have been criticized, and undoubtedly some accurate analyses

TABLE 7. ANALYSES OF METEORITES BELONGING TO DIF-
FERENT CHONDRITE GROUPS, RECALCULATED IN ATOM PER-
CENTAGES ON WATER-, CARBON-, OXYGEN-, AND SULFUR-
FREE BASIS

	1	2	3	4	5
Fe	28.52	26.32	21.85	25.72	26.18
Ni	1.65	1.74	1.27	1.38	1.41
Co	0.11	0.12	0.04	0.08	0.06
Si	34.98	33.17	36.78	32.77	31.85
Ti	0.08	0.10	0.09	0.14	0.09
Al	1.91	2.04	2.01	2.42	2.90
Mn	0.02	0.25	0.26	0.16	0.19
Mg	29.43	31.72	33.92	33.03	33.19
Ca	1.67	2.34	1.57	2.19	2.04
Na	1.13	1.37	1.30	1.25	1.40
K	0.18	0.23	0.17	0.27	0.07
P	—	0.23	0.25	0.16	0.29
Cr	0.32	0.37	0.39	0.43	0.33
	100.00	100.00	100.00	100.00	100.00

were rejected and some inaccurate analyses accepted, but their work is a major contribution to the understanding of chondrite composition. When they critically examined the 94 accepted analyses they found that they could be divided into two groups, one with high total iron (their H type) and one with low total iron (their L type). The average for the 94 analyses, and the averages for the H and L types respectively, are given in Table 8.

The similarities and differences between the two types are readily seen. Many elements are present in essentially the same amounts in the two types, i.e., Mg, Al, Ca, Na, K, Cr, Mn, Ti, P, and S. The principal difference is in total Fe; nickel and cobalt vary directly with total Fe, as might be expected. The higher total Fe in the H type is coupled with lower O and lower Si, and possibly slightly lower Mg and Cr. Urey and Craig brought out this division of chondrite analyses into two types in the form of a diagram (Fig. 28) in which Fe in silicates (i.e., oxidized iron) is plotted against Fe in metal and FeS (i.e., reduced iron). The points representing the individual

TABLE 8. AVERAGES OF 94 SUPERIOR ANALYSES OF CHONDRITES, AND OF THE H (41 ANALYSES) AND L (53 ANALYSES) TYPES RESPECTIVELY (UREY AND CRAIG, 1953)

	All	H Type	L Type
SiO_2	38.04	36.17	39.49
MgO	23.84	22.93	24.55
FeO	12.45	9.26	14.97
Al_2O_3	2.50	2.36	2.61
CaO	1.95	1.95	1.96
Na_2O	0.98	0.91	1.04
K_2O	0.17	0.17	0.18
Cr_2O_3	0.36	0.27	0.43
MnO	0.25	0.23	0.27
TiO_2	0.11	0.11	0.11
P_2O_5	0.21	0.17	0.24
Fe	11.76	17.76	7.04
Ni	1.34	1.68	1.06
Co	0.08	0.10	0.07
FeS	5.73	5.69	5.77
Total Fe	25.07	28.58	22.33

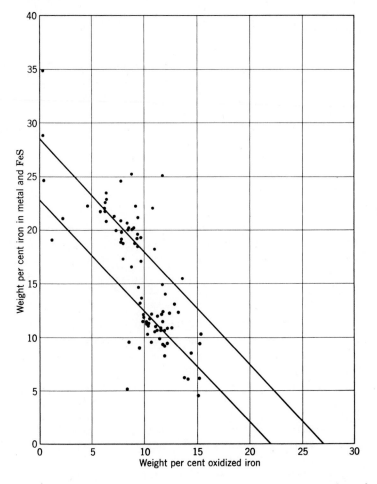

Fig. 28. Relationship between oxidized iron (present largely or entirely as ferromagnesian silicates) and iron as metal and sulfide in 94 selected analyses of chondritic meteorites (Urey and Craig, 1953).

analyses cluster around two lines, one corresponding to about 28% total iron, the other to about 22% total iron.

As can be seen from Fig. 28 the points representing the individual analyses show a considerable scatter and some overlap between the H and L types. Ringwood (1961a) and Mason (1962) have shown that the scatter and overlap are remarkably reduced if the analyses are selected according to the following criteria: (1) only falls are included, since finds may be weathered and oxidized and their analyses will not give a true picture of the relationship between metallic and oxidized iron in the meteorite; (2) the FeO/FeO + MgO ratio in the olivine and pyroxene (determined from refractive indices) must be consistent (within ±2%) with this ratio in the chemical analysis of the meteorite. The results of this procedure are shown in Fig. 29.

This diagram is exceedingly illuminating, in that it shows clearly

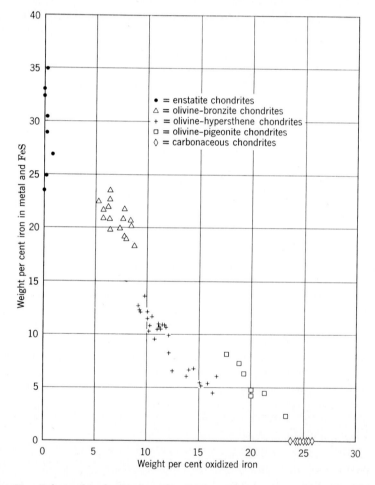

Fig. 29. Relationship between oxidized iron and iron as metal and sulfide in analyses of observed falls, illustrating the separation into distinct subgroups and the variation within the subgroups (Mason, 1962).

that each of the five groups of chondrites occupies a specific composition field, and there is essentially no overlap of the different groups. The hiatus between the enstatite chondrites and the olivine-bronzite chondrites, noted and discussed by Ringwood (1961a), is very marked. Another remarkable feature is the coincidence of L type chondrites with the olivine-hypersthene group—all olivine-hypersthene chondrites are L type, and none are H type. Carbonaceous chondrites, olivine-pigeonite chondrites, and olivine-bronzite chondrites are all H type; enstatite chondrites show a considerable range of iron content—they may be included as H type, but Wiik (1956) has suggested that the more iron-rich ones should be considered as an HH type.

Mineralogical Composition

The mineralogical composition of the chondritic meteorites is remarkably uniform and simple, especially if the carbonaceous chondrites, which contain hydrated compounds, are excluded. The other classes of chondrites are made up largely of olivine and pyroxene (the enstatite chondrites contain no olivine, only pyroxene), with lesser amounts of nickel-iron, oligoclase (sometimes maskelynite), and troilite. The nickel-iron consists of both kamacite and taenite, usually as discrete grains or as plessite, and never in the Widmanstatten intergrowth which characterizes most of the iron meteorites. The metal particles in some chondrites have been carefully described by Urey and Mayeda (1959). The usual accessory minerals are chromite and a phosphate, apatite and/or merrillite. The mineralogy of the carbonaceous chondrites is not well known, because of their fine grain and the presence of opaque carbonaceous material, which greatly obscures the minerals; they consist largely of serpentine or amorphous hydrated silicates.

The relative amounts of olivine, pyroxene, and nickel-iron in any chondrite are closely related to its chemical composition, whereas the amounts of oligoclase and troilite are practically constant. This is summarized in Table 9 and illustrated in Fig. 30, which shows in a schematic form the amounts of the different minerals in relationship to the FeO/FeO + MgO mole percentage, which is the principal variable in the bulk composition. In the olivine-pigeonite chondrites it is about 32–40, and these meteorites consist almost entirely of olivine,

TABLE 9. CHEMICAL AND MINERALOGICAL VARIATION WITHIN THE CHONDRITE GROUPS (ALL FIGURES ARE WEIGHT PER CENT, EXCEPT FeO/FeO + MgO, WHICH IS IN MOLE PER CENT)

	Enstatite	Olivine-Bronzite	Olivine-Hypersthene	Olivine-Pigeonite
Pyroxene	50–60 (Fs$_0$) *	20–35 (Fs$_{14-20}$)	25–35 (Fs$_{20-50}$)	5
Olivine	none	25–40 (Fa$_{15-22}$) *	35–60 (Fa$_{22-32}$)	65–70 (Fa$_{32-40}$)
Nickel-iron	20–28	16–21	1–10	0–6
Oligoclase	5–10	5–10	5–10	5–10
Troilite	7–15	∼5	∼5	∼5
Total Fe	23–35	27–30	20–23	24–26
FeO	<1	7–12	12–22	22–29
FeO/FeO + MgO	<1	15–22	22–32	32–40

* Fs = mole per cent FeSiO$_3$.   Fa = mole per cent Fe$_2$SiO$_4$.

with a few per cent of pyroxene (pigeonite) and little or no nickel-iron. In the olivine-hypersthene chondrites it is about 22–32, and they consist largely of olivine and hypersthene (olivine somewhat in excess of pyroxene), with between 5% and 10% of nickel-iron. In the olivine-bronzite chondrites it is 15–22; they consist largely of olivine and bronzite, with usually between 15% and 20% nickel-iron. In the enstatite chondrites it is effectively zero (i.e., no iron in the silicate phases) and they consist largely of enstatite, with more than 20% nickel-iron and usually somewhat higher troilite than the other chondritic meteorites.

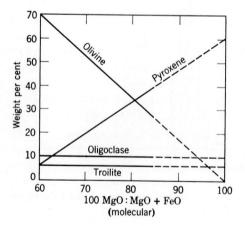

Fig. 30. Schematic representation of the variation of mineralogical composition with chemical composition in the chondritic meteorites; the dashed lines represent the hiatus between the olivine-bronzite and the enstatite chondrites (after Mason, 1960*b*).

The chemical and mineralogical hiatus between the enstatite chondrites and the olivine-bronzite chondrites was noted by Farrington (1915) and has been discussed by Ringwood (1961a). There seem to be no chondrites with FeO/FeO + MgO percentages between 1 and 15. In terms of the conventional chemical analyses, the enstatite chondrites contain practically no FeO (usually less than 0.5%), whereas the olivine-bronzite chondrites average 9–10% FeO, and it is doubtful if any of them have less than 7% FeO (analyses showing less than 7% FeO when checked against the composition of the minerals have been found erroneous).

The compositions of olivine, pyroxene, and nickel-iron in individual chondrites show a regular variation with the bulk composition, as demonstrated by Ringwood (1961a) and Kvasha (1961). Olivine and pyroxene become progressively richer in iron as the FeO/FeO + MgO ratio increases, and the nickel-iron becomes progressively richer in nickel. The writer has determined the composition of the olivine in 180 olivine-bronzite and olivine-hypersthene chondrites by X-ray methods, and his results are summarized in Fig. 31. The enstatite chondrites contain no olivine, and in the olivine-bronzite

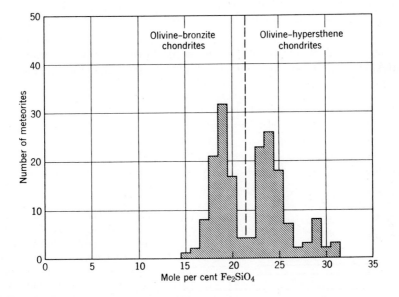

Fig. 31. Olivine composition in 180 olivine-bronzite and olivine-hypersthene chondrites, determined by X-ray diffraction.

chondrites no olivine with less than 15 mole per cent of the Fe_2SiO_4 component (Fa) has been found. The frequency of olivine composition shows peaks at 19% Fa (the commonest composition in an olivine-bronzite chondrite) and 24% (the commonest composition in an olivine-hypersthene chondrite). Comparatively few chondrites have olivine more iron-rich than 25% Fa.

Pyroxene composition also shows a regular variation with bulk composition in the chondritic meteorites. In the olivine-bronzite and olivine-hypersthene chondrites the composition of the olivine and that of the orthopyroxene shows a consistent relationship—the FeO/ FeO + MgO ratio is normally somewhat higher in the olivine than in the associated orthopyroxene. This is consistent with equilibrium relationships in the MgO-FeO-SiO_2 system as established by Bowen and Schairer (1935) and is a weighty argument for considering these meteorites to be an equilibrium association of minerals, not chance aggregates.

In the enstatite, olivine-bronzite, and olivine-hypersthene chondrites the orthorhombic pyroxene is usually associated with accessory amounts of diopside, either as discrete grains or in parallel intergrowth with the orthopyroxene. Ringwood (1961a) has pointed out that the intergrowth is parallel to the (100) plane, an orientation characteristic of diopside exsolving from primary orthopyroxene.

Structure

The essential feature of the structure of chondritic meteorites is of course the presence of chondrules or chondri, although some carbonaceous chondrites have no chondrules, and in a few stones classed as chondrites (especially some of the enstatite chondrites and the olivine-hypersthene chondrites) chondrules are poorly developed or absent. Chondrules are spheroidal bodies, commonly about 1 mm in diameter, and normally consist of olivine and/or orthopyroxene (Fig. 32). The orthopyroxene chondrules are usually made up of radiating prisms (or plates) of orthopyroxene; at their most perfect they are truly spherical, sharply bounded, and the prisms, as they appear in thin section, radiate from a point which is eccentric, not central. Sometimes the orthopyroxene is so fine-grained as to appear cryptocrystalline. The olivine chondrules may be granular, consisting of several crystals, or they may consist of a single crystal or parts of a crystal in optical continuity. A remarkable variety, the so-called barred chondrules, consists of alternate layers of olivine and dark interstitial material variously identified as glass or an aggregate of fibrous orthopyroxene. Sometimes the olivine chondrules have a border of clear olivine, parts of which may be in optical continuity with the interior. Occasionally the chondrules are bordered by a rim of nickel-iron and troilite. Chondrules of nickel-iron, and of plagioclase, have been recorded, but are rare.

Clearly the origin of the chondrules is a key to a satisfactory theory for the origin of this great group of meteorites. Many theories have been put forward, and were admirably summarized by Roy (1957) as follows:

(1) chondrules are fused drops of "fiery rain" (Sorby, 1864, 1877);
(2) chondrules are fragments of pre-existing meteorites, which have become rounded by oscillation and attrition (Tschermak, 1885);
(3) chondrules are products of a special phase of magmatic segregation, formed in place as a result of rapid, arrested crystallization in a molten mass (Brezina, 1885);
(4) chondrules originated from a dispersal of a silicate melt in a hot atmosphere, the resultant drops crystallizing from the outside inward (Wahl, 1910);
(5) chondrules are metamorphosed garnets—garnets converted to enstatite (Fermor, 1938);
(6) chondrules were produced by the cooling of liquid silicates, which fell as a molten rain during the collision of a small asteroid with a larger one (Urey and Craig, 1953).

Roy favors the formation of chondrules in place, as products of separation from a silicate melt, followed often by subsequent deformation and metamorphism. Ringwood (1959, 1961a) has discussed the origin of chondrules in considerable detail, and prefers a variant of Brezina's hypothesis; he believes that most chondrules originate by spherulitic crystallization within a homogeneous magma, but at a comparatively low temperature ($<1000°$ C), the magma having melted under high partial pessures of H_2O and CO_2.

Recently Levin and Slonimsky (1958) and Mason (1960a) have discussed current theories for the origin of chondrules and pointed out their inadequacies, particularly the supposed formation from a silicate melt. Levin and Slonimsky favor an origin by direct condensation from a cool dust cloud in which the particles were essentially in the colloidal state; they consider the original chondrules to have been amorphous, and to have been crystallized by later heating processes after aggregation into small planetary bodies. Mason has suggested

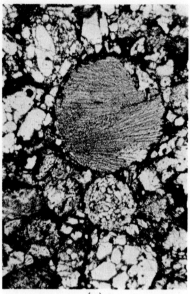
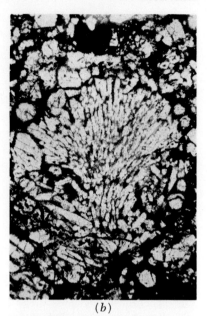

(a)   (b)

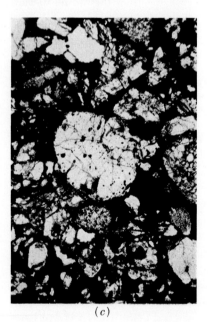
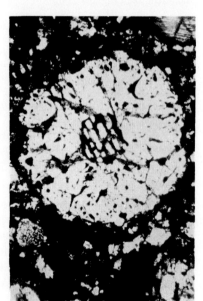

(c)   (d)

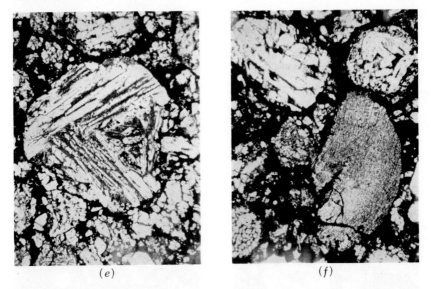

(e) (f)

Fig. 32.   Photomicrographs of thin sections of various types of chondrules; the
diameters of the chondrules are approximately 1 mm (courtesy J. Weber).
(a) A chondrule of finely fibrous or prismatic orthopyroxene together with
numerous chondrules of granular olivine, the individual olivine grains frequently
showing crystal faces (Selma meteorite).   (b) A chondrule of prismatic orthopyroxene with an excentric radiating structure; black is limonite from weathering
of nickel-iron (Selma meteorite).   (c) A chondrule which consists of a single
crystal of olivine (Yonozu meteorite).   (d) An olivine chondrule; the olivine
is a single crystal, but the core shows barred structure, the bars consisting of
turbid isotropic material (Selma meteorite).   (e) A chondrule consisting of
prismatic crystals of olivine, in three different orientations; the dark areas between the prisms consist of turbid isotropic material (Selma meteorite).   (f)
Chondrules of randomly oriented grains of olivine, and a fragmented chondrule
of finely prismatic orthopyroxene (Selma meteorite).

that chondrules result from the thermal metamorphism of carbonaceous chondrites.   A few carbonaceous chondrites consist almost
entirely of amorphous material and are structureless and without chondrules.   Most carbonaceous chondrites are made up largely of serpentine, and in them chondrules are usually small and sparse; these chondrules consist of olivine and pyroxene which is almost iron-free, and
appear to be crystallizing in the groundmass serpentine, which is consistent with a thermal metamorphism at about 400° C.   In the olivine-
pigeonite chondrites, which are closely related to the carbonaceous
chondrites in composition, the whole meteorite is a mass of chondrules,

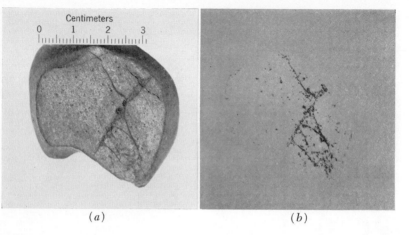

Fig. 33. (a) Section of the Harrisonville chondrite showing veins; (b) sulfur print of Harrisonville; the areas rich in troilite show up dark in the print—note that the veins are enriched in troilite (courtesy E. Anders).

which Mason interprets as the complete conversion of the original serpentine into an aggregate of chondrules of olivine and pyroxene.

The matrix of the typical chondrites is a fine-grained, compact or friable aggregate of olivine and pyroxene with interstitial nickel-iron, troilite, and plagioclase, and sometimes glass, through which the chondrules are scattered. This structure is sometimes referred to as "tuffaceous," but is no proof of an analogous origin to terrestrial tuffs. Many chondrites are seamed with narrow (<1 mm thick) black veinlets (Fig. 33). These veinlets have been extensively studied by Anders and Goles (1961), who have shown they consist of glassy silicates in which are suspended a large number of tiny globules of troilite. They point out that previous theories for the formation of these veins—frictional heating or injection of a melt—are unsatisfactory. They conclude that the veins were produced by the momentary passage of hot sulfur-containing gases or vapors through cracks in the parent body of such meteorites.

Many chondritic meteorites have a brecciated structure. Sometimes this brecciation is more apparent than real, being due to differently colored patches in an otherwise homogeneous stone; a typical example is Paragould, described by Roy and Wyant (1955). The brecciated meteorites, both chondrites and achondrites, have been carefully described by Wahl (1952), who distinguishes two types, the monomict and polymict breccias. Monomict breccias consist of fragments of a single kind, polymict breccias contain fragments of more than one kind. Wahl classifies most of the brecciated chondrites as polymict breccias, but in many of them the fragments differ only in color, and proof of gross chemical inhomogeneity is lacking. It appears that most brecciated chondrites are similar to Paragould, and are actually monomict breccias. Monomict breccias are presumably of secondary origin, the brecciation having been caused by compression or crushing of a previously homogeneous stone.

The Enstatite Chondrites

The enstatite chondrites are rare among the chondrites; the Prior-Hey catalog (1953) lists 19 of them, but some of these are wrongly classified (apparently because some investigators apply the name enstatite to all orthorhombic pyroxene in meteorites, without reference to iron content). Eleven true enstatite chondrites have been identified (Table 10), nine of them falls. Although few in number, they are of extraordinary interest as a group of very specific composition; they are separated by a complete hiatus from the olivine-bronzite chondrites, and they show some similarities with the carbonaceous chondrites.

Chemically the enstatite chondrites are characterized by a high de-

TABLE 10. ENSTATITE CHONDRITES

	Date of Fall	Weight (kg)
Abee (Alberta, Canada)	6/10/1952	107.5
Atlanta (Louisiana, U.S.A.)	Found 1938	5.5
Blithfield (Ontario, Canada)	Found 1910	1.83
Daniel's Kuil (South Africa)	3/20/1868	1.20
Hvittis (Finland)	10/21/1901	14
Indarch (U.S.S.R.)	4/17/1891	27
Jajh deh Kot Lalu (Pakistan)	5/2/1926	0.97
Khairpur (India)	9/23/1873	14
Pillistfer (U.S.S.R.)	8/8/1863	23
St. Marks (South Africa)	1/3/1903	13.8
Saint-Sauveur (France)	7/10/1914	14

gree of reduction; essentially all the iron is present in the metal and the sulfide phases (some analyses show a small amount of FeO, but this may be the result of either analytical error or oxidation prior to or during analysis). Not only is the iron totally reduced, but other elements are also: calcium, manganese, and chromium may be present in the sulfide phases, and some silicon is present in the metal phase (Ringwood, 1961b). Prior (1916) noted that the analysis of mechanically separated metal from the Khairpur enstatite chondrite showed silicon (reported as SiO_2) which could not be correlated with the basic oxides.

Other significant features of the chemical composition of the enstatite chondrites are a higher than average sulfur content (often twice that of the olivine-bronzite and olivine-hypersthene chondrites),

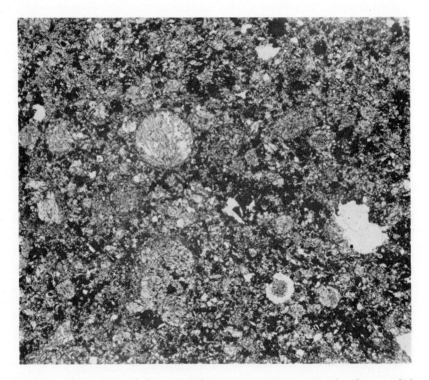

Fig. 34. Thin section of the St. Marks meteorite, an enstatite chondrite; nickel-iron and sulfides are black, enstatite is gray, white grains in central chondrule (1 mm diameter) are quartz, but other white patches are holes in the section (courtesy J. Weber).

higher total iron content (up to 35%) than other groups of chondrites, and the frequent presence of carbon in amounts up to 0.5%. Their content of minor and trace elements often deviates from that of other groups of chondrites but resembles that of the carbonaceous chondrites.

These chemical peculiarities are reflected in their mineralogy. The principal mineral is always enstatite (or clinoenstatite in part), which is pure or nearly pure $MgSiO_3$. A little diopside may be present. Olivine is normally absent; indeed, excess SiO_2 is frequently present, as accessory quartz, tridymite, or cristobalite. The high degree of reduction is also shown by the presence of calcium as oldhamite, manganese as alabandite, and chromium as daubreelite. The metal phase has a low concentration of nickel and is entirely kamacite.

Measured densities of the enstatite chondrites are 3.66 (Daniel's Kuil, St. Marks, Saint-Sauveur), 3.5 (Abee), 3.45 (Khairpur); the density is probably related to the amount of free iron present.

Some of the enstatite chondrites show well-developed chondritic structure, with prominent chondrules of radiating enstatite (e.g., St. Marks, Fig. 34), but others (Blithfield, Hvittis, Pillistfer) seem to have no chondrules at all, being granular aggregates of enstatite and other minerals (the crystalline enstatite chondrites of the Rose-Tschermak-Brezina classification).

The Olivine-Bronzite Chondrites

The olivine-bronzite chondrites are an abundant group; the Prior-Hey catalog lists 80 of them, and many of the unclassified chondrites belong to this group. With some experience they can frequently be identified on sight by their comparative richness in nickel-iron; this feature also makes them notably tougher than the olivine-hypersthene chondrites.

Chemically they are characterized by having most of their iron in the free state. The FeO content ranges from 7% to 12%; figures of less than 7% have been recorded, but when checked against the composition of the minerals these lower figures prove to be erroneous (the analysis figure for FeO is particularly liable to error where the true figure is low and the amount of free iron is high). In contrast to the enstatite chondrites, calcium, chromium, and manganese are present entirely as oxidic compounds.

Mineralogically they consist largely of olivine (25–40%), an ortho-

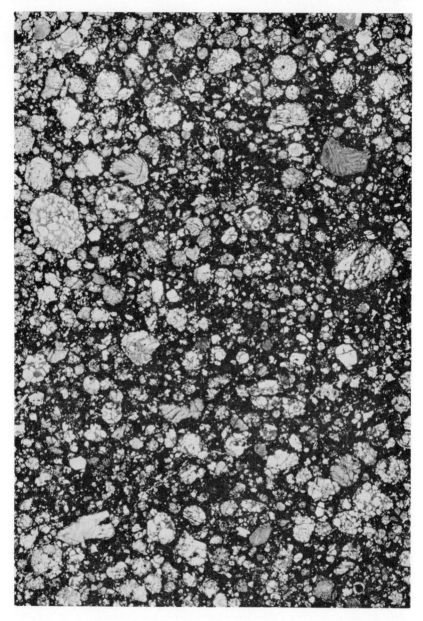

Fig. 35.   Thin section (10×) of the Selma meteorite, an olivine-bronzite chondrite; nickel-iron (partly altered to limonite) and troilite are black, olivine and
bronzite white to gray (courtesy J. Weber).

rhombic pyroxene (20–35%), together with nickel-iron (16–21%), plagioclase (usually oligoclase) or maskelynite, and troilite, with accessory amounts of a phosphate (apatite and/or merrillite), chromite, and diopside (Fig. 35). It is noteworthy that the olivine always contains 15 mole per cent or more of the Fe_2SiO_4 component, the bronzite 14 mole per cent or more of the $FeSiO_3$ component. There is evidently a cutoff in the iron content of the olivine and pyroxene below this figure.

Recorded densities of olivine-bronzite chondrites range widely, from about 3.4 to 3.9. This wide range is inconsistent with their comparative uniformity in chemical and mineralogical composition, and personal experience is that the true density of an unweathered olivine-bronzite chondrite is between 3.6 and 3.8.

The Olivine-Hypersthene Chondrites

These are evidently the commonest of the chondrites; the Prior-Hey catalog lists 159 of them, and many of the unclassified chondrites also belong to this group. With some experience they can usually be identified on sight by the comparatively small amount of nickel-iron which they contain; as a result of this they also tend to be more friable than the olivine-bronzite chondrites. Chondritic structure (Fig. 36) in many of the olivine-hypersthene chondrites is not as prominent as in the olivine-bronzite chondrites, and in some is quite obscure, apparently having been largely destroyed by partial recrystallization.

Chemically they are characterized by having a large part of their iron in the ferromagnesian silicates. The FeO content ranges from 12 to 22%; figures above 22% are erroneous or are of weathered meteorites containing free iron oxide formed from the nickel-iron or the troilite. The olivine-hypersthene chondrites are also distinguished from the other groups of chondrites by a lower total iron content, which is about 22%.

Mineralogically they are very similar to the olivine-bronzite chondrites. The principal minerals are olivine (35–60%) and hypersthene (25–35%), with lesser amounts of plagioclase (usually oligoclase) or maskelynite ($\sim$10%), nickel-iron ($\sim$8%), and troilite ($\sim$5%); accessory minerals are chromite and a phosphate (apatite and/or merrillite), and usually a little diopside. Those olivine-hypersthene chondrites relatively rich in iron may contain some pigeonite. The olivine

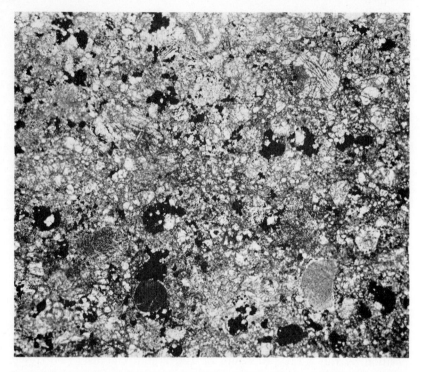

Fig. 36. Thin section (10×) of the Holbrook meteorite, an olivine-hypersthene chondrite, consisting of nickel-iron and troilite (black), and olivine and hypersthene (gray); white patches are holes in the section (courtesy J. Weber).

contains 22–32 mole per cent Fe_2SiO_4, the hypersthene 20–30 mole per cent $FeSiO_3$. The olivine and the pyroxene show the same compositional relationship as in the olivine-bronzite chondrites.

Recorded densities of the olivine-hypersthene chondrites range from 3.3 to 3.6. This range reflects the difficulty of making good density determinations, rather than a real variability in density. Personal experience indicates that the density of unweathered meteorites in this group is normally between 3.5 and 3.6.

The Olivine-Pigeonite Chondrites

When Prior drew up his classification of the chondritic meteorites he was not aware that in those with a high FeO content the pyroxene was pigeonite, not hypersthene, and hence he included these meteorites with the olivine-hypersthene chondrites. Nevertheless they form a distinct, if small, group (Table 11); they differ from the olivine-hypersthene chondrites not only in the nature of the pyroxene, but also in having a higher total iron content. Some of them are black from the presence of carbonaceous compounds (Fig. 37), although the carbon content does not exceed 0.5%. These meteorites are classed as ornansites and spherulitic carbonaceous chondrites in the Rose-Tschermak-Brezina system.

Chemically they are characterized by having most of their iron in the ferromagnesian silicates; the FeO content ranges from 22 to 29%. Mineralogically they are characterized by the predominance of olivine (about 70%), pigeonite in accessory amounts (about 5%), about 10% of plagioclase, 5–6% troilite, and accessory amounts of nickel-iron (0–5%); the nickel-iron is rich in nickel and is entirely taenite. They commonly contain a small amount of magnetite. Pentlandite instead of troilite is the predominant sulfide in one of them (Karoonda) and has also been recorded in Kaba and some others. It is usually difficult to determine the refractive indices, and hence the composition, of the olivine in these meteorites; this mineral is normally almost opaque from tiny inclusions, probably carbon. Measurements of olivine composition by the X-ray procedure of Yoder and Sahama (1957) gives compositions of from 30 to 40 mole per cent Fe_2SiO_4. The diffractom-

TABLE 11.   OLIVINE-PIGEONITE CHONDRITES

	Date of Fall	Weight (kg)	Notes
Felix (Alabama, U.S.A.)	5/15/1900	3	Carbonaceous
Chainpur (India)	5/9/1907	8	
Grosnaja (Caucasus, U.S.S.R.)	6/28/1861	3.3	Carbonaceous
Kaba (Hungary)	4/15/1857	3	Carbonaceous
Karoonda (South Australia)	11/25/1930	42	
Lancé (France)	7/23/1872	52	Carbonaceous
Mokoia (New Zealand)	11/26/1908	4	Carbonaceous
Ngawi (Java)	10/3/1883	1.39	
Ornans (France)	7/11/1868	6	
Tieschitz (Czechoslovakia)	7/15/1878	28	
Vigarano (Italy)	1/22/1910	16	Carbonaceous
Warrenton (Missouri, U.S.A.)	1/3/1877	1.6	

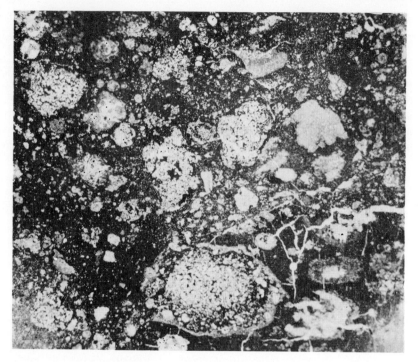

Fig. 37.   Thin section (10×) of the Mokoia meteorite, a carbonaceous olivine-pigeonite chondrite, showing incipient chondrules of finely granular olivine in a black groundmass (courtesy J. Weber).

eter peaks are frequently diffuse and irregular, indicating that the olivine is variable in composition within a single meteorite. This is in marked contrast to the olivine in the olivine-bronzite and olivine-hypersthene chondrites, which gives sharp and well-defined peaks on a diffractometer trace.

No analysis of pigeonite from an olivine-pigeonite chondrite has been made. Refractive index measurements indicate that it normally contains about 30–40 atom per cent Fe in total Ca + Fe + Mg. The presence of pigeonite in these meteorites may be of considerable significance in elucidating the conditions under which they formed. It may indicate a temperature of crystallization greater than 1100° C, which is the equilibrium transition temperature between orthorhombic and monoclinic pyroxene in this composition range (Kuno and Nagashima, 1952). However, an alternative hypothesis should be con-

sidered.   The olivine-pigeonite and the olivine-hypersthene chondrites contain approximately the same amount of calcium.   However,
in the olivine-pigeonite chondrites the total amount of pyroxene is
quite small, whereas in the olivine-hypersthene chondrites it makes up
a considerable amount of the ferromagnesian minerals.   Therefore, if
the amount of calcium in each type is similar, the *concentration* of
calcium will automatically be much higher in the pigeonite than in
the hypersthene.   In other words, the formation of pigeonite (probably metastably) may be conditioned by the concentration of calcium,
rather than by a high temperature of crystallization.

Recorded densities of the olivine-pigeonite chondrites range from
about 3.4 to 3.6.

The Carbonaceous Chondrites

The carbonaceous chondrites number comparatively few meteorites,
but in spite of their low abundance they occupy an extremely significant place, because of the peculiarities of their mineralogical and
chemical composition, especially the presence of hydrated minerals
and organic compounds.   All of them were seen to fall and were
picked up shortly afterwards; otherwise it is doubtful if they would
survive for any length of time (they are very friable and contain
water-soluble compounds)—of one of them it is recorded that when
placed in a glass of water it disintegrated and gave off a nasty smell!
Even if they did survive it would require an experienced collector to
recognize them as meteorites.

The first meteorite of this type fell at Alais in France on March 15,
1806.   When it was sent to Berzelius for chemical analysis he expressed
doubt that it was a meteorite, since its composition was so remarkably
different from all other meteorites known up to that time.   A second
one fell at Renazzo in Italy in 1824 and altogether some seventeen
meteorites of this type are now known (Table 12).   Rose in 1863
made a special grouping for "kohlige Meteorite," and in the final version of the Rose-Tschermak-Brezina classification the carbonaceous
chondrites were divided into three groups: carbonaceous chondrites,
spherulitic carbonaceous chondrites, and spherulitic veined carbonaceous chondrites.   The definition of a carbonaceous chondrite is no-
where clearly stated, but they can certainly be readily distinguished

TABLE 12.   CARBONACEOUS CHONDRITES

	Date of Fall	Weight (kg)	Notes
Alaïs (France)	3/15/1806	6	Type I
Al Rais (Arabia)	12/10/1957	0.16	Type II
Bells (Texas, U.S.A.)	9/9/1961	0.3	Type II
Boriskino (U.S.S.R.)	4/20/1930	1.17	Type II
Cold Bokkeveld (South Africa)	10/13/1838	3	Type II
Crescent (Oklahoma, U.S.A.)	8/17/1936	0.08	Type II
Erakot (India)	6/22/1940	0.11	Type II
Haripura (India)	1/17/1921	0.32	Type II
Ivuna (Tanganyika)	12/16/1938	0.70	Type I
Mighei (U.S.S.R.)	6/18/1889	8	Type II
Murray (Kentucky, U.S.A.)	9/20/1950	12.6	Type II
Nawapali (India)	6/6/1890	0.06	Type II
Nogoya (Argentina)	6/30/1879	4	Type II
Orgueil (France)	5/14/1864	10	Type I
Renazzo (Italy)	1/15/1824	5	Type II
Santa Cruz (Mexico)	9/3/1939	0.05	Type II
Tonk (India)	1/22/1911	0.01	Type I

from all other meteorites by their peculiar characteristics—dull black color, friability, generally low density, lack or almost total lack of free nickel-iron.

Wiik (1956) chemically analyzed eleven of the carbonaceous chondrites and took the analyses of three others from the literature. He showed that they could be divided into three subgroups, according to the mean values of certain constituents, as follows:

	SiO_2	MgO	C	H_2O	S
Type I	22.56	15.21	3.54	20.08	6.20
Type II	27.57	19.18	2.46	13.35	3.25
Type III	33.58	23.74	0.46	0.99	2.27

These three subgroups have characteristic physical and mineralogical differences. Type I carbonaceous chondrites have notably low density ($\sim$2.2), are largely made up of amorphous hydrated silicate, are strongly magnetic (apparently from finely divided iron-nickel spinel), and have much of their sulfur as water-soluble sulfate. Type II have densities in the range 2.5–2.9, are largely made up of serpentine, are weakly or non-magnetic, and have much of their sulfur in the free state. Type III carbonaceous chondrites have densities in the range

3.4–3.5, and are largely made up of olivine, with accessory pigeonite; they are here classified with the other (non-carbonaceous) olivine-pigeonite chondrites.

The Type I and Type II carbonaceous chondrites are never found as large stones (presumably because of the friability), the largest being the Mighei stone, which weighed about 8 kg. (One reason for the lack of research on the carbonaceous chondrites has been their rarity and lack of material.) The stones are coated with a black fusion crust, normally somewhat thicker than that on other stony meteorites. The interior is dark grey to black in color, sometimes with a greenish tinge. Type I carbonaceous chondrites contain no chondrules (an awkward contradiction); Type II contain chondrules which vary from meteorite to meteorite in size, abundance, and perfection in form (Fig. 38). These chondrules are olivine of forsterite composition, and enstatite or clinoenstatite.

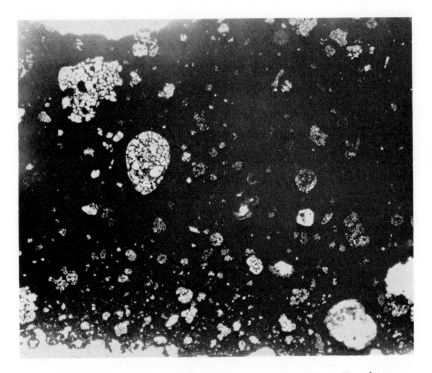

Fig. 38. Thin section (10×) of the Murray meteorite, a Type II carbonaceous chondrite, showing chondrules and irregular aggregates of olivine grains in an opaque groundmass of serpentine and carbonaceous matter (courtesy J. Weber).

Our knowledge of the chemical composition of the carbonaceous chondrites is largely due to the work of Wiik, although the earlier analyses also provide much useful information. Unfortunately Wiik's analyses of these meteorites are in part misleading because he reports all sulfur as FeS, a standard and well-founded practice, since in other meteorites the sulfur is present in this form. However, the Type I and Type II carbonaceous chondrites contain little or no FeS, and the sulfur is present largely as free S and sulfate. Wiik's analyses of these meteorites should be recast, reporting S separately and all Fe as FeO. Since Wiik determined total H_2O by heating a sample of the meteorite with an oxidizing agent (PbO_2) and condensing and weighing the water, this will include not only free and combined water and OH groups, but also H present in the organic material. Wiik reported figures for C and loss on ignition, commenting that the latter figure was total loss on ignition minus H_2O, C, and S, and was an approximate measure of the amount of organic compounds. The chemical analysis of carbonaceous chondrites presents some almost insoluble problems to the analyst. Wiik made a noteworthy contribution when he recalculated his analyses of the carbonaceous chondrites into atomic percentages on a water-, carbon-, oxygen-, and sulfur-free basis. The differences between the various types then disappear, and it is seen that they have essentially the same elemental composition for the major elements—Fe, Ni, Co, Si, Ti, Al, Mn, Mg, Ca, Na, K, P, and Cr—and they all belong to the H type of Urey and Craig.

Measurements of the content of minor and trace elements in the carbonaceous chondrites show that for many of these elements the abundances are the same as in the common chondrites. However, for a few of them—Bi, Pb, Tl, Hg, for example—the abundance in the carbonaceous chondrites is an order of magnitude or more higher than in the normal chondrites. The carbonaceous chondrites also show abnormally high contents of the inert gases, especially xenon.

Organic Material in Carbonaceous Chondrites

The occurrence of organic compounds in carbonaceous chondrites was noted as long ago as 1834 by Berzelius, when he analyzed the Alais meteorite. A considerable number of papers describing such occurrences were published during the nineteenth century, and are well summarized by Cohen (1894). Some of the organic compounds can be extracted from the carbonaceous chondrites by sublimation or by solvents such as alcohol, ether, or benzene. The amount of extractable compounds is generally small, seldom more than 1%, and with the minute amounts available little identification of the actual compounds was possible by the techniques of classical organic chemistry. Nevertheless, the work in the nineteenth century showed the presence of solid hydrocarbons, compounds containing C, H, and O, and compounds containing C, H, and S.

Cloez (1864) showed that the insoluble black carbonaceous material in the Orgueil meteorite is not graphite or amorphous carbon, but an organic compound. He separated it by dissolving the other material of the meteorite in boiling HCl followed by KOH; he obtained 6.4% of insoluble residue, which gave the following analysis: C, 63.45%; H, 5.98%; O (difference), 30.57%. The material is presumably a complex polymer of high molecular weight. The black carbonaceous material in other carbonaceous chondrites is probably similar; it is not graphite, because it is quite amorphous to X-ray diffraction.

In recent years the nature of the organic material in these meteorites has been the subject of renewed interest and investigation. Mueller (1953) made a careful study of the carbonaceous substances in the Cold Bokkeveld meteorite. Organic microanalysis gave the following figures: C, 2.20%; H, 1.53%; S, 1.99%; O, etc. (by difference), 4.84%; residue (non-organic), 89.44%; Mueller observes that part of the H and O may have been produced by the decomposition of hydrated silicates. Organic solvents (ethyl alcohol and benzene being found the most effective) extracted 1.1% of resinous material from the meteorite, consisting of organic compounds mixed with free sulfur. The sulfur (about 10–12%) was eliminated by hand picking, and the remainder gave the following analysis: C, 19.84%; H, 6.64%; N, 3.18%; S, 7.18%; Cl, 4.81%; O, etc., 40.02%; ash, 18.33%. The presence of chlorine is particularly interesting, as it has not been recorded by previous investigators, presumably because it was not looked for. A solution of the organic material in benzene showed no optical rotation, an important observation indicating that the material was formed by non-biological processes. The extracted organic material was insoluble in acids but soluble in alkali. Mueller deduced that it consisted of complex organic acids with some substituted N, S, and Cl. The material was not homogeneous, but contained compounds different in solubility.

Calvin (1961) has studied the infra-red and ultra-violet absorption spectra of extracts from the Murray and Orgueil carbonaceous chondrites. He concludes that these extracts contain a wide variety of organic compounds, including hydrocarbons and heterocyclic bases. He found no amino acids in aqueous extracts either of Murray or Orgueil. Briggs (1961) has demonstrated the presence of a variety of complex water-soluble organic compounds in Mokoia (a carbonaceous olivine-pigeonite chondrite), but was unable to identify them.

Nagy, Meinschein, and Hennessy (1961) have examined mass-spectrographically organic compounds from the Orgueil meteorite and have identified a number of paraffinoid hydrocarbon molecules in the C_{15}–C_{30} range, with peaks at C_{18} and C_{23}. They find a good correlation between the pattern of distribution of these hydrocarbons and that observed in material of biological origin such as butter and recent marine sediments.

The origin of these organic compounds is of course a question of extreme importance, as has been emphasized by Bernal (1961). Nagy and his co-workers believe that their observations indicate that the material is of biological origin, that there was living matter where these meteorites originated. In this they agree with the opinions of some of the early workers—Wöhler (1860) and Cloez (1864). On the other hand Berzelius in 1834 commented that the presence of these organic compounds in carbonaceous chondrites does not justify the conclusion that living matter existed where these meteorites originated. Mueller (1953) pointed out the significance of the fact that the extracts from the Cold Bokkeveld meteorite showed no measurable optical rotation, whereas the Earth's biologically formed organic compounds invariably show optical rotation. He writes, "In the light of modern organic chemical experience, there seems to be no great difficulty in accounting for a non-biological origin of the organic substances. The existence of CH, CN, and similar radicals in atmospheres of comets has been proved spectroscopically. It is reasonable to conjecture that under conditions of varying illumination and temperature a proportion of the constituents of such an atmosphere would polymerize into complex molecules." Such synthesis of complex organic compounds from methane, ammonia, and water has been demonstrated experimentally by Miller (1957).

Recently Claus and Nagy (1961) have presented evidence for the presence of fossil micro-organisms in the Orgueil and Ivuna meteorites. They refer to them non-committally as "organized elements," but state that they resemble fossil algae; they are roughly circular or hexagonal in form with diameters of the order of 0.01 mm. Morrison

(1962) has suggested that these "organized elements" are not micro-fossils, but are skeletal crystals (carbonaceous "snowflakes") resembling in their complexity the intricate forms of snowflakes. The nature and interpretation of these "organized elements" have been extensively discussed in a symposium by Urey and others (1962), without any consensus as to their biological or non-biological origin.

Origin of the Chondrites

The close relationships between the different chondrite groups demand explanation in any theory of the origin of these meteorites. The overall uniformity of composition in terms of most of the elements, and the sequential chemical and mineralogical relationships between the individual groups, support the theory that the chondritic meteorites were all derived from a common parent material. Prior (1920) held this view, and proposed that the different groups had been formed by the progressive oxidation of a highly reduced magma, the earliest stage being represented by the enstatite chondrites. Mason (1960a, b) and Ringwood (1961a) have theorized that the parent material was highly oxidized, its original state being similar to that of the Type I carbonaceous chondrites, the other groups of chondrites having been produced from this material by dehydration and progressive reduction. Mason suggested the following reaction:

$$Mg_4Fe_2Si_4O_{10}(OH)_8 \rightarrow 2(Mg,Fe)_2SiO_4 + 2(Mg,Fe)SiO_3 + 4H_2O$$

$$\text{serpentine} \qquad\qquad \text{olivine} \qquad\qquad \text{pyroxene}$$

$$\downarrow +2C$$

$$4MgSiO_3 + 2Fe + 2CO_2$$

$$\text{enstatite} \qquad \text{iron}$$

Urey and Craig (1953), from the occurrence of H and L types of chondrites, have argued that these types must have been derived from at least two asteroids of different composition. Urey (1961) has recently criticized the theory that material similar to that of the carbonaceous chondrites could be the parent material of all the chondritic meteorites, because of differences in chemical composition between the different groups. Fish, Goles, and Anders (1960) favor an initial material similar in composition to the carbonaceous chondrites, and the development of the other meteorite groups from this material in bodies of asteroidal size.

The origin of the characteristic chondritic structure is clearly part of the problem of the origin of these meteorites. Practically all investigators have accepted that chondrules were once molten drops, which requires a high temperature and a liquid state of the meteoritic material at one stage in its development. Ringwood (1961a) suggests that the required temperature may have been reduced considerably (to below 1000° C) by a high pressure of H_2O and CO_2. Mason (1960a) has argued from textural relations that the chondrites have never been molten, and that chondrules have formed from serpentine or amorphous hydrated silicates by solid-state recrystallization at comparatively moderate temperatures.

Wiik (1956) refused to speculate on the origin of the chondrites. However, he did present the following scheme of chemical evolution:

$$\text{Type I carbonaceous chondrites} \xrightarrow[\text{organic matter}]{-H_2O,\ S,\ \text{and}} \text{Type II carbonaceous}$$

$$\text{chondrites} \xrightarrow[\text{organic matter}]{-H_2O,\ S,\ O,\ \text{and}} \text{olivine-pigeonite chondrites} \xrightarrow{-O} \text{H group normal}$$

$$\text{chondrites (olivine-bronzite chondrites)} \xrightarrow{-O} \text{enstatite chondrites}$$

He writes "This is intended only to give a picture of the chemical relations between the subgroups, and not intended to suggest the genesis." Nevertheless, it does present a reasonable genetic sequence, representing essentially a progressive thermal metamorphism of the material of the Type I carbonaceous chondrites. In this connection it is significant that chondrules first appear in the Type II carbonaceous chondrites and that these chondrules consist of pure or nearly pure Mg_2SiO_4, despite the presence of much iron in these meteorites. The thermal decomposition of serpentine can take place at about 400° C (Bowen and Tuttle, 1949) and produces pure Mg_2SiO_4. The appearance of the chondrules in the Type II carbonaceous chondrites suggests spherulitic crystallization in a solid medium. Had the process gone in the reverse direction one would expect to find abundant chondrules of serpentine, formed by the hydration of olivine, in the carbonaceous chondrites. This is not the case. It is therefore plausible that the Type I carbonaceous chondrites represent a primitive material from which the other types of chondrites have been formed by thermal processes involving dehydration and reduction. This hypothesis is strongly supported by the work of Ringwood (1961a).

However, other investigators have argued that the evolutionary process has gone in the opposite direction, and that the carbonaceous chondrites are secondary objects produced by the alteration of olivine-pyroxene chondrites. Urey (1961) suggested this as a process of hydration and the addition of carbon and sulfur. Stulov (1960) has shown that the process does not necessarily involve the presence of water, and postulates the following reaction:

$$3Mg_2SiO_4 + Fe_2SiO_4 + 2CO + 2CH_4 = Mg_6Si_4O_{10}(OH)_8 + 4C + 2Fe$$

$$\underbrace{}_{\text{olivine}} \qquad\qquad\qquad\quad \text{serpentine}$$

It should be noted, however, that this reaction liberates free iron in the formation of the carbonaceous chondrites, but free iron is con-spicuously absent from these meteorites.

On the whole, the available data support the concept of a common source material for the chondritic meteorites. The chemical differ-ences between the different groups are of second-order magnitude in comparison to the overall uniformity of composition. However, if we start from a uniform parent material of carbonaceous chondrite composition, it is clear that the formation of the different chondrite groups can hardly have been a simple sequential process. The proc-esses of dehydration and reduction operated to produce two abundant groups, the olivine-bronzite and olivine-hypersthene chondrites, dif-fering somewhat in degree of reduction and markedly in their total iron content. The olivine-pigeonite chondrites are closely related to the carbonaceous chondrites and represent dehydration with compara-tively little reduction or chemical differentiation. The enstatite chon-drites are clearly marked off from all other groups by their high degree of reduction. These differences are not readily explained on the model of a single planet as expounded by Ringwood. The close chem-ical and mineralogical relationships between the different chondrite groups do not agree with these meteorites being chance aggregates of debris from collision between asteroids, as maintained by Urey and Craig. The theory of Fish, Goles, and Anders that these meteorites formed in asteroidal bodies seems most in accordance with the avail-able data.

7

The Achondrites

Introduction

The achondrites are a somewhat heterogeneous group of stony meteorites, considered together because they lack the characteristic chondrules of the chondritic stones. They commonly are much more coarsely crystallized than the chondrites, and show closer analogies in chemical and mineralogical composition to some terrestrial rocks. Nickel-iron is almost or completely lacking in most of them.

Prior divided the achondrites into two groups, the calcium-poor (0–3% CaO) and the calcium-rich (5–25% CaO) achondrites, a division which is followed here. He subdivided the calcium-poor achondrites into aubrites, ureilites, amphoterites and rodites, diogenites, and chassignites. Kvasha (1958) has shown that the amphoterites contain chondrules and belong to the olivine-hypersthene chondrites, and the rodites are closely related to, or identical with the diogenites, thus eliminating the subgroup of amphoterites and rodites. Prior subdivided the calcium-rich achondrites into angrites, nakhlites, eucrites, howardites, and shergottites. This subdivision is followed here, but the eucrites, howardites, and shergottites are considered as a single subgroup, since they are similar in chemical and mineralogical composition.

The individual achondrites are set out in Table 13. It will be noticed that they are nearly all falls. The rarity of achondrites as finds is partly due to their absolute rarity, but is certainly conditioned

TABLE 13. ACHONDRITES

A. Calcium-Poor Achondrites

1. Enstatite achondrites (aubrites)

	Date of fall	Weight (kg)
Aubres (France)	9/14/1836	0.8
Bishopville (U.S.A.)	3/25/1843	6
Bustee (India)	12/2/1852	2
Cumberland Falls (U.S.A.)	4/9/1919	24
Khor Temiki (Sudan)	4/8/1932	3
Norton County (U.S.A.)	2/18/1948	1070
Pena Blanca Spring (U.S.A.)	8/2/1946	70
Pesyanoe (U.S.S.R.)	10/2/1933	3.4
Shallowater (U.S.A.)	Found 1936	4.7

2. Hypersthene achondrites (diogenites)

	Date of fall	Weight (kg)
Ellemeet (Holland)	8/28/1925	1.5
Garland (U.S.A.)	1950	0.1
Ibbenbuhren (Germany)	7/16/1870	2
Johnstown (U.S.A.)	7/6/1924	40
Manegaon (India)	6/29/1843	0.04
Roda (Spain)	1871	0.4
Shalka (India)	11/30/1850	4
Tatahouine (Tunisia)	7/27/1931	12

3. Olivine achondrites (chassignites)

	Date of fall	Weight (kg)
Chassigny (France)	10/3/1815	4

4. Olivine-pigeonite achondrites (ureilites)

	Date of fall	Weight (kg)
Dyalpur (India)	5/8/1872	0.3
Goalpara (India)	Found 1868	2.2
Novo-Urei (U.S.S.R.)	9/4/1886	2.1

B. Calcium-Rich Achondrites

1. Pyroxene-plagioclase achondrites [eucrites (Eu) and howardites (Ho)]

	Date of fall	Weight (kg)	Type
Adalia (Turkey)	Found 1883	0.01	Eu?
Bereba (West Africa)	6/27/1924	18	Eu

TABLE 13. ACHONDRITES (*Continued*)

	Date of fall	Weight (kg)	Type
Bholghati (India)	10/29/1905	2.5	Ho?
Bialystok (Poland)	10/5/1827	4	Eu
Binda (Australia)	Found 1912	6	Ho
Brient (U.S.S.R.)	4/19/1933	5.5	Eu
Bununu (Nigeria)	1942	0.35	Ho
Cachari (Argentina)	Found 1916	23.5	Eu
Chaves (Portugal)	5/3/1926	2.7	Ho
Chervony Kut (U.S.S.R.)	6/23/1939	1.8	Eu
Frankfort (U.S.A.)	12/5/1868	0.6	Ho
Haraiya (India)	1878	1	Eu
Jodzie (U.S.S.R.)	6/17/1877	0.05	Ho?
Jonzac (France)	6/13/1819	5	Eu
Juvinas (France)	6/15/1821	91	Eu
Kapoeta (Sudan)	4/22/1942	11.34	Ho
Lakangaon (India)	11/24/1910	0.2	Eu?
Le Teilleul (France)	7/14/1845	0.8	Ho
Luotolax (Finland)	12/13/1813	0.9	Eu
Macibini (South Africa)	9/23/1936	2	Eu
Mässing (Germany)	12/13/1803	1.6	Eu
Medanitos (Argentina)	7/14/1953	0.03	Eu?
Moore County (U.S.A.)	4/21/1913	2	Eu
Nagaria (India)	4/24/1875	12	Eu?
Nobleborough (U.S.A.)	8/7/1823	2	Eu
Nuevo Laredo (Mexico)	5/1926	0.5	Eu
Padvarninkai (U.S.S.R.)	2/9/1929	3.8	Eu
Pampa del Infierno (Argentina)	Found 1895	0.9	Ho?
Pasamonte (U.S.A.)	3/24/1933	4	Eu
Pavlovka (U.S.S.R.)	8/2/1882	2.1	Ho
Peramiho (Tanganyika)	10/24/1899	0.16	Eu
Petersburg (U.S.A.)	8/5/1855	2	Eu
Serra de Mage (Brazil)	10/1/1923	1.5	Eu
Shergotty (India)	8/25/1865	5	Eu
Sioux County (U.S.A.)	8/8/1933	4.1	Eu
Stannern (Czechoslovakia)	5/22/1808	52	Eu
Washougal (U.S.A.)	7/21/1939	0.2	Ho
Yurtuk (U.S.S.R.)	4/2/1936	1.5	Ho
Zmenj (U.S.S.R.)	8/1858	0.2	Ho

2. Augite achondrites (angrites)

	Date of fall	Weight (kg)
Angra dos Reis (Brazil)	1/30/1869	1.5

3. Diopside-olivine achondrites (nakhlites)

	Date of fall	Weight (kg)
Lafayette (U.S.A.)	Found 1931	0.6
Nakhla (Egypt)	6/28/1911	40

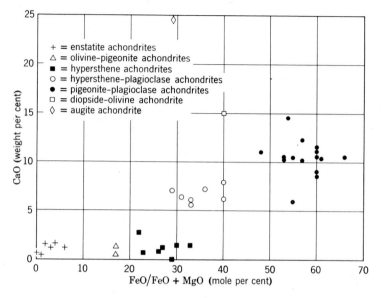

Fig. 39. Plot of CaO (weight per cent) against FeO/FeO + MgO (mole per cent) for the achondrites.

in part by the difficulty of distinguishing these meteorites from terrestrial rocks.

The achondrites may be characterized chemically by their CaO content and the relative proportions of FeO and MgO. When their analyses are plotted with respect to those components (Fig. 39), the different subgroups fall into distinct fields, with marked hiatuses between them. It is noteworthy that the FeO/FeO + MgO mole percentage, which does not exceed 50 in the chondrites, is higher than this in the eucrites, reaching 66.

The Enstatite Achondrites

The enstatite achondrites are generally referred to as aubrites, after the first member of the group to fall—Aubres. They are sometimes known as bustites, from the Bustee meteorite. They have been included with the hypersthene achondrites as a single group known as chladnites. However, just as there is a chemical and mineralogical hiatus between the enstatite chondrites and the other chondrite types, a similar hiatus exists between the enstatite achondrites (in which the pyroxene is essentially iron-free) and the hypersthene achondrites.

Chemically the enstatite achondrites are characterized by consisting of SiO_2 and MgO almost to the exclusion of other components. The molecular proportion of SiO_2 to MgO is close to 1 and as a result these meteorites consist largely of enstatite, sometimes with a little forsterite or diopside. The enstatite occasionally shows areas of intergrown clinoenstatite. A little oligoclase may be present. Nickel-iron, low in nickel (about 6%) and hence usually kamacite, is commonly present in accessory amount, as is troilite. Schreibersite inclusions in the nickel-iron are recorded from the Norton County aubrite. Oldhamite is present in Norton County and Bustee.

The structure of the enstatite achondrites is normally brecciated, coarse angular fragments of enstatite up to 20–30 mm across occurring in a groundmass of crushed and broken enstatite. The only unbrecciated aubrite is Shallowater, in which individual enstatite crystals up to 45 mm long were noted.

Included here with the aubrites is Cumberland Falls, which has been distinguished as a unique type, called a whitleyite, because of its having inclusions of a black chondrite (Fig. 40). However, the

Fig. 40. Polished surface of the Cumberland Falls meteorite, showing angular pieces of a black chondrite in a matrix of fragmental enstatite and clinoenstatite (white); the specimen is 10 cm long (courtesy The American Museum of Natural History).

main material of Cumberland Falls is an enstatite achondrite indistinguishable from other meteorites of this class. Nevertheless the presence of these fragments of a chondrite within the Cumberland Falls meteorite poses a pretty problem of origin.

The problem of origin of the enstatite achondrites as a group is a difficult one. The following statement by Foshag (1940) on the Shallowater meteorite is equally applicable to other meteorites of this class:

> The silicate portion of the Shallowater meteorite, like the terrestrial enstatolites and other similar pyroxenites, is difficult to interpret in the light of the equilibrium relations found in the system MgO-SiO$_2$ as worked out by N. L. Bowen and Olaf Anderson and the system MgO-FeO-SiO$_2$ as worked out by N. L. Bowen and J. F. Schairer. Clinoenstatite is the stable form at high temperatures; its inversion to enstatite takes place at 1140°. From the data furnished by these equilibrium studies it is not to be expected that an orthorhombic enstatite of the nature of the Shallowater meteorite should form directly by crystallization of its melt, or magma, without the intervention of the monoclinic form. For terrestrial enstatolites, Bowen and Schairer have been led to conclude that these rocks are the result of local accumulations of crystals of one kind from a magma of complex constitution.
>
> Yet the extraordinarily coarse crystallinity of the enstatite, the total lack of any evidence of its derivation from a pre-existing form, and the reticulated fabric of the crystals, as well as the relation of the forsterite to the enstatite, suggest that this meteorite may, indeed, be a direct crystallization from a magma. The evidence of orthorhombic pyroxenes in the chondrules of chondritic meteoric stones, too, should not be overlooked. There is perhaps some mechanism that has as yet escaped attention by which orthorhombic pyroxenes can result directly from melts.

Foshag's statement is equally valid today, with the substitution of protoenstatite for clinoenstatite in the second sentence. It is conceivable that the enstatite achondrites are related in origin to the enstatite chondrites, which they resemble in their mineralogy (except for the presence of considerable amounts of nickel-iron and troilite in the enstatite chondrites). Melting of a large body of enstatite chondrite composition, with gravitational segregation of the nickel-iron and troilite, would leave a magma of approximately enstatite composition. The problem still remains to crystallize such a magma directly to enstatite. However, Boyd and England (1961) have noted that the complicated polymorphism of MgSiO$_3$ is eliminated at moderate pressures (about 6 kilobars and higher); under these circumstances enstatite will crystallize directly from a melt of appropriate composition.

The Hypersthene Achondrites

The hypersthene achondrites number eight in all, if we include the so-called rodites Ellemeet and Roda, which are not essentially different in composition. They are all witnessed falls. The chemical analyses show a very limited range in composition: SiO_2, 49.83–54.94%; MgO, 23.32–28.35%; FeO, 13.64–20.81%; Al_2O_3, up to 2.86%; CaO, 0.08–2.61%; Na_2O, less than 1%; Cr_2O_3, up to 1.82%; FeS, up to 1.73%; free nickel-iron, traces to less than 1%. Some of these variations, especially in minor constituents, may be more apparent than real, as a result of analytical error.

Mineralogically, these meteorites consist of hypersthene, with only accessory amounts of other minerals—plagioclase (bytownite in Johns-

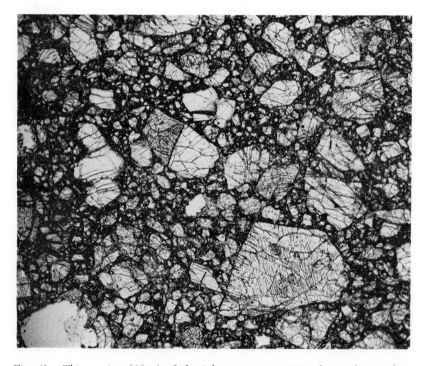

Fig. 41. Thin section (10×) of the Johnstown meteorite, a hypersthene achondrite, showing angular fragments of hypersthene in a matrix of comminuted hypersthene (courtesy J. Weber).

town), olivine, troilite, nickel-iron, and chromite. Structurally, they are similar to the enstatite achondrites in being crushed and brecciated, with large angular fragments of hypersthene in a groundmass of crushed and broken hypersthene (Fig. 41). In Johnstown some of the large fragments are up to 50 mm across.

The origin of the hypersthene achondrites, as essentially monomineralic rocks composed of coarsely crystalline orthopyroxene, presents problems similar to those outlined in the discussion of the enstatite achondrites. The complete hiatus in composition between these two groups of achondrites is even more marked than the hiatus between the enstatite chondrites and the olivine-bronzite chondrites.

The Olivine Achondrites

The only representative of this group is Chassigny, a stone weighing about 4 kg which fell in France on October 3, 1815. This meteorite is very similar in composition and structure to a terrestrial dunite, except that the FeO content is higher in the meteorite. It consists of more than 95% olivine, with accessory amounts of chromite, plagioclase (probably oligoclase), and a little nickel-iron rich in nickel. The chemical analysis of the stone indicates that the olivine contains about 33 mole per cent Fe_2SiO_4, a composition confirmed by the gamma refractive index, which is 1.733.

In composition Chassigny resembles the olivine-pigeonite chondrites, but differs from them in the absence of chondrules and in its allotriomorphic-granular texture. Possibly it represents a recrystallized olivine-pigeonite chondrite.

The Olivine-Pigeonite Achondrites

The ureilites form a unique group of three meteorites, quite distinct in composition from all other achondrites. They are especially noteworthy for the presence of diamond in two of them (Novo-Urei and Goalpara), and they are the only achondrites with an appreciable amount of nickel-iron.

The original analysis of the Novo-Urei meteorite is as follows: SiO_2, 39.51%; MgO, 35.80%; FeO, 13.35%; CaO, 1.40%; Al_2O_3, 0.60%; Cr_2O_3,

0.95%; MnO, 0.43%; P, 0.02%; Ni, 0.20%; Fe, 5.25%; C, 2.26%; S, 0.15%. Ringwood (1960a) has subsequently determined Na_2O (0.45%) and TiO_2 (0.09%). The analysis shows that the meteorite consists almost entirely of ferromagnesian silicates, with a small amount of nickel-iron, the nickel-iron being unusually low in nickel, about 4%.

Mineralogically and structurally the three ureilites are closely similar. They consist of grains of olivine and clinopyroxene in a black carbonaceous matrix. The nickel-iron occurs as small granules around the grains of silicate. A small amount of troilite, corresponding to the S in the analysis, is present. In Novo-Urei about 1% of diamond is present, and graphite also occurs. According to Ringwood the refractive indices of the olivine in Novo-Urei are $\alpha = 1.676$, $\gamma = 1.712$, and of the clinopyroxene $\alpha = 1.676$, $\gamma = 1.691$. X-ray examination shows that the clinopyroxene is pigeonite. The refractive indices show that the olivine contains 21 mole per cent Fe_2SiO_4, the pigeonite 20% Fe of total Ca + Mg + Fe atoms. No feldspar has been detected in Novo-Urei, and the small amount of Na_2O and Al_2O_3 in the analysis is possibly in the pigeonite.

The composition of Novo-Urei resembles that of an olivine-hypersthene chondrite; it differs in that nickel, sulfur, iron, sodium, and aluminum are relatively deficient, magnesium relatively increased: Ringwood remarks that the deficient elements are those which would be concentrated in the liquid phase if a chondrite had been subjected to a small degree of partial melting, and suggests such an origin. However, Novo-Urei and the other ureilites differ from the olivine-hypersthene chondrites in their considerable carbon content. In this respect their closest relatives are the carbonaceous chondrites. Possibly the ureilites represent some line of descent from the carbonaceous chondrites marked by rather special conditions of temperature, pressure, and chemical differentiation.

The presence of diamonds in the ureilites has been argued as proving their origin deep within a body of lunar or planetary dimensions. However, Lipschutz and Anders (1961) have shown that diamonds can be formed by extreme shock such as produced by impact at high speeds, in which case the diamonds in the ureilites could be formed in this way. It is noteworthy that the grain size of diamonds in these meteorites is very small.

The Pyroxene-Plagioclase Achondrites

These meteorites are the commonest type of achondrites; of the 63 achondrites listed in Table 13, 39 belong to this subgroup. The names applied to these meteorites—eucrites and howardites—were originally introduced by Rose in 1863; he defined the eucrites as consisting of augite and anorthite, the howardites of olivine and anorthite. Tschermak (1872a) showed that the mineral identified by Rose as olivine is actually orthopyroxene, and Wahl (1907) that the so-called augite was a calcium-poor clinopyroxene now known as pigeonite. Hence the modern version of Rose's definitions would be: eucrites—pigeonite and anorthite; howardites—hypersthene and anorthite. These criteria are used here, and the designations in Table 13 are made on this basis, although they differ in some instances from those given in the Prior-Hey catalog. The subdivision of the pyroxene-plagioclase achondrites into eucrites and howardites has not been consistently followed, partly because of lack of precise mineral identification, partly because of confusion in the criteria of distinction. Lacroix (1926) decided that the howardites were only a textural variety of the eucrites and did not merit a special name, and this has been accepted by some later workers. However, Rose's definitions, when modernized, are quite logical and clearcut, and Fig. 39 shows that the howardites and eucrites are distinct chemically; howardites are in the FeO/FeO + MgO range 29–40, eucrites in the range 48–66, and the howardites show a generally lower CaO content than the eucrites.

Tschermak (1872b) described the Shergotty meteorite as a variety of eucrite in which the plagioclase was represented by maskelynite. Brezina (1904) elevated it to a distinct type, named shergottite. However, the utility of such a distinction is not obvious, and Shergotty and the only other meteorite of this type, Padvarninkai, are here classed as eucrites.

Chemically the pyroxene-plagioclase achondrites are notably similar in composition; if we leave out an exceptional one (Serra de Mage) the range in composition shown by analyses is: SiO_2, 47.21–53.11%; MgO, 6.50–17.59%; FeO, 13.19–21.85%; Al_2O_3, 5.90–15.57%; CaO, 5.79–12.18%; Na_2O, 0.15–2.04%; FeS, 0.05–1.40%; a small amount of free nickel-iron is recorded in some of them. Serra de Mage is exceptional in being very low in FeO and MgO and high in CaO and Al_2O_3; its analysis is: SiO_2, 43.42%; TiO_2, 0.18%; MgO, 3.18%; Fe_2O_3, 2.07%; FeO, 4.79%; Al_2O_3, 27.20%; CaO, 14.53%; Na_2O, 1.59%; K_2O, 0.20%; Cr_2O_3, 0.33%; MnO, 0.58%; S, 0.04%; H_2O+, 1.71%; H_2O-, 0.01%. The exceptional composition of Serra de Mage is due to its having an unusually high plagioclase and low pyroxene content.

Mineralogically the pyroxene-plagioclase achondrites consist almost entirely of these two minerals; usually pyroxene somewhat exceeds plagioclase in amount. The plagioclase is bytownite or anorthite, the composition being near An_{90}. In Shergotty the maskelynite has the composition of labradorite. The pyroxene in the howardites is hypersthene, sometimes with minor pigeonite; in the eucrites it is pigeonite, sometimes with minor hypersthene. Hess and Henderson (1949) have carefully examined the pigeonite in the Moore County eucrite, and have shown that it has undergone a complex series of exsolution processes; they deduce a sequence of subsolidus reactions involving the separation of five different pyroxenes from the original homogeneous pigeonite. It is noteworthy that in the pyroxene-plagioclase achondrites there is an almost perfect balance between SiO_2 and basic oxides; sometimes there is a slight excess of SiO_2 which appears as accessory tridymite or quartz, and rarely a slight deficiency, which results in accessory olivine. The only other accessory minerals are chromite, and in some a little nickel-iron, ilmenite, and troilite.

The structure of some of the pyroxene-plagioclase achondrites is similar to that of terrestrial gabbros (Fig. 42). Hess and Henderson (1949) have made a petrofabric study of the Moore County eucrite and report that the fabric of this meteorite indicates a dimensional orientation of the plagioclase and pyroxene. The plagioclase b and c crystallographic axes and the pyroxene c axis tend to lie in one plane. This fabric is considered to represent primary layering developed by crystal accumulation on the floor of a magma chamber. They interpret this as crystallization differentiation in an original planetary body.

Many of the pyroxene-plagioclase achondrites are brecciated. Foshag (1938) has shown that in the Pasamonte meteorite the individual fragments differ somewhat in composition. Wahl (1952) classifies many of these meteorites as polymict breccias because of the variety of the individual fragments; besides the fragments of eucrites and howardites he identified fragments of other achondrite types in them.

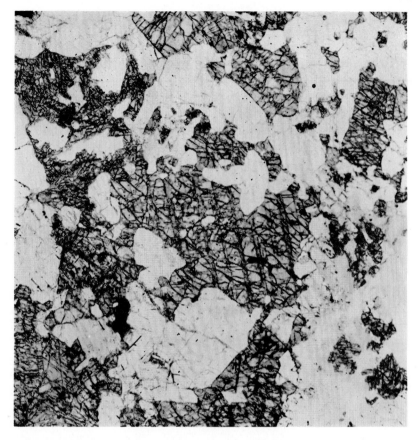

Fig. 42. Thin section (10×) of the Moore County meteorite, showing pigeonite (gray) and bytownite (white); note augite lamellae parallel to the 001 plane in pigeonite (courtesy the U.S. National Museum).

The Augite Achondrites

The sole representative of this type is the Angra dos Reis meteorite, which fell near Rio de Janeiro, Brazil, on January 30, 1869. It was a single stone weighing about $1\frac{1}{2}$ kg, of which much has been lost; Wülfing in 1897 could account for only 397 grams.

The chemical analysis is: SiO_2, 44.58%; MgO, 10.05%; FeO, 8.50%; Fe_2O_3, 1.81%; Al_2O_3, 8.86%; CaO, 24.51%; Na_2O, 0.26%; K_2O, 0.19%; Cr_2O_3, trace; TiO_2, 2.39%; P_2O_5, 0.13%; FeS, 1.26%. The analysis is noteworthy in showing more CaO and TiO_2 than any other meteorite.

Mineralogically the meteorite consists of more than 90% of augite, together with a little olivine and troilite; no feldspar was observed, so the small amount of sodium and potassium is presumably in the pyroxene. The small amount of P_2O_5 shown by the analysis suggests the presence of accessory apatite. The optical properties of the augite were carefully described by Wahl (1907).

This unique stone shows no close relationship to any other achondrite. It is the only meteorite which contains true augite, an aluminum-rich member of the diopside-hedenbergite series.

The Diopside-Olivine Achondrites

The diopside-olivine achondrites or nakhlites are represented by two meteorites, Lafayette (Indiana, U.S.A.) and Nakhla (Egypt). Little is known about Lafayette except that it is a nakhlite; it was recognized by O. C. Farrington in 1931 in the collections of Purdue University, a single hemispherical stone weighing some 600 grams, with a well-developed glassy crust and a very fresh appearance; it must have been a recent fall. The Nakhla fall was a shower of stones, about 40 in all, with a total weight of 40 kg; it has been described in detail by Prior (1912).

The bulk composition of Nakhla is as follows: SiO_2, 48.96%; TiO_2, 0.38%; Al_2O_3, 1.74%; Cr_2O_3, 0.33%; Fe_2O_3, 1.29%; FeO, 19.63%; MnO, 0.09%; CaO, 15.17%; MgO, 12.01%; Na_2O, 0.41%; K_2O, 0.14%; S, 0.06%; $H_2O + 110°$, 0.07%; $H_2O - 110°$, 0.17%. The density of the meteorite is 3.47. After Angra dos Reis it is the meteorite richest in CaO. Mineralogically the stone consists of about 75% diopside, 15% olivine, with a small amount of plagioclase (oligoclase-andesine) and a little magnetite. The calculated composition of the diopside is 50 mole per cent $CaMgSi_2O_6$, 25 mole per cent $CaFeSi_2O_6$, and 25 mole per cent $MgFeSi_2O_6$. The olivine is notably rich in the Fe_2SiO_4 component, about 66%, which is much higher than any other olivine from a meteorite.

Origin of the Achondrites

The mineralogy and texture of most of the achondrites suggests that they originally crystallized from a magma. The petrochemistry of the achondrites has been extensively discussed by Moore (1962). Some of the major groups—the diogenites, the howardites, and the eucrites—show a sequential relationship in mineralogy and chemical composition which closely parallels that of certain igneous rocks, and which can be interpreted in terms of the information available from laboratory studies of silicate melts. Composition-wise these groups fall in the system anorthite-forsterite-silica, except for the presence of iron replacing some of the magnesium. The phase relations in this system were worked out by Andersen (1915) and are illustrated in Fig. 43. An initial melt of meteoritic composition might be represented by point O. A melt of this composition on cooling begins to crystallize at about 1500° C with the separation of olivine, and the liquid changes composition in the direction of T. At T(1375° C) olivine reacts with the liquid and pyroxene begins to crystallize. As cooling continues, the composition of the liquid changes along the boundary curve T-1260°. When the temperature has fallen to 1260° anorthite begins

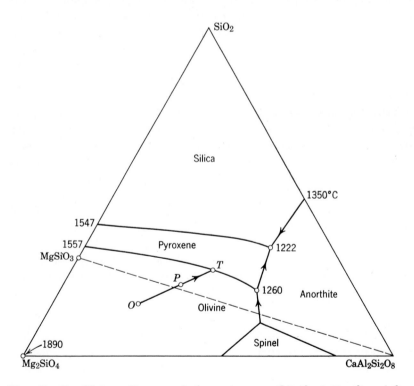

Fig. 43. Equilibrium diagram of the system anorthite-forsterite-silica (after Andersen, 1915).

to separate. The temperature then remains constant at 1260°, with the continued crystallization of anorthite and pyroxene, liquid and olivine decreasing in amount, until all the liquid disappears. The completely crystalline mass now consists of pyroxene, anorthite, and olivine.

If the original melt had the composition P, again olivine would be the first mineral to crystallize. The same course would be followed, but at 1260° some liquid would remain after all the olivine had been resorbed. This liquid would continue to crystallize with the separation of pyroxene and anorthite, and would change in composition along the 1260°–1222° line. At 1222° tridymite would begin to crystallize, and the remaining liquid would solidify as a mass of anorthite, pyroxene, and tridymite. It should be noted that the early formed olivine is completely resorbed during the latter crystallization of the liquid.

Such a crystallization process provided a ready explanation of the sequence from the diogenites (hypersthene achondrites) to the howardites and eucrites (pyroxene-plagioclase achondrites) and the presence of accessory olivine in some of the diogenites and howardites and of accessory tridymite in some of the eucrites. The composition of an initial melt was presumably near P, since pure olivine achondrites are essentially unknown (Chassigny being the only representative); however, it is conceivable that the pallasites may represent an earlier stage of crystallization in the sequence outlined above, as suggested by Ringwood (1961a). In this connection a comparison of the average compositions of different groups is illuminating. Table 14 shows that the average of these three groups of pyroxene-plagioclase achondrites, hypersthene achondrites, and pallasites is similar to the average composition of the chondrites. A melt of chondritic composition if crystallized under the conditions outlined here could give rise to meteorites ranging from pallasites through diogenites and howardites to eucrites.

In the above discussion the nature of the pyroxene has not been considered. However, the pyroxene in these meteorites shows a regular change, increasing in iron content from an Fe/Fe + Mg atom percentage of 20–30 in the diogenites to 30–40 in the howardites to 40–60 in the eucrites, with a changeover from hypersthene to pigeonite at an Fe/Fe + Mg percentage of about 35. This is consistent with the trend of pyroxene crystallization in basic magmas, as discussed by Hess (1960). With an initial melt at about 1100° and an initial Fe/Fe + Mg percentage of about 20, hypersthene will crystallize, and

TABLE 14.   AVERAGE COMPOSITIONS OF THE PYROXENE-PLAGIOCLASE ACHONDRITES, HYPERSTHENE ACHONDRITES, PALLASITES, AND CHONDRITES (YAVNEL AND DYAKONOVA, 1958)

	SiO_2	MgO	FeO	Al_2O_3	CaO	Na_2O	Fe
Pyroxene-plagioclase achondrites	49	11	17	11	10	0.5	0.9
Hypersthene achondrites	53	26.5	17	1.5	1.4	—	0.8
Pallasites	18	21	6.5	0.1	—	—	48
Sum	120	58.5	40.5	12.6	11.4	0.5	49.7
Average	40	19.5	13.5	4.2	3.8	0.2	16.6
Chondrites	37	23.6	13.5	2.4	1.9	0.9	11.2

as crystallization proceeds this mineral becomes richer in iron. At an Fe/Fe + Mg percentage between 30 and 40 the crystallization curve crosses the hypersthene-pigeonite inversion curve, and beyond this the pyroxene will be a pigeonite with increasing iron content as crystallization proceeds.

8

The Stony-Irons

Introduction

The stony-irons are a minor group of meteorites, 64 in all according to Table 15, or 4% of all meteorites. Of these 11 are falls and 53 finds. They are divided into two major groups according to the nature of the silicate minerals, the pallasites (olivine stony-irons) and mesosiderites (pyroxene-plagioclase stony-irons), with two other types, lodranite (olivine-bronzite stony-iron) and siderophyre (bronzite-tridymite stony iron), each represented by a single meteorite.

The designation of a separate division of stony-irons was proposed by Maskelyne in 1863 and has been widely adopted. Nevertheless some classifications omit this division, placing the pallasites as a separate group within the irons, and the mesosiderites as a separate group within the achondrites. The division of stony-irons is a rather artificial one at best, since the pallasites and mesosiderites have little in common save the presence of an appreciable amount of nickel-iron. The lodranite and siderophyre resemble the pallasites rather than the mesosiderites.

TABLE 15.   THE STONY-IRONS

	Find or Fall	Weight (kg)
1. Pallasites		
Admire (U.S.A.)	Find	50
Ahumada (Mexico)	Find	53
Albin (U.S.A.)	Find	37
Anderson (U.S.A.)	Find	1.5
Antofagasta (Chile)	Find	14
Argonia (U.S.A.)	Find	34
Bendock (Australia)	Find	27
Bitburg (Germany)	Find	1600
Brahin (U.S.S.R.)	Find	700
Brenham (U.S.A.)	Find	1000
Calderilla (Chile)	Fell 1883?	0.02
Cold Bay (Alaska)	Find	0.32
Eagle Station (U.S.A.)	Find	36
Finmarken (Norway)	Find	77.5
Giroux (Canada)	Find	4.7
Glorieta Mountain (U.S.A.)	Find	146
Gran Chaco (Argentina)	Find	1.6
Huckitta (Australia)	Find	1415
Ilimaes (Chile)	Find	95
Imilac (Chile)	Find	240
Itzawisis (Southwest Africa)	Find	0.35
Krasnoyarsk (U.S.S.R.)	Find	687
Lipovskii (U.S.S.R.)	Find	3.8
Marjalahti (Finland)	Fell 6/1/1902	45
Molong (Australia)	Find	105
Mount Dyrring (Australia)	Find	11
Mount Vernon (U.S.A.)	Find	160
Newport (U.S.A.)	Find	5.6
Ollague (Bolivia)	Find	6.7
Pavlodar (U.S.S.R.)	Find	4.5
Phillips County (U.S.A.)	Find	1.3
Pojoaque (U.S.A.)	Find	0.08
Port Orford (U.S.A.)	Find	0.03
Salta (Argentina)	Find	27.1
Singhur (India)	Find	14.2
Somervell County (U.S.A.)	Find	12
South Bend (U.S.A.)	Find	2.5
Springwater (Canada)	Find	67
Sterling (U.S.A.)	Find	0.7
Zaisho (Japan)	Fell 2/1/1898	0.33

TABLE 15. THE STONY-IRONS (*Continued*)

	Find or Fall	Weight (kg)
2. Siderophyre		
Steinbach (Germany)	Find	98
3. Lodranite		
Lodran (Pakistan)	Fell 10/1/1868	0.97
4. Mesosiderites		
Barea (Spain)	Fell 7/4/1842	3.2
Bencubbin (Australia)	Find	54
Clover Springs (U.S.A.)	Find	7.7
Crab Orchard (U.S.A.)	Find	49
Dalgaranga (Australia)	Find	1.1
Dalgety Downs (Australia)	Find	—
Dyarrl Island (New Guinea)	Fell 1/31/1933	0.17
Enon (U.S.A.)	Find	0.76
Estherville (U.S.A.)	Fell 10/5/1879	340
Hainholz (Germany)	Find	16.5
Lowicz (Poland)	Fell 3/12/1935	59
Lujan (Argentina)	Find	0.03
Mincy (U.S.A.)	Find	90
Morristown (U.S.A.)	Find	16
Patwar (Pakistan)	Fell 7/29/1935	37.4
Pinnaroo (Australia)	Find	39.4
Simondium (South Africa)	Find	1.2
Udei Station (Nigeria)	Fell 1927	103
Vaca Muerta (Chile)	Find	37.2
Veramin (Iran)	Fell 5/3/1880	54
Weatherford (U.S.A.)	Find	2.0
Winona (U.S.A.)	Find	24

The Pallasites

In the Rose-Tschermak-Brezina classification the pallasites are sub-divided into four groups on the physical nature (rounded, angular, brecciated, etc.) of the olivine crystals (Figs. 44, 45). However, they form a homogeneous group, both chemically and mineralogically, although Yavnel (1958) has divided them on chemical composition into

Fig. 44. Polished surface of the Ollague pallasite, showing rounded grains of olivine (black) in a matrix of nickel-iron; the specimen is 10 cm across (courtesy The American Museum of Natural History).

two subgroups. In one of the larger subgroups, the olivine averages about 13% FeO (range 10–16%), and in the other the olivine averages about 19% FeO (range 16–21%). These two groups show corresponding differences in the composition and amount of nickel-iron; the first group averages about 55% nickel-iron, with a nickel content averaging 10%, whereas the second group has a considerably lower nickel-iron content (about 30–35%) with a higher nickel content (about 15%). However, the amount of nickel-iron may vary considerably from specimen to specimen of the same pallasite, and even within individual specimens; for example, most specimens of Brenham are typical pallasite, but some are entirely nickel-iron, and some shows patches of pallasite and nickel-iron in the same specimen (Fig. 46).

The mineralogy of the pallasites is comparatively simple. For the nickel-iron both kamacite and taenite are present, commonly in Widmanstatten intergrowth. Small inclusions of troilite and schreibersite are often present in the nickel-iron. The olivine occurs in angular or rounded grains, normally 5–10 mm across, but sometimes considerably larger; its composition varies as mentioned above, ranging from about 10–20 mole per cent of the Fe_2SiO_4 component. The only other accessory mineral is farringtonite, $Mg_3(PO_4)_2$, recognized in 1960 in

Fig. 45. Polished surface of the Eagle Station pallasite, showing angular and brecciated grains of olivine in a matrix of nickel-iron; the specimen is 10 cm across (courtesy The American Museum of Natural History).

Fig. 46. Polished surface of the Brenham meteorite; most specimens of Brenham are typical pallasite, but this shows a large patch of nickel-iron with Widman-statten structure; the specimen is 18 cm long (courtesy The American Museum of Natural History).

the Springwater pallasite; it is probably present in other pallasites but has been overlooked, since it resembles the olivine closely, and is always associated with it.

Siderophyre

The single siderophyre is the Steinbach meteorite (also known as Breitenbach or Rittersgrün), which has been known since 1724. It consists of a network of nickel-iron which encloses granular aggregates of orthopyroxene and minor tridymite, the nickel-iron and silicate being present in approximately equal amounts. Accessory minerals are schreibersite (in the nickel-iron), chromite, and troilite. The nickel-iron contains about 10% Ni and shows the Widmanstatten structure. The orthopyroxene contains about 20 mole per cent $FeSiO_3$ and is therefore on the boundary between bronzite and hypersthene. Its optical properties are: $\alpha = 1.673$, $\beta = 1.681$, $\gamma = 1.688$; optically negative, $2V = 86°$. The optical properties of the tridymite are: $\alpha = 1.471$, $\beta = 1.472$, $\gamma = 1.474$; optically positive, $2V = 76°$ (Heide, 1923).

Lodranite

The single example of this type is the Lodran meteorite, which fell near Multan, Pakistan, on October 1, 1868. It was described by Tschermak (1870). It consists of a friable aggregate of granular olivine and orthopyroxene in a discontinuous aggregate of nickel-iron, these three principal phases being present in approximately equal amounts by weight. The nickel-iron contains about 9% nickel; the olivine contains about 13 mole per cent Fe_2SiO_4, the orthopyroxene about 17 mole per cent $FeSiO_3$. Accessory minerals are chromite, troilite, and possibly a little plagioclase.

The Mesosiderites

Some 20 mesosiderites are known, considerably fewer than the pallasites (40), but 7 mesosiderites are observed falls, against only 2

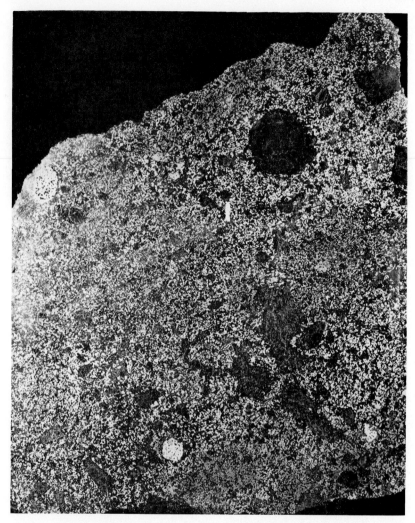

Fig. 47. Polished surface of the Mincy mesosiderite, showing nickel-iron (white) in silicate matrix (gray to black); the specimen is 20 cm across (courtesy The American Museum of Natural History).

pallasites, so that the mesosiderites may have a greater absolute abundance. They are probably less likely to be recognized as meteorites than the pallasites.

In the Rose-Tschermak-Brezina classification a separate group of grahamites is recognized among the stony-irons; they are supposed

to differ from the mesosiderites by the presence of plagioclase in the
grahamites and its absence in the mesosiderites. However, Prior
(1918) has shown that structurally, mineralogically, and chemically
there are no real distinctions between the two groups, and they are
here treated as a single group.

The mesosiderites are composed of approximately equal amounts
of nickel-iron and silicates. The nickel-iron does not generally form
a continuous network, as in the pallasites, but is usually irregularly
distributed in grains of different sizes throughout the meteorite (Figs.
47, 48). The silicates (plagioclase and pyroxene) frequently show
a cataclastic structure, fragments of pyroxene and plagioclase crystals
being scattered through a granulated mass of the same minerals (Fig.
49).

The nickel-iron normally contains about 7% nickel; it does not show
Widmanstatten structure, except when it is present as rather large
nodules. The silicates are mainly pyroxene and plagioclase, the
pyroxene being in greater amount than the plagioclase, the composition of which is anorthite or bytownite. The pyroxene is normally
hypersthene with about 20–30 mole per cent of the $FeSiO_3$ component;

Fig. 48. Polished surface of the Estherville meteorite; in this mesosiderite the
nickel-iron (white) tends to occur in aggregates and nodules, instead of being
disseminated throughout the meteorite as in Mincy; the specimen is 30 cm long
(courtesy The American Museum of Natural History).

Fig. 49. Thin section (10×) of the Veramin mesosiderite, consisting of nickel-iron (black), orthopyroxene (light gray) and plagioclase (white) (courtesy J. Weber).

pigeonite may be present as an accessory, and in the Crab Orchard mesosiderite is the dominant pyroxene. Accessory minerals are troilite, chromite, schreibersite, apatite and/or merrillite, and olivine. The last mineral occurs in small amount (usually less than 2%) in comparatively large isolated grains; it is much richer in magnesium than the associated pyroxene, usually having about 10 mole per cent of the Fe_2SiO_4 component.

A few mesosiderites (e.g., Bencubbin, Patwar) have almost pure $MgSiO_3$ as the pyroxene; in these meteorites nickel-iron is predominant, and they should probably be classed as irons with silicate inclusions.

Prior (1918) pointed out that the silicate phases of the mesosiderites are similar to those of the eucrites and howardites. He writes, "The curiously uneven distribution of the iron and the rather sporadic occurrence of the olivine suggest that both these constituents are in some way foreign to the main mass of stony matter consisting of anorthite and pyroxene, and to this idea the peculiar structural features of these meteorites lend support. . . . From the author's point of view of a genetic relationship of meteorites, therefore, there is considerable *a priori* evidence in favor of the idea that the characters of this group of meteorites may be most reasonably explained as the result of a mixture of two types, to one of which belong the pyroxene and anorthite, and to the other the iron and olivine; a eucritic magma . . . having been invaded by a pallasitic magma."

Lovering (1962) has re-examined some of the mesosiderites and considers it more likely that a solid mass of eucritic composition was invaded by molten nickel-iron carrying with it the olivine. The great difference in magnesium content between the olivine and pyroxene, noted above, supports the belief that these two minerals originated in different chemical environments.

9

The Irons

Introduction

In numbers the iron meteorites are the second largest group of meteorites, there being a total of 545 iron meteorites to 932 stones (Prior-Hey catalog, 1953). In total mass the iron meteorites far outweigh the stones, since all large meteorites are irons, and the average mass of an iron is much greater than that of a stone. However, in terms of falls the irons are clearly subordinate, there being only 41 witnessed falls of irons to 628 witnessed falls of stones, which undoubtedly reflects their abundance relative to the stones.

The irons may be grouped into a sequence, based on structure, and closely linked with the nickel content. This sequence is:

	Falls	Finds	Total
Hexahedrites, 4–6% Ni	6	49	55
Octahedrites, 6–14% Ni	27	364	391
Nickel-rich ataxites, >12% Ni	—	36	36

The Prior-Hey catalog distinguishes a group of metabolites (2 falls, 12 finds), which have the same composition range as the octahedrites but do not show Widmanstatten structure; they appear to be recrystallized octahedrites. In addition, the catalog lists 6 falls and 36 finds as unclassified irons. One unique meteorite which fell near Soroti in

Uganda in 1945 consists of approximately equal amounts of nickel-iron and troilite, and has been honored with the name sorotiite (Henderson and Perry, 1958).

Chemical Composition

Numerous calculations have been made of the average composition of the iron meteorites. That of Brown and Patterson (1947), based on 107 analyses, the average recalculated to 100 (after eliminating the small amounts of P, S, and C shown in many analyses) is: Fe, 90.78%; Ni, 8.59%; Co, 0.63%. Lovering (1957a) has pointed out that when the masses of the individual meteorites are taken into account the average will be displaced towards a higher nickel content, since the individual nickel-rich irons tend to be heavier than the nickel-poor irons. He believes that the absolute value for the nickel content of the total mass of iron meteorites is about 11%.

The frequency of occurrence of specific nickel contents shows some significant features. Figure 50 is a plot of nickel content against number of analyses (Yavnel, 1958). The first feature to note is that no iron meteorite contains less than 4% nickel—actually, most modern analyses (e.g., Henderson, 1941) show at least 5% nickel, and some of the analyses with lower nickel content are probably erroneous. The next feature is the sharp peak at 5.5% Ni, which is the composition of many of the hexahedrites. Another peak at 8% Ni corresponds to a large number of octahedrites. Very few iron meteorites contain more than 20% Ni; these are:

Freda (U.S.A.)	23.49%
Wedderburn (Australia)	23.95%
San Cristobal (Chile)	25.44%
Twin City (U.S.A.)	29.91%
Lime Creek (U.S.A.)	29.99%
Santa Catharina (Brazil)	33.97%
Oktibbeha County (U.S.A.)	62.01%

Analyses of meteoritic iron show, besides Fe, Ni, and Co, small amounts of P, S, Cr, and C, as a result of the presence of included schreibersite, troilite, daubreelite, cohenite, and graphite or other form of carbon. Iron meteorites sometimes contain inclusions of silicate

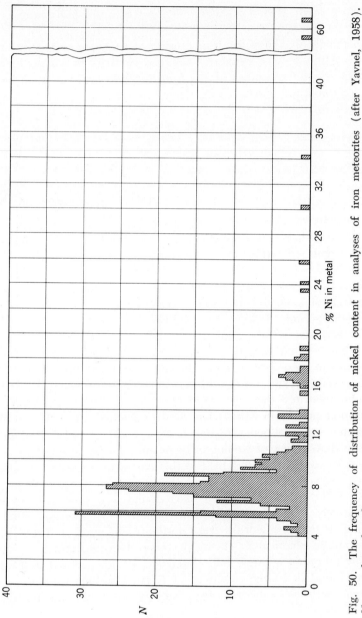

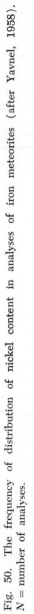

Fig. 50. The frequency of distribution of nickel content in analyses of iron meteorites (after Yavnel, 1958). N = number of analyses.

minerals, usually enstatite and/or olivine which are practically iron-free.

Mineralogically the nickel-iron consists of kamacite or taenite or a mixture of these. The structures assumed by these two minerals are the basis for the groupings of the iron meteorites. They have been well described and illustrated by Perry (1944), and will be discussed separately for each group.

The Hexahedrites

The hexahedrites are so-called because they normally consist of large crystals of kamacite, which are cubic (cube = hexahedron). These crystals have cleavage parallel to the faces of a cube and on etching a polished surface show fine lines (Neumann lines, or bands) as a result of twinning on a trapezohedron face (Fig. 51). Table 16 lists 55 hexahedrites, of which 6 are falls. Most hexahedrites are single crystals of kamacite, but some, inaccurately called "brecciated," are actually granular hexahedrites consisting of aggregates of crystals, often of large size. The granulation is conspicuous because these irons often separate along the crystal boundaries. The orientation of Neumann lines in these grains shows the differing orientation of the different crystals. The so-called nickel-poor ataxites are here included in the hexahedrites; they are identical in chemical and mineralogical composition, and Perry (1944) has shown that they cannot be readily demarcated. Nickel-poor ataxites have a finely granular structure, and may show traces of Neumann lines and cubic cleavage; they are believed to have originated by the thermal metamorphism of hexahedrites, probably during periods of close approach to the Sun.

Most of the hexahedrites have been found in a small number of comparatively limited geographical regions. Henderson (1941) showed that the hexahedrites from northern Chile (12 in Table 16) are essentially identical in chemical composition and structure, and probably represent a single fall. Similarly, 10 others listed in Table 16 were found in contiguous areas of North Carolina, Georgia, and Alabama; and the hexahedrites from Mexico and Texas may also represent a single fall.

Uhlig (1955) has discussed the significance of Neumann bands in meteoritic nickel-iron. They are lamellae of mechanically twinned

Fig. 51. Polished and etched surface of the Bennett County meteorite, a hexa-hedrite (Ni = 5.25%); it consists of a single crystal of kamacite, and shows Neumann lines, the delicate series of parallel bands (courtesy U.S. National Museum).

metal, produced by twinning of the body-centered cubic structure of kamacite along the (112) planes. Such twins do not readily form in the face-centered cubic structure of taenite. In meteorites Neumann bands are practically ubiquitous in the hexahedrites, and can be observed in the kamacite bands of the octahedrites and in the kamacite particles of stony meteorites. Uhlig has shown that the presence of Neumann bands in meteoritic nickel-iron is the result of strong mechanical deformation at relatively low temperatures, presumably below 300° C and not above 600° C. In the case of the iron meteorites he interprets this to mean that sometime in their history the body or bodies of which they formed a part were subjected to violent impact or explosion.

TABLE 16. HEXAHEDRITES AND NICKEL-POOR ATAXITES

(Observed falls are indicated with an asterisk)

	Date of Fall or Find	Weight (kg)
Aragon (Georgia, U.S.A.)	1898	0.05
Aswan (Egypt)	1955	12
Auburn (Alabama, U.S.A.)	1867	4
*Avce (Italy)	3/31/1908	1.2
Bellsbank (South Africa)	1955	38
Bennett County (South Dakota, U.S.A.)	1934	89
Bingera (Australia)	1880	6.6
*Boguslavka (U.S.S.R.)	10/18/1916	256
*Braunau (Czechoslovakia)	7/14/1847	39
Bruno (Canada)	1931	13
Cachiyuyal (Chile)	1874	2.5
Cedartown (Georgia, U.S.A.)	Before 1898	11.3
Coahuila (Mexico)	1837	~1200
Coya Norte (Chile)	1927	17.9
Dorofeevka (U.S.S.R.)	1910	12.5
Edmonton (Canada)	1939	7.3
El Burro (Mexico)	1939	36
Filomena (Chile)	Before 1941	21.1
Hex River Mountains (South Africa)	1882	60
Holland's Store (Georgia, U.S.A.)	1887	12
Indian Valley (Virginia, U.S.A.)	1887	14
Iredall (Texas, U.S.A.)	1898	1.5
Keen Mountain (Virginia, U.S.A.)	1950	6.7
Kendall County (Texas, U.S.A.)	1887	21
Lick Creek (North Carolina, U.S.A.)	1879	1.2
Lombard (Montana, U.S.A.)	1953	7
Mayodan (North Carolina, U.S.A.)	1920	15
Mejillones (Chile)	Before 1875	15
Mount Joy (Pennsylvania, U.S.A.)	1887	380
Murphy (North Carolina, U.S.A.)	1899	8
Navajo (Arizona, U.S.A.)	1921	220
Negrillos (Chile)	Before 1936	28.5
Nenntmannsdorf (Germany)	1872	12.5
New Mexico (New Mexico, U.S.A.)	1935	0.1
*Okano (Japan)	4/7/1904	4.7
Opava (Czechoslovakia)	1925	14.3
Otumpa (Argentina)	1576	>8000
Puripica (Chile)	1929	19

TABLE 16. HEXAHEDRITES AND NICKEL-POOR ATAXITES (*Continued*)

	Date of Fall or Find	Weight (kg)
Quillagua (Chile)	1938	78
Richland (Texas, U.S.A.)	1951	13.6
Rio Loa (Chile)	1915	4
Sandia Mountains (New Mexico, U.S.A.)	1925	15
San Martin (Chile)	Before 1924	29
Scottsville (Kentucky, U.S.A.)	1867	10
Sierra Gorda (Chile)	1898	22
*Sikhote-Alin (U.S.S.R.)	2/12/1947	70,000
Smithonia (Georgia, U.S.A.)	1940	70
Summit (Alabama, U.S.A.)	1890	1
*Tandil (Argentina)	1916?	1
Tocopilla (Chile)	1927	75
Tombigbee River (Alabama, U.S.A.)	1859	40
Union (Chile)	1930	22
Uwet (Nigeria)	Before 1903	50
Walker County (Alabama, U.S.A.)	1932	70
Yarroweyah (Australia)	1903	10

The hexahedrites are remarkably uniform in chemical composition, comprising about 93.5% Fe, 5.5% Ni, and 0.5% Co, the remainder being P, S, Cr, and C. As a result of their uniformity in composition, they show a uniformity in density; Henderson and Perry (1954) have shown that the density of the metal phase in the hexahedrites is 7.90 ± 0.02. Lower values have been recorded, but are due to erroneous measurements or samples contaminated with alteration products.

As mentioned previously, hexahedrites consist essentially of kamacite. Accessory minerals are schreibersite, both as macroscopic inclusions and as minute plates (rhabdites); troilite, usually in rounded nodules; daubreelite, commonly adjacent to troilite or intergrown with it; and graphite, as nodules, or in association with troilite.

With increasing nickel content ($\sim$6% Ni) hexahedrites grade into coarsest octahedrites. When the nickel content exceeds its maximum solubility in kamacite, the nickel-rich phase taenite segregates along the boundaries of the kamacite crystals. The initial segregation of taenite theoretically marks the transition between the hexahedrites and the octahedrites. For some meteorites whose composition lies close to the boundary the classification as a hexahedrite or coarsest octahedrite may be a matter of opinion.

The Octahedrites

The octahedrites are by far the commonest type of iron meteorite. They are so-called because they show an orientation of kamacite and taenite bands parallel to octahedral planes—the Widmanstatten structure.

The Widmanstatten structure is a pattern of bands crossing one another in two, three, or four directions (Figs. 52, 53, 54). The broader parts of bands are kamacite, and are bordered by thin lamel-

Fig. 52. Polished and etched surface of the Arispe meteorite, a coarse octahedrite (Ni = 6.77%); the broad bands are kamacite (frequently showing Neumann lines), and are bordered by microscopically thin and discontinuous lamellae of taenite (courtesy U.S. National Museum).

Fig. 53. Polished and etched surface of the Merceditas meteorite, a medium octahedrite (Ni = 7.33%); the kamacite bands (bordered by thin taenite lamellae) intersect almost at right angles, indicating that the section is cut almost parallel to a (100) plane in the originally homogeneous crystal of gamma-iron; the specimen is 22 cm long (courtesy The American Museum of Natural History).

lae of taenite; the angular interstices between the bands are composed of plessite. The pattern of the Widmanstatten structure is illustrated in Fig. 55, which shows the differing appearance of the structure, depending upon the orientation of the section. If the section is parallel to an octahedral plane, three systems of bands appear, at 60° to each other. If the section is parallel to a cubic plane, two systems of bands intersecting at right angles are seen. If the section is parallel to a dodecahedral plane, three systems of bands are visible, two at an angle of 109° to each other, and the third bisecting this angle. A random section shows four systems of bands with different angles of intersection.

In the Rose-Tschermak-Brezina classification five types of octa-hedrites are recognized, based on the width of the kamacite bands. These are as follows (numbers of each type are from the Prior-Hey catalog):

Name	Band Width of Kamacite (mm)	Number
Coarsest octahedrites	>2.5	21
Coarse octahedrites	1.5–2.5	86
Medium octahedrites	0.5–1.5	181
Fine octahedrites	0.2–0.5	59
Finest octahedrites	<0.2	22

Lovering et al. (1957) have measured the width of the kamacite bands in 63 octahedrites and propose a simplification of the above classification into three types, coarse (kamacite bands >2.0 mm), medium (0.5–2.0 mm) and fine (<0.5 mm) octahedrites. There is a direct relationship between structure and composition, the coarse octahedrites having 6–8% Ni, the medium 7–9% Ni, and the fine 8–14% Ni. The coarse octahedrites grade into the hexahedrites, the fine octahedrites into the nickel-rich ataxites. Massalski (1962) has also discussed the relationship between the Widmanstatten structure and the nickel content.

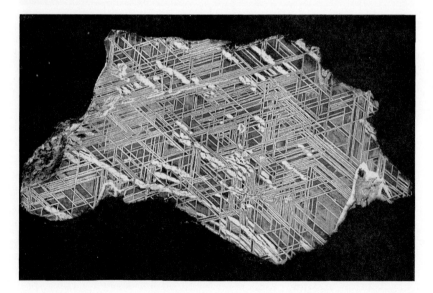

Fig. 54. Polished and etched surface of the Edmonton (Kentucky) meteorite, a fine octahedrite (Ni = 12.57%); the narrow white bands are kamacite, and the gray angular areas enclosed by these bands are plessite; the irregular white bands cutting across the octahedral pattern are also kamacite; the specimen is 12 cm long (courtesy U.S. National Museum).

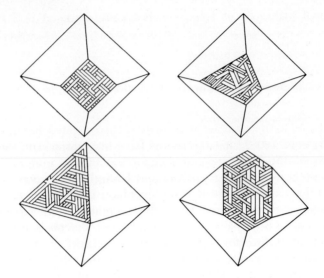

Fig. 55. The appearance of the Widmanstatten structure as controlled by the crystallographic orientation of the section.

Accessory minerals in the octahedrites include schreibersite, troilite, cohenite (in the coarsest octahedrites), and graphite. Diamonds have been recorded in Canyon Diablo and Magura (the latter record needs confirmation). Lawrencite may be present. Chromite is of widespread occurrence in small amounts, generally in association with troilite and cohenite.

The Nickel-Rich Ataxites

As the nickel content of the octahedrites increases the bands of kamacite become narrower and narrower. Eventually, at 12–14% Ni, they become extremely narrow and discontinuous, and the Widmanstatten structure disappears. Meteorites of this kind are classified as nickel-rich ataxites (Fig. 56). Some 36 are known (Table 17), all of them finds; unlike the other classes of meteorites, no nickel-rich ataxite has been observed to fall. They consist essentially of plessite, except for the few with more than 25% Ni, which consist of taenite with small inclusions of kamacite commonly arranged in a trigonal pattern.

The Iron Meteorites in Terms of the Fe-Ni System

The Fe-Ni system has been extensively investigated because of its metallurgical interest, and the results have been applied to the interpretation of the structure and composition of the iron meteorites, most recently by Lovering (1957a) and Uhlig (1954). Some caution is called for in the application of the phase relations in the simple Fe-Ni system to meteorites, since they contain additional elements in small amounts, specifically Co, C, S, and P; cobalt presumably has much the same effect as nickel, but the effect of the other elements cannot be readily predicted. In addition, all the work on the simple system has been done at 1 atmosphere pressure, whereas the

Fig. 56. Polished and etched surface of the Dayton meteorite, a nickel-rich ataxite (Ni = 18.10%); it consists essentially of fine-grained plessite (courtesy U.S. National Museum).

TABLE 17. NICKEL-RICH ATAXITES

Name	Date of Find	Weight (kg)
Babb's Mill (Tennessee, U.S.A.)	1842	143
Botetourt County (West Virginia, U.S.A.)	1850	—
Cape of Good Hope (South Africa)	1793	136
Chinga (U.S.S.R.)	1913	80
Dayton (Ohio, U.S.A.)	1892	26.3
Deep Springs (North Carolina, U.S.A.)	1846	11.5
El Qoseir (Egypt)	1921	2.4
Freda (North Dakota, U.S.A.)	1919	0.27
Guffey (Colorado, U.S.A.)	1907	310
Hoba (Southwest Africa)	1920	60,000
Illinois Gulch (Montana, U.S.A.)	1899	2.5
Iquique (Chile)	1871	12.5
Klondike (Canada)	1901	16.5
Kokomo (Indiana, U.S.A.)	1862	1.8
Lime Creek (Alabama, U.S.A.)	1834	0.65
Linville (North Carolina, U.S.A.)	1882	0.44
Monahans (Texas, U.S.A.)	1938	27.9
Morradal (Norway)	1892	2.75
Nordheim (Texas, U.S.A.)	1932	15.2
Oktibbeha County (Mississippi, U.S.A.)	1854	0.16
Ottsjö (Sweden)	1951	—
Pinon (New Mexico, U.S.A.)	1928	17.9
Rafruti (Switzerland)	1886	18.2
San Cristobal (Chile)	1882	5
Santa Catharina (Brazil)	1875	7000
Shingle Springs (California, U.S.A.)	1869	38.5
Smithland (Kentucky, U.S.A.)	1839	5
South Byron (New York, U.S.A.)	1915	6
Tawallah Valley (Australia)	1939	75.8
Ternera (Chile)	Before 1891	0.65
Tlacotepec (Mexico)	1903	70.6
Tucson (Arizona, U.S.A.)	Before 1850	975
Washington County (Colorado, U.S.A.)	1927	5.75
Weaver Mountains (Arizona, U.S.A.)	1898	38.8
Wedderburn (Australia)	Before 1953	0.21
Wiley (Colorado, U.S.A.)	1938	3.5

iron meteorites may have crystallized at much higher pressures. Nevertheless the data on the simple system can be correlated with the phase relation observed in the meteorites, and useful deductions can be made regarding the conditions of their formation.

The solid-liquid relations in the Fe-Ni system are illustrated in Fig. 57. Pure iron melts at 1539° C, and the melting point is lowered by the addition of nickel. The liquidus curve reaches a minimum of 1430° at a nickel content of 68%, and then rises again to the melting point of pure nickel. The solidus curve is complicated by the occurrence of the delta phase at low nickel concentrations, but this can be ignored when dealing with iron meteorites, since they all contain sufficient nickel to form the gamma phase, with the structure of taenite, which crystallizes from all melts of meteoritic composition.

Lovering has shown that the relative weights and abundances of the iron meteorites of different types indicates an average composition of about 11% Ni. If an iron-nickel melt of this composition (A, Fig. 57) is crystallized under equilibrium conditions, the first phase to crystallize will be gamma phase with 5.5% Ni (B, Fig. 57). Continued crystallization will produce an increasing amount of this phase with an increasing Ni content, while the liquid decreases in volume but also increases in Ni content. At point C the last drop of liquid (composition D, approximately 20% Ni) crystallizes and we have a solid mass of gamma phase with homogeneous nickel content equal to that of the original melt (11% Ni).

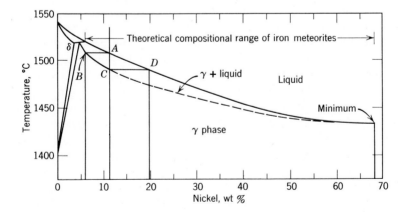

Fig. 57.   Solidus-liquidus relations in the iron-nickel system (Lovering, 1957a).

However, it is readily conceivable that under non-equilibrium conditions crystal fractionation could occur, with the production of solid phases with differing nickel contents. If the first solid phase (composition B, 5.5% Ni) is withdrawn from the system and thereby rendered incapable of reacting with the remaining melt, then this melt will be richer in nickel than under equilibrium conditions. Progressive crystallization with the removal of the solid phase from the remaining melt could continue in this manner until the minimum on the solidus and liquidus curves at 68% Ni is reached. The nickel content of the crystallizing phase of a melt with 11% Ni can thus vary, under non-equilibrium conditions, from 5.5% Ni to 68% Ni. It is significant that the observed range in nickel content of iron meteorites is from 5% Ni to approximately 62% Ni. Lovering therefore concludes that the observed range in nickel content of iron meteorites may be explained by their having differentiated during the crystallization of an originally homogeneous iron-nickel melt containing 11% Ni, this melt having formed the core of a parent meteorite body.

The subsolidus relations in the Fe-Ni system are illustrated in Fig. 58 (Owen and Liu, 1949). On cooling, pure iron changes at 918° C from the face-centered cubic structure of the gamma phase to the body-centered cubic structure of the alpha phase. The addition of nickel decreases the temperature of the gamma-alpha transformation and introduces a two-phase region in which a low-nickel alpha phase coexists with gamma phase richer in nickel. This two-phase region broadens at lower temperatures; as the temperature falls the nickel content of both phases increases, but that of the gamma phase increases much more rapidly than that of the alpha phase. The amount of each phase varies to accommodate the change in composition of the individual phases, and if during the cooling process the alpha phase reaches the same nickel content as the original gamma phase, the amount of the latter will diminish to zero. Thus, if we start with an alloy containing 6.5% Ni at say 1000° C and cool it under equilibrium conditions, it will be homogeneous gamma phase until 750° C, when alpha phase containing 2% Ni will begin to separate. On further cooling the amount of alpha phase steadily increases, as does its nickel content; the amount of gamma phase progressively decreases, while its nickel content increases. At a little above 400° C the alloy will consist almost entirely of alpha phase containing slightly less than 6.5% Ni, together with a little gamma phase containing 42% Ni. At 400° the gamma phase is completely resorbed, and the alloy consists entirely of alpha phase containing 6.5% Ni.

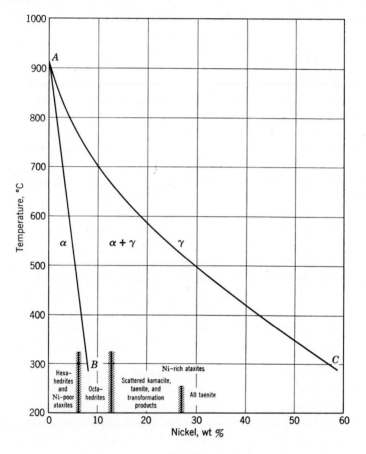

Fig. 58. Phase diagram for iron-nickel alloys at 1 atmosphere pressure, combined with iron meteorite classification (Uhlig, 1954).

The relationship of this phase equilibrium diagram to the interpretation of the composition and structure of the iron meteorites is readily seen. The hexahedrites and the nickel-poor ataxites (consisting entirely of alpha phase kamacite) fall in the field of the alpha phase at temperatures below about 500° C; the majority of the iron meteorites (octahedrites and nickel-rich ataxites, consisting of a mixture of alpha and gamma phase kamacite and taenite) fall in the two-phase field in the same temperature region; a few extremely nickel-rich ataxites consist entirely of taenite and fall in the field of the gamma phase.

When a nickel-iron alloy is cooled slowly into the two-phase field
the alpha phase precipitates preferentially along the octahedral planes
of the gamma phase. This is the explanation for the Widmanstatten
structure, with kamacite bands bordered by taenite lamellae following
the octahedral planes of the originally homogeneous gamma phase.
The Widmanstatten pattern is good evidence for the extremely slow
cooling of the octahedrites within the alpha plus gamma field. In
most octahedrites the Widmanstatten pattern is continuous throughout
the meteorite, showing that it originally consised of a large single
crystal of gamma phase. The size of these crystals is also important
evidence of very slow crystallization. Widmanstatten structures have

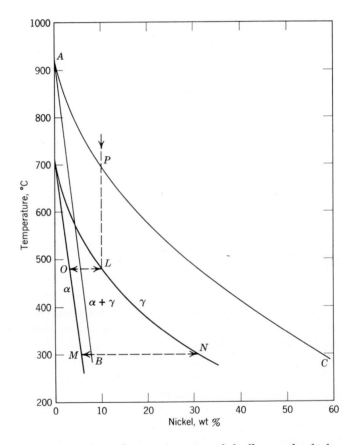

Fig. 59. Estimated phase diagram for iron-nickel alloys under high pressure;
light lines trace phase boundaries at 1 atmosphere (Uhlig, 1954).

been produced in artificial iron-nickel alloys by very slow cooling, but these structures are only visible on high magnification, in contrast to the macroscopic structure of the octahedrites. Iron meteorites presumably cooled so much more slowly that the separated phases achieved larger dimensions, making them visible to the naked eye.

The nickel-rich ataxites have more than about 14% Ni, and do not show the Widmanstatten structure, but consist of scattered fields of kamacite in a groundmass of plessite; ataxites containing more than about 27% Ni are all taenite. Uhlig (1954) points out that from the subsolidus phase diagram of the Fe-Ni system there is no obvious reason for the absence of Widmanstatten structure in iron meteorites containing more than 14% Ni. A meteorite containing 15% Ni, for example, enters the alpha plus gamma field at 640° C, and given sufficient time should develop a Widmanstatten structure as readily as a 12% alloy, which enters this field at 675° C. Uhlig presents evidence indicating that crystallization under high pressure is responsible for these discrepancies. The phase diagram of Owen and Liu was established for 1 atmosphere pressure. Application of the Clapeyron-Clausius equation indicates that high pressures will lower the temperature of the gamma-alpha transformation, and diminish the two-phase region. Uhlig's suggested phase diagram for high pressures is given in Fig. 59. An alloy cooling from high temperatures begins to segregate alpha phase at L instead of P, producing taenite of composition L and kamacite of composition O. As the alloy is slowly cooled, the taenite and kamacite eventually reach compositions of N and M at 300° C, below which any further change will be extremely slow because of restricted diffusion, as shown by laboratory experiments and also by calculations of the diffusion rates at this temperature.

From considerations of this kind Uhlig concludes that the composition and structure of iron meteorites indicates an equilibrium reached at about 300° C and pressures of the order of 10^5 atmospheres. This of course is good evidence for their formation in the interior of a body of planetary dimensions.

10

The Elemental Composition
of Meteoritic Matter

ONE of the principal stimuli to the study of meteorites is the fact that they are the only tangible samples of the universe beyond our own planet. By analyzing them we may hope to arrive at some conclusions regarding the composition of the universe as a whole, and the relative and absolute abundances of the chemical elements. With this purpose in mind many investigators have grappled with the problem of the analysis of meteorites, not only for the major constituents, but also for the minor and trace elements. Many data are available in the literature, but the interpretation of these data is often fraught with difficulty and uncertainty.

There are various practical difficulties in obtaining reliable data. The selection of material is one of these—what class of meteorite shall be analyzed—an iron, a stony-iron, a chondrite, or an achondrite (and within each of these classes there are distinct groups of different compositions)? There is good evidence that the chondrites are both the commonest and the least differentiated of the various meteorite types, and that, therefore, analyses of chondrites should best approximate the average composition of meteoritic matter. Hence in arriving at the elemental composition of meteoritic matter analyses of chondrites are generally preferred. But there are enstatite chondrites, olivine-bronzite chondrites, olivine-hypersthene chondrites, olivine-pigeonite chondrites, and carbonaceous chondrites. The olivine-bronzite chondrites and olivine-hypersthene chondrites are by far the commonest of the chondrites, and most analyses have been made on them, but they differ to some degree in total iron content (respectively H and L groups of Urey and Craig, 1953). It has been suggested that the other groups of chondrites have been formed by the thermal metamorphism of carbonaceous chondrites at temperatures above 400° C; hence for elements readily volatilized at this temperature, as for example mercury, analyses of carbonaceous chondrites are more likely to give true abundance figures.

Sampling is another problem in the analysis of meteorites, especially for minor and trace elements. Meteorites are notably inhomogeneous, the principal phases being nickel-iron, troilite, and silicate (the silicate usually consisting of more than one mineral). It is seldom possible to obtain pure phases for analysis, and it is difficult to prepare and analyze a true sample of such inhomogeneous material. Some of the minor and trace elements may be very irregularly distributed as discrete grains of rare phases. The small amount of copper normally present in chondrites (about 0.01%) is evidently present largely as grains of native copper, but a random polished surface of a chondrite only occasionally intersects one of these grains. If a small sample is taken chance will probably determine whether or not copper is present in that particular sample. The average amount of gold in iron meteorites is only about 1 ppm, yet two small grains of gold were observed in the Wedderburn iron—clearly a determination of the gold content of this meteorite will vary greatly according to the location of the sample.

A further problem is the quality of the determinative methods available for a specific element, and the quality of the analytical work itself. For some elements the methods available are highly specific and very sensitive, and the results may be expected to be correspondingly accurate. For other elements no very satisfactory methods may be known. In this respect great advances have been made in analytical techniques with the introduction and elaboration of spectrographic, colorimetric, isotope dilution, and neutron activation analysis, and with improved methods of extraction and separation of minor and trace elements.

A serious problem is the possibility of the contamination of the meteorite by terrestrial material between the time of its fall and the time of its analysis. A meteorite may be accidentally contaminated between the time of its fall and the time it is prepared for an analysis. Even specimens in museum collections are rarely kept in perfectly dust-free and sterile conditions, and meteorites may also have been contaminated by such procedures as the making of casts, the determination of density, the cutting of slices, and so on. It is to be hoped that care will be taken with future meteorite falls to preserve at least some of the material in as clean a state as possible, perhaps by sealing it in plastic containers. This is particularly important for the carbonaceous chondrites, with their content of organic compounds.

In this connection attention should be drawn to the fact that many analytical data have been determined on finds. Such data are automatically suspect if they disagree with corresponding data determined on falls. Weathering is an insidious attacker of meteorites, especially the stones and stony-irons, and the chance of introduction of terrestrial material is very great. This is well brought out by the work of Moore and Brown (pers. comm.), who found over ten times as much barium in the average of 45 chondrite finds as in 43 falls—presumably the barium was introduced by groundwater and precipitated by sulfate ions from the weathering of troilite.

In spite of all these problems there are certainly many reliable figures for the content of major, minor, and trace elements in specific meteorites. A summary of recent work has been provided by Ehmann (1961). Various attempts have been made to integrate these figures into comprehensive tables of the abundances of the elements in meteoritic matter. A major problem in preparing such tables has been to decide the proportions of nickel-iron, troilite, and silicate to assume for the overall composition of meteoritic matter. If one were to assume that the Type I carbonaceous chondrites represented primordial undifferentiated meteoritic matter this problem would not arise, since these meteorites contain no nickel-iron and little if any troilite; they are certainly the most homogeneous of the stony meteorites. Unfortunately they are exceedingly rare, and hence few determinations of minor and trace elements have been made on them. However, in bulk composition of the major non-volatile elements they are similar to the H group chondrites. As a working hypothesis it may be assumed that the proportions of nickel-iron, troilite, and silicate in the H group chondrites are representative of meteoritic matter as a whole.

Table 18 presents the compilations of elemental abundances in meteoritic matter presented by Goldschmidt (1937), Urey (1952), and Levin et al. (1956), together with one prepared from the latest

TABLE 18. THE AVERAGE COMPOSITION OF METEORITIC MATTER

		Goldschmidt (1937) ppm	Urey (1952) ppm	Levin et al. (1956) ppm	This Book	
					ppm	atoms per 10^6 atoms Si
3	Li	4	5	3.2	2	47
4	Be	1	1	0.09	1?	18?
5	B	1.5	1.5	2.6	2?	30?
8	O	323,000	—	346,000	330,000	3,420,000
9	F	28	40	40	30?	260?
11	Na	5950	7500	7000	6800	49,000
12	Mg	123,000	135,500	139,000	138,600	945,000
13	Al	13,800	14,300	14,000	11,000	68,000
14	Si	163,000	179,600	178,000	169,500	1,000,000
15	P	1050	1500	1600	1300	6950
16	S	21,200	20,100	20,000	20,700	107,000
17	Cl	1000–1500?	470	800	100?	500?
19	K	1540	900	900	1000	4300
20	Ca	13,300	14,300	16,000	13,900	57,600
21	Sc	4	5	5	9	33
22	Ti	1320	580	700	800	2800
23	V	39	50	80	65	210
24	Cr	3430	2700	2500	3000	9600
25	Mn	2080	2400	2000	2000	6000
26	Fe	288,000	241,000	256,000	286,000	849,000
27	Co	1200	1100	900	1000	2800
28	Ni	15,680	14,500	14,000	16,800	47,400
29	Cu	170	170	(40)	100	260
30	Zn	138	76	20	50	125
31	Ga	4.2	4.6	8	5	12
32	Ge	79	53	(40)	10	23
33	As	—	18	70	2	4
34	Se	7	6.7	9	9	19
35	Br	20	25	(22)	10?	21?
37	Rb	3.5	8	8	3	6
38	Sr	20	23	22	11	21
39	Y	4.72	5.5	5	4	7
40	Zr	73	80	90	33	75
41	Nb	—	0.41	0.5	0.5	0.9
42	Mo	5.3	3.6	5	1.6	2.8
44	Ru	2.23	1.4	2	1	1.6
45	Rh	0.80	0.47	0.6	0.2	0.3
46	Pd	1.54	0.92	0.5	1?	1.6?

TABLE 18.   THE AVERAGE COMPOSITION OF METEORITIC MATTER (*Cont.*)

		Goldschmidt (1937) ppm	Urey (1952) ppm	Levin et al. (1956) ppm	This Book	
					ppm	atoms per 10^6 atoms Si
47	Ag	2.0	1.35	0.5	0.1	0.15
48	Cd	—	1.6	2	0.5?	0.7?
49	In	0.15	0.2	0.2	0.001	0.001
50	Sn	20	14	20	1	1.4
51	Sb	—	0.64	0.4	0.1	0.14
52	Te	0.1?	0.13	0.14	1	1.3
53	I	1	1.25	1	0.04	0.05
55	Cs	0.08	1.1	0.08	0.1	0.12
56	Ba	6.9	2.9	7	3.4	4.1
57	La	1.58	1.9	200	0.33	0.40
58	Ce	1.77?	2.1	2	0.51	0.62
59	Pr	0.75	0.88	0.8	0.12	0.15
60	Nd	2.59	3.0	3	0.63	0.74
62	Sm	0.95	1.1	1	0.22	0.25
63	Eu	0.25	0.27	0.3	0.083	0.097
64	Gd	1.42	1.7	1.6	0.34	0.36
65	Tb	0.45	0.52	0.5	0.051	0.056
66	Dy	1.80	2.1	2	0.37	0.39
67	Ho	0.51	0.60	0.6	0.075	0.078
68	Er	1.48	1.7	1.7	0.21	0.21
69	Tm	0.26	0.31	0.3	0.038	0.039
70	Yb	1.42	1.7	1.6	0.19	0.19
71	Lu	0.46	0.54	0.5	0.036	0.036
72	Hf	1.6	1.6	0.8	1.4	1.4
73	Ta	—	0.28	0.3	0.02	0.019
74	W	15	16	17	0.14	0.13
75	Re	0.0020	0.08	0.0018	0.08	0.08
76	Os	1.92	1.2	1.1	1.0	1.0
77	Ir	0.65	0.38	0.6	0.5	0.43
78	Pt	3.25	1.9	3	5?	4.3?
79	Au	0.65	0.25	0.26	0.3	0.25
80	Hg	—	<0.01	(0.009)	0.1?	0.8?
81	Tl	—	0.15	(0.14)	0.0004?	0.0003?
82	Pb	11	—	(2)	0.15	0.12
83	Bi	—	0.02	(0.16)	0.003?	0.002?
90	Th	0.8	—	0.2	0.04	0.028
92	U	0.36	—	0.05	0.014	0.097

data available, as set out in detail in this chapter. The assumed percentages of silicate, troilite, and nickel-iron in average meteoritic matter are as follows:

	Silicate	Troilite	Nickel-Iron
Goldschmidt	77	7.7	15.3
Urey	85	5.5	9.5
Levin et al.	85.7		14.3
This book *	74.7	5.7	19.6

* Average of 41 superior analyses of H group chondrites (Urey and Craig, 1953).

In the following paragraphs the data for the individual elements will be summarized and discussed, in order of atomic number. In general only the latest or most reliable data are used, no attempt being made to quote all the determinations in the literature.

Hydrogen (1): The amount of hydrogen inherent to meteoritic matter is peculiarly difficult to estimate, since in analyses of stony meteorites it is reported as H_2O, most of which is probably terrestrial, acquired since the meteorite entered the Earth's atmosphere. The carbonaceous chondrites contain hydrogen in a number of forms— water of crystallization in compounds such as epsomite and gypsum, OH groups in serpentine, hydrogen in a variety of organic compounds, and presumably acquired terrestrial H_2O as well. Nevertheless, a good part of the hydrogen reported as H_2O in their analyses is presumably extra-terrestrial, since this H_2O has the highest deuterium content ever found in natural material (Boato, 1954). It is noteworthy that the Type I carbonaceous chondrites Orgueil and Ivuna show the highest concentration of deuterium. If all the H_2O reported in analyses of these meteorites (Wiik, 1956) is extra-terrestrial, the amount of hydrogen is 2.28% in Orgueil, 2.09% in Ivuna.

Edwards (1955a) extracted hydrogen from fourteen iron meteorites, and found a range of 0.7–54 ppm.

Helium (2): Helium in meteorites has four possible sources: helium incorporated when the meteorite was formed; radiogenic helium; helium produced by cosmic-ray spallation; helium absorbed from the Earth's atmosphere. The last can probably be omitted from consideration as insignificant. The relative proportions of the other three types will vary from one meteorite to another, and the total amount of helium may be altered by diffusion losses.

Some years ago it was believed that the helium in iron meteorites was produced practically entirely by the decay of uranium and thorium, and hence the amount of helium would give at least a minimum age for these meteorites. Many determinations of helium in iron meteorites were made (Arrol, Jacobi, and Paneth, 1942). However, Bauer (1947) suggested that much of this helium had been produced by cosmic-ray spallation, and this was later proved by the presence of He^3 in meteoritic helium, since He^3 cannot be produced from uranium and thorium but only through spallation reactions. Chackett et al. (1953) measured total helium in sixty-eight samples of iron meteorites and found contents ranging from 0 to 40×10^{-6} cc/gram.

Gerling and Levskii (1956) found a large content of inert gases in the enstatite achondrite Pesyanoe. The content of helium and other inert gases was higher by a factor of 100 than that of other stony meteorites analyzed up to that time. The uranium and thorium content of Pesyanoe is not abnormally high, thus accounting for only a small fraction of the He^4, and the isotopic composition of the inert gases approaches the primordial ratios rather than those produced by cosmic-ray spallation. It is therefore believed that a great part of the helium and other inert gases in Pesyanoe was incorporated in the meteorite when it was formed. Subsequent work by other investigators has shown that Pesyanoe is not a freak, other meteorites, especially carbonaceous chondrites, having been found to have high contents of primordial inert gases. Reynolds et al. (1962) have found large amounts of primordial helium and neon in the Washington County iron.

Lithium (3): Pinson, Ahrens, and Franck (1953) analyzed nineteen chondrites (olivine-bronzite, olivine-hypersthene, and one olivene-pigeonite chondrite) for lithium spectrographically. They found a range of values from 1 to 3.7 ppm, the average being 2.7 ppm. Fireman and Schwarzer (1957) have measured lithium by neutron activation in several meteorites, with the following results (in ppm): Nakhla (diopside-olivine achondrite), 4; Sioux County (pigeonite-plagioclase achondrite), 8; St. Michel (olivine-hypersthene chondrite), 2; Shelburne (olivine-hypersthene chondrite), 2; Bur-Gheluai (olivine-bronzite chondrite), 1; they found less than $\frac{1}{100}$ of these amounts in several iron meteorites. The figure of 2 ppm is probably a reasonably good value for the average content of lithium in meteoritic matter. Since lithium is a strongly lithophile element it presumably is present almost entirely in the silicate minerals; its ionic size indicates that it is probably associated with magnesium in olivine and pyroxene.

Beryllium (*4*): Goldschmidt (1937) gave a figure of 1 ppm for the beryllium content of stony meteorites.

Boron (*5*): Goldschmidt and Peters (1932) investigated the geo-chemistry of boron, and gave the following figures for its abundance in meteorites: irons, 0.9 ppm; stones, 1.6 ppm. Vilcsek (1959) reports 5 ppm in the Breitscheid chondrite.

Carbon (*6*): It is obviously difficult to arrive at a figure for the average content of carbon in meteoritic matter. When present in small amount it is often omitted from the analysis; when present in larger amount it is usually very irregularly distributed and difficult to sample adequately. In the common chondrites (olivine-bronzite and olivine-hypersthene chondrites) its amount seldom exceeds 0.1% and is usually considerably less. The enstatite chondrites are notably richer and usually contain 0.3–0.5% C, as do some of the olivine-pigeonite chondrites. The carbonaceous chondrites contain up to 5% C, and organic compounds in addition. Probably the maximum figure for carbon in the carbonaceous chondrites should be taken as the average amount in primordial meteoritic matter, since all the processes of chemical evolution of meteorites are likely to cause loss of carbon as gases such as CO and CO_2.

The carbon in meteorites is usually recorded as graphite (except for the rare occurrence of diamonds), but much of the black carbonaceous material does not give an X-ray pattern; it is either amorphous carbon or a highly polymerized organic complex.

Boato (1954) has measured C^{13}/C^{12} ratios of carbon from chondrites, with the following results ($\delta\ C^{13}\%$): carbonaceous chondrites, -3.7 to -11.4; olivine-pigeonite chondrites (Type II of Boato), -12.9 to -18.8; olivine-bronzite chondrites, -24; one enstatite chondrite (Indarch), 12.9. These figures show a consistent sequence from carbonaceous chondrites through olivine-pigeonite chondrites to olivine-bronzite chondrites, with the enstatite chondrite showing a close relationship to the carbonaceous chondrites. Boato remarks, "A correlation between carbon content and the C^{13}/C^{12} ratio was found, possibly representing preferential loss of C^{13} during the process in which the volatiles were lost from the original material from which the various groups of chondrites were formed. Type I carbonaceous chondrites are probably closest in bulk composition to this original material. On the other hand, accumulation in varying proportions of isotopically different carbon compounds cannot be ruled out as an explanation."

Nitrogen (7): Little work has been done on the nitrogen content of meteorites. Nash and Baxter (1947) recorded an average of 0.5 mm³/gram in eight iron meteorites. Analyses of gases from meteorites made in the last century (summarized by Cohen, 1894) show that nitrogen usually makes up less than 5% of the total gas content. Combined nitrogen is present in the carbonaceous chondrites, as organic compounds and as water-soluble ammonium compounds, probably NH_4Cl and/or $(NH_4)_2SO_4$; Cloez (1864) records 0.1% NH_3 in his analysis of Orgueil. Recent unpublished analyses (Wiik, pers. comm.) show the following amounts of combined nitrogen in carbonaceous chondrites: Alais, 0.29%; Orgueil, 0.24%; Erakot, 0.26%. Mueller (1953) records 4% nitrogen in the organic material extracted from the Cold Bokkeveld meteorite. Lipman (1932) determined combined nitrogen in several olivine-bronzite and olivine-hypersthene chondrites, with the following results (in ppm): Forest City, 52; Long Island, 64; Tilden, 36; Gilgoin, 48; Holbrook (2 samples), 16, 25; Pultusk, 34.

The only nitrogen mineral recorded from meteorites is osbornite, TiN, a rare accessory known only from Bustee (an enstatite achondrite).

Oxygen (8): We have no measurement for the amount of oxygen in any meteorite. Oxygen is always a calculated figure, arrived at by allotting the requisite amount to form the standard oxides of those elements more electropositive than iron, and adding the amount required to form FeO from the iron not present as sulfide or nickel-iron. This procedure is reasonably satisfactory with the common types of stony meteorites, but is unsatisfactory for the carbonaceous chondrites (which contain organic compounds, ferric iron, and oxidized sulfur compounds) and the enstatite chondrites (in which some of the Si, Ca, Cr, and Mn may not be present as oxidic compounds).

If we take the H group chondrites as representative of the overall composition of meteoritic matter, the average amount of oxygen is about 33%.

Vinogradov, Dontsova, and Chupakhin (1960) have studied the isotope ratios of oxygen in meteorites and igneous rocks. They find average O^{16}/O^{18} ratios as follows: pallasites (3 samples), 490.4; chondrites (4 samples), 490.3; achondrites (5 samples), 490.1; carbonaceous chondrites (4 samples), 488.9. Terrestrial igneous rocks gave the following averages: dunites (5 samples), 490.0; basalts and diabases (6 samples), 489.2; granites (5 samples), 488.0. From these figures it is evident that meteorites cannot be distinguished from igneous rocks on their O^{16}/O^{18} ratios.

Fluorine (9): Goldschmidt (1937) gave a figure of 28 ppm for the average fluorine content of meteoritic matter.

Neon (10): Neon in meteorites has three possible sources: trapped gas of the atmosphere in which the meteorite originally formed; cosmogenic, the product of cosmic-ray spallation; and neon absorbed from the Earth's atmosphere. Gerling and Levskii (1956) demonstrated the presence of primordial neon in Pesyanoe, an enstatite achondrite, and this work has been extended by later investigators. Stauffer (1961) has published a summary of the results; the contents of primordial Ne^{20} (in 10^{-8} cc STP/gram) are as follows: Pesyanoe, 1886; Kapoeta (howardite), 2400; Mokoia (olivine-pigeonite chondrite), 309; Murray (carbonaceous chondrite), 53.8, 63.2; Ivuna (carbonaceous chondrite), 20.9; Abee (enstatite chondrite), 6.3; Felix (olivine-pigeonite chondrite), 5.6; Lancé (olivine-pigeonite chondrite), 3.3; Novo Urei (ureilite), 1.3; Goalpara (ureilite), 1.0.

Schaeffer and Zähringer (1960) have measured Ne^{21} (which is almost entirely cosmogenic) in seven iron meteorites, finding amounts of 0.1–6.0 cc $\times 10^{-8}$/gram. Eberhardt and Eberhardt (1961) found the following amounts (in 10^{-8} cc/gram) in some stones: in four chondrites, 4.45–9.50; Norton County (enstatite achondrite), 58.5; Goalpara (ureilite), 8.8; Novo Urei (ureilite), 2.7; olivine from Brenham pallasite, 36.5.

Sodium (11): Sodium is determined as a matter of course in all analyses of stony meteorites, but there is good evidence that many of these Na_2O determinations are unreliable. Urey and Craig's compilation of 94 selected analyses of chondrites shows a range for Na_2O from 0.41% to 2.29%, which is not consistent with the comparative uniformity of these meteorites. Later Edwards and Urey (1955) and Edwards (1955b) extracted sodium from many meteorites by high-temperature distillation and determined it by flame photometry; they found a range of values for Na from thirty falls (olivine-bronzite, olivine-hypersthene, and one enstatite chondrite) of 0.61% to 0.75%, with an average of 0.68%. (Finds gave generally lower values, evidently because of leaching by weathering.) The figure of 0.68% can be accepted as a reliable value for the average sodium content of meteoritic matter; this is equivalent to approximately 1% Na_2O, and chondrite analyses deviating greatly from this figure should be viewed with suspicion.

Edwards and Urey found lower and more variable figures for carbonaceous chondrites—usually about 0.5% Na, but one (Murray) had only 0.16% Na. Achondrites gave variable contents, generally much lower than chondrites, although one (Bishopville, an enstatite achondrite) gave 1.0% Na.

Magnesium (12): Magnesium is determined as a matter of course in analyses of stony and stony-iron meteorites. In the olivine-bronzite and olivine-hypersthene chondrites it shows little variation in good analyses; Urey and Craig's calculations give an average of 22.93% MgO in H group chondrites and 24.55% MgO in L group chondrites. Accepting the H group chondrites as typifying meteoritic matter as a whole, this results in a figure of 14% for the average magnesium content.

Magnesium is normally present in meteorites as olivine and/or pyroxene; in the carbonaceous chondrites, however, it may be present largely as serpentine. Spinel ($MgAl_2O_4$) has been recorded as a rare accessory in two olivine-pigeonite chondrites (Kaba and Vigarano), and magnesium sulfate and magnesium carbonate have been recorded in the carbonaceous chondrite Orgueil and may be present in other meteorites of this group.

Although magnesium is usually considered entirely lithophile in character, Yavnel (1950) records 10–30 ppm in the metal phase of the Sikhote-Alin iron, and 10 ppm in the troilite.

Aluminum (13): Aluminum is determined as a matter of course in all analyses of stony meteorites. However, it is notoriously difficult to obtain accurate values for Al_2O_3 in the usual chemical analysis, and a wide range of values is shown by otherwise satisfactory analyses. Urey and Craig rejected as unreliable all analyses of chondrites with less than 1% or greater than 5% Al_2O_3. Actually the true range is probably quite small, since recent analyses by Wiik and others give about 2.0–2.2% Al_2O_3 in chondritic meteorites. This indicates that Urey and Craig's average of 2.36% Al_2O_3 in the selected anlyses of H group chondrites is probably higher than the true value. A figure of 2.1% Al_2O_3, equivalent to 1.1% Al, is probably acceptable as the average amount of this element in meteoritic matter as a whole.

Aluminum in a meteorite is normally present entirely in the silicate phases, mainly in the plagioclase, although some is also present in the pyroxene. Spinel ($MgAl_2O_4$) has been recorded as a rare accessory in two olivine-pigeonite chondrites (Kaba and Vigarano).

Silicon (14): The amount of SiO_2 is determined as a matter of course in any analysis of a meteorite containing silicate minerals. In

Urey and Craig's selection of 94 analyses of chondrites SiO_2 ranges from 30.32% to 46.06%, but the extreme values are certainly inaccurate. However, their averages for the H(36.17%) and L(39.49%) groups are probably fairly close to the true figures. Using the value for the H group as typifying meteoritic matter as a whole, the average content of Si is 17%.

Silicon is normally present in meteorites as silicate minerals. However, Ringwood (1961b) has shown that in the enstatite chondrites some of this element is reduced to the elemental state and alloyed with the nickel-iron. This possibility should be borne in mind in analyzing other meteorites showing a high degree of reduction.

Tiller (1961) determined the isotopic composition of silicon in two chondrites and found it to be the same as that for terrestrial dunites.

Phosphorus (15): Phosphorus is always determined in complete analyses of meteorites, but was frequently omitted in older analyses. Urey and Craig found an average of 0.21% P_2O_5 in their compilation of 94 analyses of chondrites, but the range of values was considerable, from nothing to 0.68%. A series of recent analyses by Wiik (1956 and unpublished) shows a much smaller range, and the following averages: carbonaceous chondrites, 0.30% P_2O_5; olivine-pigeonite chondrites, 0.29%; olivine-hypersthene chondrites, 0.26%; olivine-bronzite chondrites, 0.33%. The figures do not vary much from one group to another, and the overall average is 0.30% P_2O_5, equivalent to 1300 ppm phosphorus, which can be taken as the average amount of this element in meteoritic matter.

In the stony meteorites, phosphorus is largely a lithophile element, occurring mainly as the phosphates apatite and merrillite. In the irons and the metal phase of the stony-irons it may be classed as siderophile, since it is present as the iron-nickel phosphide schreibersite.

Sulfur (16): Sulfur is probably present in all meteorites, although there may be only traces of it in some achondrites. It is usual to take the average amount in chondrites as the average for meteoritic matter as a whole. There is essentially no difference in the averages for the H(2.07%) and L(2.11%) groups of Urey and Craig, and a figure of 2.1% may be accepted as a good average. However, it should be noted that carbonaceous chondrites show much higher sulfur contents (up to 6.6%); if they represent the most primitive and least differentiated meteoritic material, the average sulfur content is much higher than the above figure.

Sulfur is normally present entirely as troilite, FeS. However, daubreelite ($FeCr_2S_4$), oldhamite (CaS), pentlandite ($(Fe,Ni)_9S_8$, and some rarer sulfides have been recorded from some meteorites, and the carbonaceous chondrites contain free sulfur, sulfates, and possibly other sulfur compounds.

The isotopic composition of sulfur in meteoritic troilite is remarkably uniform, the S^{32}/S^{34} ratio being 22.22.

Chlorine (17): The chlorine content of meteoritic material is not well known, although two chlorine-bearing minerals are known from meteorites—lawrencite and chlorapatite. If all the phosphate (0.3%) in the average chondrite were present as chlorapatite the amount of chlorine would be 0.05%; however, this assumption is not justified, since some phosphate has been shown to be present as merrillite.

Behne (1953) has measured chlorine in two chondrites, finding 110 ppm in Mocs and 100 ppm in Chateau-Renard (these are both olivine-hypersthene chondrites, and are falls). Mueller (1953) studied the Cold Bokkeveld carbonaceous chondrite, and found that the organic material extracted by solvents (about 1% by weight) contained 4.8% Cl, so the meteorite as a whole contained 480 ppm extractable chlorine. This suggests that the carbonaceous chondrites are considerably richer in chlorine than the other chondrite types.

Salpeter (1952) measured chlorine in twenty meteorites by spectrochemical analysis. He found a range of values from 100 ppm (Bluff) to 2500 ppm (Lancé), except for the Admire pallasite, for which he found 6400 ppm; the latter is a find and the high figure suggests contamination. The average of the other nineteen was 824 ppm.

Hoering and Parker (1961) determined chlorine in ten chondrites (all finds) and report a range of values from 150 to 560 ppm.

Argon (18): The argon in meteorites will be in part primordial (incorporated in the meteorite at the time of formation), in part radiogenic (from K^{40}), in part produced by cosmic-ray spallation; and this inherent argon may be contaminated by terrestrial argon. Stauffer (1961) has shown that the ureilites and carbonaceous chondrites contain large amounts of trapped primordial argon and neon. For argon the striking results are the unusually high abundances of Ar^{36} and Ar^{38}. The ratios Ar^{36}/Ar^{38} are all very close to that of atmospheric argon. However, the low values for the ratios Ar^{40}/Ar^{36} show that only a small fraction of the Ar^{36} and Ar^{38} could be due to atmospheric contamination, and therefore their extra-terrestrial origin is proved. No nuclear processes are known to produce them in meteorites in such quantities and in such a ratio, and Stauffer concludes that they are mostly primordial.

Potassium (*19*): Potassium has normally been determined in analyses of stone meteorites; however, most analyses in the literature are by the Lawrence Smith method, which is not reliable for the small amounts in meteorites, and usually gives figures that are too high. Therefore the average (0.17% K_2O) of the values in analyses of H group chondrites (Urey and Craig) should not be accepted as an accurate figure. The work of Edwards (1955*b*) and Edwards and Urey (1955), using high-temperature distillation to separate the potassium and flame photometry to measure it, showed that the common chondrites have a remarkably uniform potassium content, which averaged 0.088% for thirty-two falls, with a range from 0.075% to 0.105%. The carbonaceous chondrites showed lower figures for potassium, ranging from 0.032% to 0.060%.

Wänke (1961) has determined potassium in a number of chondrites by neutron activation analysis and obtained a narrow range of values from 0.087% to 0.116%, with an average value of 0.10%. He found 0.038% in Pasamonte and 0.033% in Sioux County (both pyroxene-plagioclase achondrites) and 0.001% in Johnstown (a hypersthene achondrite). Vinogradov, Zadorozhnii, and Knorre (1960) record 0.047% in Chervony Kut, 0.057% in Stannern, 0.043% in Yurtuk (all pyroxene-plagioclase achondrites), and 0.023% in Norton County (an enstatite achondrite). The achondrites are notably depleted in potassium and the other alkali metals in comparison to the chondrites.

Calcium (*20*): Calcium is always determined in a good analysis of a stone meteorite. Most chondrites give figures between 1 and 2.5% CaO (enstatite chondrites may have slightly less than 1%). Urey and Craig rejected analyses showing more than 4% CaO as inaccurate and their averages are 1.96% for L group chondrites and 1.95% for H group chondrites. Using these figures as a base, the average content of calcium in meteoritic matter is 1.4%.

Calcium is normally present in the silicate minerals plagioclase and pyroxene. In the highly reduced enstatite chondrites and enstatite achondrites it may be present in part as oldhamite (CaS).

Scandium (*21*): Bate, Potratz, and Huizenga (1960) have determined scandium in a number of meteorites by neutron activation analysis. Their results are as follows (in ppm): Nuevo Laredo, 45, 41; Johnstown, 17; Modoc, 9.2; Richardton, 9.9, 9.6; Forest City, 8.9; Holbrook, 9.7; Beardsley, 9.2. All these meteorites are falls; Nuevo Laredo and Johnstown are achondrites, the others chondrites. There is no clear relationship of scandium to any of the major constituents, except perhaps aluminum and calcium; Nuevo Laredo is much higher than the other meteorites in these elements. The chondrites have a nearly constant scandium content, averaging 9.4 ppm. These results are confirmed by those of Kemp and Smales (1960b) on the following chondrites: Hendersonville, 7.9 ppm; Dhurmsala, 8.1 ppm; Eli Elwah, 8.4 ppm; Chateau-Renard, 8.8 ppm; Felix, 9.7 ppm.

Titanium (22): Titanium is always determined in complete analyses of stony meteorites, but was frequently omitted in older analyses. Urey and Craig found an average of 0.11% TiO_2 in their compilation of 94 analyses of chondrites, but the range of values was considerable, from nothing to 0.37%. A series of recent analyses by Wiik (1956 and unpublished) shows a much smaller range, and the following averages: carbonaceous chondrites, 0.08% TiO_2; olivine-pigeonite chondrites, 0.16%; olivine-bronzite chondrites, 0.13%; olivine-hypersthene chondrites, 0.15%. Accepting a figure of 0.14% TiO_2 for the average amount in meteoritic matter, this corresponds to 800 ppm Ti. Moore and Brown (1962) report an average of 640 ppm Ti on the basis of spectrographic analysis of forty-three chondrite falls.

Titanium is probably entirely lithophile in its behavior in meteorites, being present in the silicate minerals and frequently as ilmenite also.

Vanadium (23): There are few determinations of vanadium in stony meteorites. Kemp and Smales (1960a) give the following figures (in ppm) for these chondrites: Hendersonville, 62; Dhurmsala, 66; Eli Elwah, 63; Chateau-Renard, 65; Felix, 77. These results indicate a fairly constant value for vanadium in the chondrites of about 65 ppm. They examined two irons (Canyon Diablo and Carlton), and found less than 0.2 ppm. Vanadium is evidently strongly lithophile in meteorites and probably occurs in the silicate minerals in the trivalent state.

Nichiporuk and Chodos (1959) determined vanadium in troilite from twelve irons, one stony-iron, and one chondrite, by X-ray fluorescence analysis. The results ranged from <13 ppm to 99 ppm, with one value of 414 ppm. (Some of the troilites were impure, containing one or more of the following minerals: nickel-iron, schreibersite, daubreelite, graphite, chromite.) The troilite from the chondrite had <13 ppm, which supports the above statement that vanadium is probably lithophile in these meteorites. Stauffer and Honda (1961) have found an upper limit of 0.02 ppm for primordial vanadium in the iron meteorite Aroos (an additional amount has been formed by cosmic-ray spallation).

Chromium (24): Chromium is normally determined as a matter of course in analyses of stony meteorites, and sometimes in analyses of other types also. Urey and Craig (1953) give an average of 0.43% Cr_2O_3 in 53 analyses of L group chondrites, 0.27% Cr_2O_3 in 41 analyses of H group chondrites, and an overall average of 0.36% Cr_2O_3 in the total of 94 analyses. It is probable that these averages do not give a true figure for chromium, since individual analyses range from 0.02% to 1.02% Cr_2O_3. Considering a series of analyses made by a single analyst, such as those of Wiik (1956 and unpublished), we find a much smaller range, and an average of 0.51% Cr_2O_3, or 3500 ppm Cr.

Bate et al. (1960) have determined chromium in a number of meteorites by neutron activation analysis. Their results are as follows (in ppm): Nuevo Laredo, 1200, 1000; Johnstown, 3200; Modoc, 2200, 2400; Richardton, 2400; Forest City, 2000; Holbrook, 2100, 2200; Beardsley, 2300. All these meteorites are falls; Nuevo Laredo and Johnstown are achondrites, the remainder chondrites. From these figures it appears that the chromium content of chondrites is essentially constant, with an average value of 2200 ppm. Bate and his co-workers state that this may be somewhat low. Possibly the figure derived from Wiik's analyses, 3500 ppm, may be more nearly correct for the true abundance of chromium in meteoritic matter.

Lovering et al. (1957) determined an average of 37 ppm Cr in irons and stony-irons. Smales et al. (1958) found a range of from 5 to 185 ppm in 15 irons. In the Sikhote-Alin iron Yavnel (1950) found 0.01% in the kamacite, 0.01% in the schreibersite, 1.0% in the troilite, and 40–50% in the chromite.

Nichiporuk and Chodos (1959) have determined chromium in troilite from twelve irons, one stony-iron, and one chondrite by X-ray fluorescence analysis. The range of values is extremely wide, and is evidently due largely to the presence of variable amounts of chromite and daubreelite included in the troilite. The minimum value, 79 ppm, was observed in troilite from the chondrite.

In most groups of stony meteorites and even in many irons and stony-irons chromium is a lithophile element, being present as chromite and in the silicate minerals, especially pyroxene. In some irons and in the enstatite chondrites, however, it is chalcophile, occurring as the sulfospinel daubreelite, $FeCr_2S_4$.

Manganese (25): Manganese is always determined in modern analyses of meteorites, but was frequently omitted in older analyses. Urey and Craig found an average of 0.25% MnO in their compilation of 94 analyses of chondrites, but the range was great, from nothing to

1.21%. A series of recent analyses by Wiik (1956 and unpublished) shows a much smaller range, and the following averages: carbonaceous chondrites, 0.20% MnO; olivine-pigeonite chondrites, 0.20% MnO; olivine-bronzite chondrites, 0.31% MnO; olivine-hypersthene chondrites, 0.32% MnO. This corresponds to 1500 ppm Mn in the first two groups, and 2400 ppm in the last two groups. The true abundance for manganese in meteoritic matter probably lies between these two figures. Moore and Brown (1962) report an average of 2600 ppm Mn on the basis of spectrographic analysis of forty-three chondrite falls.

In most of the stony meteorites manganese is lithophile, diadochic with iron in the ferromagnesian silicates; in the highly reduced enstatite chondrites, however, it is largely or entirely chalcophile, being present in oldhamite, probably in troilite, and in one meteorite (Abee) as the manganese sulfide alabandite. In the Sikhote-Alin iron Yavnel (1950) found <0.001% in the kamacite, 0.001% in the schreibersite, 0.01% in the troilite, and 0.8% in the chromite.

Iron (26): The iron content of meteorites varies greatly from group to group, ranging from essentially nothing in the enstatite achondrites to about 94% in the hexahedrites. Within the chondrites the range is much less, and as Urey and Craig showed, they can be divided in two groups, H and L, according to their iron content. The L group averages 22% Fe, and the H group 28% Fe; some of the enstatite chondrites show a rather higher iron content, up to 34%, and should perhaps be separated as an HH group. As shown previously, there are good grounds for considering the H group chondrites as representing average meteoritic matter, and on this basis the average iron content can be taken as 28%. Its distribution between metal, silicate, and sulfide phases will be controlled by the amounts of available oxygen and sulfur.

Cobalt (27): In chemical properties cobalt is closely related to nickel, and its amount in different types of meteorites may be expected to vary directly with the nickel content. The analytical data support this. If we accept the H group chondrites as representative of average meteoritic matter, then their cobalt content (average 0.10%, according to Urey and Craig's computations) may be taken as the true average content of meteoritic matter. This makes the weight proportion of nickel to cobalt 17:1. Smales et al. (1957) determined cobalt by radioactivation analysis in seven chondrites and report a range of values from 104 to 961 ppm, giving an average of 635 ppm, considerably lower than the 1000 ppm from Urey and Craig's computations. In an essentially iron-free enstatite achondrite (Khor Temiki) they found the cobalt content very low, only 4 ppm.

Cobalt in meteorites does not form individual minerals, but is normally present entirely or almost entirely in the metal phase. Lovering et al. (1957) determined cobalt in eighty-eight iron meteorites and found a range of values from 0.38% to 0.92%, with an average of 0.51%. In the Sikhote-Alin iron Yavnel (1950) found 0.47% in the kamacite, 0.03% in the schreibersite, 0.01% in the troilite, and 0.01% in the chromite.

Nichiporuk and Chodos (1959) have determined cobalt in troilite from twelve irons, one stony-iron, and one chondrite. The range of values is extremely wide, from 18 to 6000 ppm, and varies considerably in different samples from the same meteorite. The range is due in part at least to the presence of variable amounts of other phases, such as nickel-iron and schreibersite, included in the troilite. Troilite from the one chondrite had 547 ppm Co. In view of the small amount of troilite in a chondrite ($\sim$5%), this supports the previous statement that cobalt in stone meteorites must be largely in the metal phase. Smales et al. (1958) found 20 and 800 ppm in two samples of troilite from the Canyon Diablo iron.

Nickel (28): Nickel shows the same variability from one meteorite group to another as does iron. However, using the same evidence as previously presented, we may take the average amount of nickel in H group chondrites as representative for meteoritic matter as a whole. Urey and Craig found an average of 1.7% Ni in the analyses of H group chondrites. This makes the average weight proportion of iron to nickel 17:1.

The nickel in meteorites is normally entirely or almost entirely in the metal phase, alloyed with the free iron. However, in the carbonaceous chondrites with no free iron some of it is in a nickeliferous magnetite phase, and in some olivine-pigeonite chondrites it is present as the nickel-iron sulfide pentlandite.

Nichiporuk and Chodos (1959) have determined nickel in troilite from twelve irons, one stony-iron, and one chondrite. The range of values is extremely wide, from 0.017% to 6.61%, and varies considerably in different samples from the same meteorite; the range is due in part at least to the presence of variable amounts of other phases, such as nickel-iron and schreibersite, included in the troilite. Troilite from the one chondrite had 1.22% Ni. In view of the small amount of troilite in a chondrite ($\sim$5%), this does not conflict with the statement that nickel is essentially siderophile in meteorites.

Copper (*29*): Copper is not usually determined in analyses of meteorites. However Wiik (unpublished) has determined this element
in eight chondrites (all falls). For seven of these the range is quite
small (90–119 ppm) and the average is close to 100 ppm; in the
eighth (St. Marks, an enstatite chondrite) the amount is 204 ppm.
Smales et al. (1957, 1958) have found 72–111 ppm in chondrites,
the average being around 90 ppm; and a range of 8–434 ppm in the
irons, with a similar average. Lovering et al. (1957) found a range
of 95–253 ppm and an average of 152 ppm in irons. Nichiporuk and
Chodos (1959) have determined copper in troilite from twelve irons,
one stony-iron, and one chondrite. The range of values is extremely
wide, 66–3400 ppm, and varies considerably in different samples
from the same meteorite. Copper in meteorites is present largely as
minute grains of the native metal, usually irregularly distributed in
association with nickel-iron and troilite; the wide range of recorded
values is certainly due, in part at least, to this irregular distribution.
The figure of 100 ppm is probably a reasonable estimate of the amount
of copper in meteoritic matter.

Smales et al. (1957) found 8 ppm in Khor Temiki, an enstatite
achondrite practically free of nickel-iron and troilite.

Zinc (*30*): Noddack and Noddack (1934) give the following figures for zinc in meteoritic matter: chondrites, 76 ppm; irons, 115 ppm;
troilite, 1530 ppm. Nichiporuk and Chodos (1959) have determined
zinc in troilite from twelve irons, one stony-iron, and one chondrite.
The range of values is from $<$50 ppm, the lower limit of detection,
to 521 ppm with one extreme value of 3300 ppm. (The last value
is suspect because of possible contamination.) The troilite from the
chondrite contained 61 ppm. Nishimura and Sandell (1962) report
an average of 50 ppm in common chondrites, with a range from about
30 to 70 ppm, most of the zinc being in the silicate; the troilite contains about 10 ppm, and the metal phase even less. Some enstatite
chondrites contain much more zinc than common chondrites. Iron
meteorites are low in zinc, the average of eight octahedrites being
about 20 ppm, with a range from 3 to about 40 ppm.

Gallium (*31*): Onishi and Sandell (1956) have studied the gallium content of chondrites, using a photometric method of analysis.
They determined this element in nineteen olivine-bronzite and olivine-
hypersthene chondrites (all finds), and found a narrow range of values, from 4.2 to 6.8 ppm, with an average of 5.3 ppm. The last
figure can probably be taken as the gallium content of average me-

teoritic matter. They also separated composite samples of these chondrites into metal, sulfide, and silicate phases, and found the following average values: silicate, 3.2 ppm; sulfide, 12 ppm; metal, 15 ppm. These figures show that gallium is about as strongly chalcophile as siderophile in meteorites, and also has minor lithophile properties.

Lovering and co-workers (1957) measured gallium in 88 iron meteorites and found values ranging from 1 to 93 ppm, with a clear division into four groups: group I, 80–100 ppm; group II, 40–65 ppm; group III, 8–20 ppm; group IV, 1–3 ppm.

Germanium (32): Wardani (1957) and Onishi (1956) have investigated the geochemistry of germanium, using a photometric method for the determination of this element. Their results on meteorites are generally in excellent agreement. Wardani analyzed two composite samples, each of seven chondrites, and five chondrites individually (these meteorites were all finds); he obtained values ranging from 6.6 to 12.0 ppm, with an average of 9.4 ppm. One composite sample he separated into magnetic and non-magnetic fractions, and found 29.0 ppm in the magnetic fraction and 2.5 ppm in the non-magnetic fraction. This indicates that germanium must be almost entirely siderophile in meteoritic matter. Cohen (1960) found from 7 to 12 ppm in five chondrites, and 0.2 ppm in Norton County, an enstatite achondrite with very little metal phase.

Taking the above results together, a figure of 10 ppm for germanium in average meteoritic matter seems well established. It would be interesting to have a determination of germanium in a carbonaceous chondrite.

Iron meteorites show a remarkable variation in germanium content (Lovering et al. 1957), ranging from <1 ppm to 410 ppm in measurements on eighty-eight meteorites; the germanium content of the metal phase of eight stony-iron meteorites ranged from 18 to 63 ppm. They divided the iron meteorites into four groups with different germanium contents: group I, 300–420 ppm; group II, 130–320 ppm; group III, 15–80 ppm; group IV, <1–1 ppm. There is some correlation with nickel content, low germanium content (groups I and II) being generally associated with low nickel content (<7%). Smales et al. (1958) confirmed this wide variation in iron meteorites; in fifteen irons they found a range from 0.2 to 359 ppm, also with a tendency for the values to fall into four distinct groups. In two samples of troilite from the Canyon Diablo iron they found 32 and 19 ppm. In the Sikhote-Alin iron Yavnel (1950) found 300 ppm in the kamacite, 30 ppm in the schreibersite, 30 ppm in the troilite, and 100 ppm in the chromite.

Arsenic (*33*): The abundance of arsenic in meteoritic matter has been extensively studied by Onishi and Sandell (1955a). In the Canyon Diablo iron they found an average of 8.1 ppm, in the Henbury iron an average of 3.6 ppm. In fourteen olivine-bronzite and olivine-hypersthene chondrites (all finds) they found an average of 2.2 ppm. They also separated composite samples of the chondrites into silicate, sulfide, and metal phases, and found an average of 0.3 ppm in the silicate phase, 12 ppm in the metal phase, and 10 ppm in the sulfide phase. These data indicate that in meteorites arsenic is strongly chalcophile and siderophile, to about the same extent quantitatively.

In view of the known volatility of arsenic at moderate temperatures it would be of great interest to have arsenic determinations for some of the carbonaceous chondrites.

Smales et al. (1958), using neutron activation analysis, report a range of 0.6–30 ppm in fifteen irons, with an average of 9 ppm. They report 0.03–0.07 ppm in troilite from the Canyon Diablo iron, a remarkably low figure in view of the amount recorded from chondritic troilite.

Selenium (*34*): Selenium has been determined in a considerable number of chondritic meteorites by DuFresne (1960), using a spectrophotometric method. She found the values for finds consistently lower than for falls, indicating that finds lose selenium, presumably through leaching by groundwater. The average for twenty-one falls was 7.9 ppm; the values ranged from 5.3 to 15.1 ppm. No consistent relationship between selenium and sulfur is observable, although the highest value for selenium is in Indarch, an enstatite chondrite which contains about twice as much sulfur as the other meteorites examined, which are all olivine-bronzite or olivine-hypersthene chondrites.

Selenium has been measured in four chondrites (all falls) by neutron activation analysis by Schindewolf (1960); his results are as follows (in ppm): Beardsley, 10.8; Forest City, 8.6; Holbrook, 13.3; Modoc, 6.5. These figures are consistent with those of DuFresne and give an average of 9.8 ppm. A figure of 9 ppm for selenium in chondritic meteorites appears to be well established, although determinations on carbonaceous chondrites would be desirable.

Schindewolf also measured selenium in two achondrites: Johnstown, 0.007 ppm; Nuevo Laredo, 0.0016 ppm. The very low value for selenium in these meteorites correlates with their very low troilite content, indicating that selenium is concentrated in the sulfide phase of meteorites.

Bromine (*35*): The bromine content of meteoritic material is very poorly known. Behne (1953) found 11.4 ppm in the Mocs olivine-hypersthene chondrite (a fall) and believes that a figure of 10 ppm is probably reasonable for the average bromine content of stony meteorites. Selivanov (1940) found 0.47 ppm in the Saratov meteorite, an olivine-hypersthene chondrite.

Krypton (*36*): Krummenacher et al. (1962) have measured the isotopic composition of krypton from the following meteorites: Orgueil, Murray (carbonaceous chondrites), Bruderheim (olivine-hypersthene chondrite), Richardton (olivine-bronzite chondrite), St. Marks, Indarch (enstatite chondrites). They found no significant anomalies in the isotopic composition. They report 5.8×10^{-11} gram Kr^{84} per gram of the Murray meteorite, which, assuming terrestrial isotopic composition, corresponds to 1×10^{-10} gram Kr per gram of meteorite.

Rubidium (*37*): Rubidium in meteorites has been determined by Herzog and Pinson (1956), Schumacher (1956), Webster, Morgan, and Smales (1957), and Gast (1960a). For fourteen olivine-bronzite and olivine-hypersthene chondrites (some measured more than once) the range is from 1.0 to 4.9 ppm, with an average of 3.0 ppm. Smales (pers. comm.) reports 2.3 ppm in Ivuna and 1.7 ppm in Mighei, both carbonaceous chondrites.

Considerably lower figures, ranging from 0.16 to 0.66 ppm, are reported from four pyroxene-plagioclase achondrites. Rubidium is thus strongly impoverished in these meteorites, as is cesium and (to a lesser degree) potassium.

Strontium (*38*): Pinson, Ahrens, and Franck (1953) analyzed twenty-one chondrites (one olivine-pigeonite chondrite, the remainder olivine-bronzite and olivine-hypersthene chondrites) for strontium spectrographically. They found a range of values from 7 to 18 ppm, and an average of 11 ppm. For a carbonaceous chondrite (Orgueil) they found less than 1 ppm, a curiously low value.

Calcium-rich achondrites (Moore County, Nuevo Laredo, Pasamonte, and Sioux County) contain 69–95 ppm, according to the results of Herzog and Pinson (1956) and Gast (1960b). Webster, Morgan, and Smales (1957) found 2.1 ppm in Johnstown, a calcium-poor achondrite. Strontium is a strongly lithophile element and its abundance generally shows a direct proportionality to that of calcium.

Gast (1960*b*) has shown that the Sr^{87}/Sr^{86} ratio is essentially constant in the three achondrites he examined, ranging from 0.7004 to 0.7027; this ratio varies considerably in the chondrites, from 0.739 to 0.811.

Yttrium (*39*): Noddack (1935) gives a figure of 6.13 ppm for yttrium in stony meteorites. Mason and Wiik (1961*b*) report 2.3 ppm in the Holbrook chondrite.

Zirconium (*40*): Pinson, Ahrens, and Franck (1953) analyzed twenty-one chondrites (olivine-bronzite, olivine-hypersthene, and one olivine-pigeonite chondrite) for zirconium spectrographically. They found a range of values from 22 to 47 ppm (omitting one value of 76 ppm) and an average of 33 ppm. This figure is probably a reasonably good value for the average content of zirconium in meteoritic matter. For pallasitic olivine they found 1 ppm; for a hypersthene achondrite (Johnstown), 30 ppm; and for a carbonaceous chondrite (Orgueil), <1 ppm; the very low value for the carbonaceous chondrite is curious. Zirconium is presumably a strongly lithophile element in meteorites, but the mineral or minerals in which it is concentrated cannot be told from the available data.

Merz (1962) has determined zirconium by neutron activation analysis in five chondrites, with the following results (in ppm): Plainview, 33; Morland, 36; Potter, 48; Pultusk, 30; Mocs, 20. In two irons (Canyon Diablo and Henbury) he found 0.3–0.4 ppm.

Niobium (*41*): Rankama (1948) found 0.5 ppm in stony meteorites, and states that this element is completely absent from meteoritic iron.

Molybdenum (*42*): Kuroda and Sandell (1954) have studied the geochemistry of molybdenum, using a colorimetric method of analysis. They determined this element in fourteen chondrites (all falls) and found a rather uniform abundance, 1.2–2.0 ppm, with an average of 1.6 ppm; this can be taken as a good figure for the average content of molybdenum in meteoritic matter. For the individual phases of the chondrites they found the silicate to contain an average of 0.6 ppm, the nickel-iron 8.0 ppm, and the troilite 5.7 ppm. Thus molybdenum is siderophilic and chalcophilic in meteorites, with little or no lithophilic tendency.

The chondrites analyzed were all olivine-bronzite or olivine-hypersthene chondrites; it would be interesting to have a measurement of molybdenum in carbonaceous chondrites.

Kuroda and Sandell found 17 ppm in the Canyon Diablo iron, 10 ppm in the Henbury iron, figures of the same order of magnitude as those for the metal phase of the chondrites.

Ruthenium (44): The amount of ruthenium in meteoritic matter has been extensively studied by Hara and Sandell (1960), using a colorimetric (spectrophotometric) method. In analyses of seventeen iron meteorites they found a wide range of values, from 1 to 15 ppm, and comment that the average of 7 ppm can have little exact significance. They note a general tendency for ruthenium content to decrease as nickel content increases, but no direct relationship between ruthenium content and the gallium-germanium groups of Lovering and co-workers (1957). Analyses of fourteen chondrites (all finds) range narrowly from 0.7 to 1.3 ppm Ru, with an average of 0.95 ppm, which can be rounded off to 1 ppm. The chondrites were divided into two composite samples, from which metal and troilite phases were separated and analyzed; the metal gave 4.3 and 5.3 ppm, the troilite 6.3 and 5.2 ppm. Ruthenium is evidently about equally siderophilic and chalcophilic in meteorites, and is probably almost or completely absent from the silicate phases.

Rhodium (45): Schindewolf and Wahlgren (1960) have measured the abundance of rhodium in five chondrites by neutron activation analysis. The meteorites used (all falls) and the results obtained are as follows: Beardsley, 0.21 ppm; Forest City, 0.21 ppm; Hessle, 0.20 ppm; Holbrook, 0.15 ppm; Modoc, 0.16 ppm. The lower content in Holbrook and Modoc can be correlated with a lower amount of metal phase in these meteorites, since the rhodium is presumably concentrated in this phase. The average of the above figures is 0.186 ppm. However, the absolute abundance of rhodium in meteoritic matter containing 20% metal phase will be approximately 0.22 ppm. Yavnel (1950) found 0.9 ppm in the Sikhote-Alin iron.

Palladium (46): Goldberg, Uchiyama, and Brown (1951) determined palladium by neutron activation analysis in 45 iron meteorites, and found a comparatively small range of values, from 1.44 to 9.88 ppm; the average is 3.7 ppm. There is a positive correlation between nickel content and palladium content. Yavnel (1950) found 6.9 ppm in the Sikhote-Alin iron. Noddack and Noddack (1930) give a figure of 4.5 ppm for palladium in troilite. These figures indicate that palladium is almost equally siderophile and chalcophile in meteorites; it probably has no lithophile properties.

Silver (47): Schindewolf and Wahlgren (1960) have measured the abundance of silver in five chondrites by neutron activation analysis. The meteorites used (all falls) and the results obtained are as follows:

Beardsley, 0.12 ppm; Forest City, 0.13 ppm; Hessle, 0.06 ppm; Holbrook, 0.04 ppm; Modoc, 0.12 ppm. There is no apparent correlation between these figures and the phase composition of these meteorites; from the geochemical nature of silver this element should be present in the nickel-iron and the troilite. The average of the above figures is 0.094 ppm.

Hess, Marshall, and Urey (1957) have measured silver (by a colorimetric method) in the Toluca and Canyon Diablo irons. They found less than 0.2 ppm in the metal phase of Canyon Diablo, and less than 3 ppm in the troilite. Lovering (1957b) found less than 0.5 ppm in three troilites, including Toluca. From these data it appears that silver is essentially chalcophile in meteoritic matter, being concentrated in troilite. However, Yavnel (1950) found 6.2 ppm in the Sikhote-Alin iron.

Cadmium (48): Noddack and Noddack (1930) gave the following figures for cadmium in meteoritic matter: chondrites, 1.6 ppm; nickel-iron, 8 ppm; troilite, 30 ppm. Onishi and Sandell (1957) consider the figure for chondrites of questionable reliability and estimate that the true value is about 0.5 ppm.

Indium (49): Schindewolf and Wahlgren (1960) have measured the abundance of indium in five chondrites by neutron activation analysis. The meteorites used (all falls) and the results obtained are as follows: Beardsley, 0.0013 ppm; Forest City, 0.0010 ppm; Hessle, 0.0008 ppm; Holbrook, 0.0003 ppm; Modoc, 0.0006 ppm. There is a general trend towards higher indium content with higher content of metal phase, but the trend is not very regular (Holbrook has about the same amount of metal phase as Modoc). The average of the above figures is 0.001 ppm. Schindewolf and Wahlgren remark on the apparent low abundance of indium in these meteorites and speculate that indium has been depleted by some chemical or physical fractionation. In this connection it would be interesting to know the indium content of a carbonaceous chondrite.

Tin (50): Onishi and Sandell (1957) have made an extensive study of the geochemistry of tin, using a colorimetric or photometric method of analysis. They analyzed two composite samples of chondrites, each of seven meteorites (all finds), and found 1 ppm in each composite. In the metal phase separated from these composites they found 5 ppm, and from the amount of metal phase (approximately 12%) this indicates that at least half of the tin in chondrites resides in this phase. The non-magnetic fraction (which includes the troilite) averages 0.4 ppm tin; it is not unlikely that most of this is in the sulfide phase. It appears that in meteorites tin is about equally siderophile and chalcophile and has little lithophile tendencies. However, Goldschmidt and Peters (1933) found an average of 0.0015% in troilite, and 0.01% in nickel-iron, a ratio of 1:7, which would indicate that tin is largely siderophile rather than chalcophile.

Onishi and Sandell found that different iron meteorites varied greatly in their tin contents, ranging from 0 to 10 ppm, with an average of 2.3 ppm for nineteen specimens. Winchester and Aten (1957) analyzed eight iron meteorites for tin, and obtained values ranging from less than 1 to 22 ppm, with an average of 6.7 ppm. The tin content of iron meteorites is evidently non-uniform, but the reason for this is not obvious.

Antimony (51): The geochemistry of antimony has been studied by Onishi and Sandell (1955b), using a photometric method for the analysis of this element. They analyzed two composite samples of chondrites, each made up of seven meteorites (all finds), and found 0.1 ppm Sb in each sample. The metal phase separated from these samples averaged 0.6 ppm Sb; since the metal phase comprised about 12% of the samples, most of the antimony must reside in this phase, and the remainder is probably in the troilite. Thus antimony is largely siderophilic in meteorites. The Canyon Diablo iron averaged 0.8 ppm Sb, the Henbury iron 0.5 ppm Sb.

Smales et al. (1958) determined antimony in fifteen iron meteorites by neutron activation analysis and found a considerable range in values, from 0.01 to 0.78 ppm; in a troilite nodule from the Canyon Diablo iron they found 0.64 ppm in the inner part and 0.11 ppm in the outer part.

Tellurium (52): Tellurium has been determined in a considerable number of chondritic meteorites by DuFresne (1960), using a spectrophotometric method. The average for twenty-one finds is 1.34 ppm; the individual values range from 0.23 ppm to 3.17 ppm, but most are between 1 and 2 ppm. No consistent relationship between tellurium content and the amount of troilite or nickel-iron is observable, although the highest value is for Indarch, an enstatite chondrite with unusually high nickel-iron and troilite content; the other meteorites analyzed were all olivine-bronzite or olivine-hypersthene chondrites.

Schindewolf (1960) has measured tellurium in four chondrites by neutron activation analysis; his results are: Beardsley, 0.88 ppm; Forest City, 0.46 ppm; Holbrook, 0.62 ppm; Modoc, 0.46 ppm; the

average is 0.61 ppm, about half that found by DuFresne. From these
results it appears that the abundance of tellurium in the chondritic
meteorites is of the order of 1 ppm.

Schindewolf also determined tellurium in one achondrite, Johnstown, and found 0.007 ppm. This very low value can be correlated
with the almost complete absence of nickel-iron and troilite in this
meteorite.

Goles and Anders (1962) have determined tellurium in a number
of chondrites by neutron activation analysis, with the following results (in ppm): Richardton, 0.73, 0.44, 0.52; Plainview, 0.49, 0.42;
Bruderheim, 0.46, 0.20, 0.50; Mocs, 0.46; Ergheo, 0.48; Stalldalen,
0.50; Indarch, 1.82, 3.4; Abee, 2.25, 2.14; St. Marks, 1.31, 1.55; Murray, 1.23; Mighei, 2.63, 1.88. These results show that enstatite and
carbonaceous chondrites (the last five) have consistently higher tellurium contents than the olivine-bronzite and olivine-hypersthene
chondrites. In the Toluca iron the metal phase contained about 0.05
ppm, the troilite about 1.7 ppm; in the Canyon Diablo iron the metal
had about 0.09 ppm, the troilite about 5 ppm. These figures show
that tellurium is predominantly chalcophile in meteorites.

Iodine (53): Iodine has been determined by neutron activation
analysis in fifteen samples of chondrites by Goles and Anders (1962).
Their results are as follows (in parts per billion): Beardsley, 60, 65;
Richardton, 31, 21, 33; Plainview, 47, 50; Bruderheim, 16, 27, 5; Mocs,
50; Ergheo, 90; Ställdalen, 570; Indarch, 210, 300, 300; Abee, 140, 150;
St. Marks, 64, 100; Murray, 150, 300, 230; Mighei, 350, 270. The first
seven are olivine-bronzite and olivine-hypersthenes chondrites; Indarch, Abee, and St. Marks are enstatite chondrites; Murray and Mighei
carbonaceous chondrites (Type II). Although variation in iodine
content among different samples of the same meteorite is considerable, the greater abundance of iodine in enstatite and carbonaceous
chondrites is clearly shown. The averages are: olivine-bronzite and
olivine-hypersthene chondrites (omitting Ställdalen), 34 ppb; enstatite
chondrites, 180 ppb; carbonaceous chondrites, 260 ppb.

Goles and Anders also measured iodine in nickel-iron and troilite
from iron meteorites, with the following results (all in ppb)—for
nickel-iron: Toluca, 170, 320; Canyon Diablo, 28; Grant, 11; for
troilite: Toluca, 1030; Canyon Diablo, 62; Grant, 24; Sardis, 3590;
Soroti, 50.

Goles and Anders found a marked positive correlation between the
abundances of iodine and tellurium in chondrites, and suggest that a
large fraction of both elements are in the same or several associated

phases, probably troilite and other sulfides. They found that most of the iodine in Richardton and Bruderheim and at least one-third of that in Murray is water-soluble.

Xenon (54): The occurrence of xenon in meteorites has been the subject of intensive investigation since Reynolds (1960*a*) showed that some chondrites contain a notable amount of xenon of anomalous isotopic composition, especially Xe^{129} in excess. This has been shown beyond reasonable doubt to be due to radioactive decay of extinct I^{129}. Xenon shows a preferential concentration in the carbonaceous chondrites. Other xenon isotopes also show anomalous abundances, and several theories have been suggested to explain this, in particular the spontaneous fission of Pu^{244}. The xenon content is of the order of 10^{-10}–10^{-11} gram/gram.

Cesium (55): Cesium in stone meteorites has been measured by a number of investigators. Webster, Morgan, and Smales (1958), using isotope dilution and neutron activation analysis on twelve chondrites, obtained a range of values from 0.01 to 0.28 ppm, with an average of 0.09 ppm. Ahrens, Edge, and Taylor (1960) determined cesium in six chondrites by an ion exchange enrichment procedure followed by spectrochemical analysis and found a much smaller range, from 0.10 to 0.18 ppm, with an average of 0.12 ppm. Gast (1960*a*) reports a range of 0.088 to 0.193 ppm in five chondrites by isotope dilution analysis, with an average of 0.12 ppm. The overall average of the above results is 0.11 ppm; all these determinations were made on olivine-bronzite and olivine-hypersthene chondrites. Smales (pers. comm.) reports 0.18 ppm in Ivuna and 0.12 ppm in Mighei, both carbonaceous chondrites.

Gast reports the following figures (in ppm) for the following pyroxene-plagioclase achondrites: Pasamonte, 0.011; Nuevo Laredo, 0.019; Sioux County, 0.012; Moore County, 0.005. Thus the abundance of cesium in these meteorites is approximately one-tenth of that in chondrites, a depletion which is noted in rubidium and potassium also.

Barium (56): The chemistry of barium indicates that it will be present almost entirely in the silicate phases of meteorites. The abundance of barium in stony meteorites has been determined by neutron activation analysis by Reed et al. (1960). They found the following amounts (in ppm) in different meteorites: Forest City, 3.3; Modoc, 3.8; Richardton, 3.2; Holbrook, 3.6; Beardsley, 3.0; Abee, 1.8; Indarch, 1.9; Mighei, 2.5; Orgueil, 2.4; Nuevo Laredo, 44. The first five are olivine-bronzite or olivine-hypersthene chondrites; Abee and Indarch are enstatite chondrites; Mighei and Orgueil carbonaceous chondrites; Nuevo Laredo a calcium-rich achondrite. The barium content shows a positive correlation with the calcium content. Assuming the olivine-bronzite and olivine-hypersthene chondrites are representative of meteoritic matter as a whole, this makes the average content of barium 3.4 ppm.

Reed and his co-workers also analyzed for barium in three samples of Canyon Diablo troilite (0.4, <0.006, <0.3 ppm) and one sample of Toluca troilite (<0.1 ppm). These figures indicate that barium does not tend to go into the sulfide phase; the single high figure of 0.4 ppm in one sample of Canyon Diablo troilite may be the result of contamination.

Reed and co-workers report that the isotopic composition of meteoritic barium is consistent with that of terrestrial barium to within an accuracy of 5%, a finding confirmed by Krummenacher et al. (1962). However, Umemoto (1962) claims to have detected small but real differences in the relative abundances of the barium isotopes between terrestrial and meteoritic material.

Rare earth elements (57–71): The abundances of the rare earth elements in four chondrites and two achondrites have been determined by Schmitt et al. (1960, 1961). They used neutron activation analysis, combined with an ion exchange procedure for the separation of the rare earth elements. Their results are given in Table 19. The figures indicate that the rare earth content of a meteorite is directly related to its calcium content, and these elements presumably reside in the calcium minerals.

Europium has been determined in a number of meteorites by Bate et al. (1960), also by neutron activation analysis. Their results are as follows (in ppm): Nuevo Laredo (plagioclase-pigeonite achondrite), 0.75, 0.77; Johnstown (hypersthene achondrite), 0.0098; Modoc (olivine-hypersthene chondrite), 0.080, 0.079; Richardton (olivine-bronzite chondrite), 0.079, 0.080; Forest City (olivine-bronzite chondrite), 0.073; Holbrook (olivine-hypersthene chondrite), 0.081; Beardsley (olivine-bronzite chondrite), 0.074. The figures for the chondrites are in good agreement with that given by Schmitt and his co-workers.

Umemoto (1962) looked for but failed to detect any differences in isotopic abundances of cerium between terrestrial and meteoritic material.

Hafnium (72): Merz (1962) has determined hafnium by neutron activation in five chondrites, with the following results (in ppm):

TABLE 19. ABUNDANCES (IN PPM) OF THE RARE EARTH
ELEMENTS IN METEORITES (SCHMITT AND CO-WORKERS,
1960, 1961)

	1	2	3	4	5	6
La	0.33	0.32	0.25	0.39	4.03	3.21
Ce	0.54	0.48	0.66	1.04	10.7	8.08
Pr	0.12	0.12	0.13	0.15	1.47	1.26
Nd	0.65	0.61	0.36	0.62	8.0	5.10
Sm	0.24	0.20	0.14	0.21	2.19	1.90
Eu	0.087	0.080	0.045	0.072	0.75	0.68
Gd	0.34	0.34	0.15	0.27	2.45	2.69
Tb	0.049	0.053	0.036	0.049	0.59	—
Dy	0.39	0.34	0.21	0.32	4.14	3.06
Ho	0.082	0.068	0.046	0.079	0.84	0.69
Er	0.22	0.21	0.14	0.21	2.87	1.65
Tm	0.043	0.033	0.024	0.037	0.48	0.30
Yb	0.20	0.19	0.14	0.19	2.34	1.67
Lu	0.038	0.033	0.027	0.030	0.30	0.50
Ca(%)	1.24	1.54	0.87	1.37	7.43	7.34

1. Allegan (olivine-bronzite chondrite)
2. Richardton (olivine-bronzite chondrite)
3. St. Marks (enstatite chondrite)
4. Murray (carbonaceous chondrite)
5. Nuevo Laredo (pigeonite-plagioclase achondrite)
6. Pasamonte (pigeonite-plagioclase achondrite)

Plainview, 1.7; Morland, 1.8; Potter, 2.0; Pultusk, 1.2; Mocs, 0.44.
The average is 1.4 ppm, which is probably a reasonable figure for
hafnium in meteoritic matter. In two irons (Canyon Diablo and
Henbury) Merz found 0.02 ppm.

Tantalum (73): Atkins and Smales (1960) have determined tantalum by neutron activation analysis in a number of olivine-hypersthene and olivine-bronzite chondrites, with the following results (in
ppm): Bjurbole, 0.021; Chandakpur, 0.020; Chateau Renard, 0.027;
Forest City, 0.023; Holbrook, 0.025; Long Island, 0.027; Ness County,
0.022; and Ochansk, 0.018. The figures show little variation, and
give an average of 0.023 ppm. Ehmann (pers. comm.) reports the
following results for chondrites (in ppm): Plainview, 0.022; Elenovka,
0.012; Forest City, 0.027; Cynthiana, 0.021; Ioka, 0.035; Kunashak,

0.032; Murray, 0.037, 0.040; he also reports 0.004 ppm in troilite from the Canyon Diablo iron.

Atkins and Smales also report 0.008 ppm in the Johnstown meteorite, a hypersthene achondrite.

Tungsten (74): Amiruddin and Ehmann (1962) have determined tungsten in meteorites by neutron activation analysis. They report 0.14 ppm as an average for sixteen chondrites (range 0.08–0.19 ppm); a wide range for different achondrites, from 0.006 ppm for Johnstown (diogenite) to 0.12 ppm for Shallowater (aubrite); an average of 1.16 ppm for five irons (range 0.78–1.45 ppm); and an average of 0.017 ppm for two samples of troilite. From these figures it appears that tungsten is almost entirely siderophile in meteorites, and its amount in any meteorite is directly related to the nickel-iron content.

Atkins and Smales (1960) determined tungsten in five chondrites by neutron activation analysis. They reported a range from 0.08 to 0.17 ppm, with an average of 0.14 ppm, in excellent agreement with the above results. For irons they give the following figures: Canyon Diablo, 1.6 ppm; Henbury, 0.76 ppm; San Martin, 2.6 ppm.

Rhenium (75): Brown and Goldberg (1950) found a range of 0.34–1.95 ppm in five irons by neutron activation analysis. Herr et al. (1961) determined rhenium in twenty-eight irons and found a range of 0.002–4.80 ppm; the extreme range of these figures is comparable to that found for osmium, but the Os/Re ratio is fairly uniform, ranging from 5 to 20. They found 0.188 ppm in the metal phase of the Ramsdorf chondrite, and 0.291 ppm in the metal phase and 0.031 ppm in the silicate phases of the Mocs chondrite.

Osmium (76): Goldschmidt (1937) gave the abundance of osmium in meteoritic material as follows: silicate, 0; nickel-iron, 8 ppm; troilite, 9 ppm. Bate (unpublished) has found an average of 0.8 ppm in six chondrites by neutron activation analysis. Herr et al. (1961) found a remarkable variation in the osmium content of iron meteorites, the figures ranging from 0.025 to 50.4 ppm. They found 2.57 ppm in the metal phase of the Ramsdorf chondrite, and 3.67 ppm in the metal phase and 0.35 ppm in the silicate phases of the Mocs chondrite.

Iridium (77): Goldschmidt (1937) gave the abundance or iridium in meteoritic material as follows: silicate, 0; nickel-iron, 4 ppm; troilite, 0.4 ppm. Rushbrooke and Ehmann (1962) and Ehmann (pers. comm.) report that the iridium content of stony meteorites is directly related to the nickel-iron content, and that iridium is thus essentially siderophile. They report an average of 0.46 ppm in twelve chondrites (range 0.21–0.57 ppm). For other meteorite types they give the following results (in ppm): Sikhote-Alin (iron), 0.014; Canyon Diablo (iron), 1.49; Odessa (iron), 2.02; Johnstown (hypersthene achondrite), 0.008; Cumberland Falls (enstatite achondrite), 0.002; Shallowater (enstatite achondrite), 0.14; troilite (from Canyon Diablo iron), 0.001 and 0.002.

Platinum (78): Goldschmidt (1937) gave the abundance of platinum in meteoritic material as follows: silicate, 0; nickel-iron, 20 ppm; troilite, 2 ppm. Yavnel (1950) found 4.6 ppm in the Sikhote-Alin iron.

Gold (79): Gold, being a siderophile element, may be expected to occur entirely in the metal phase of meteorites. The abundance of gold in iron meteorites has been determined by neutron activation analysis in forty-five iron meteorites by Goldberg, Uchiyama, and Brown (1951). For individual meteorites they obtained gold contents ranging from 0.094 to 8.744 ppm (these are two extreme values —the nearest on the low side is 0.452 ppm and on the high side 2.54 ppm). Goldberg and his co-workers remark that the concentration of gold in general increases with the nickel content of the meteorite, but this trend is not marked. The average of all determinations is 1.44 ppm. Yavnel (1950) found 1.8 ppm in the Sikhote-Alin iron.

Vincent and Crocket (1960) have determined the gold content in four chondrites: Limerick, 0.29 ppm; Ochansk, 0.14 ppm; Bjurbole, 0.10 ppm; and Chateau Renard, 0.13 ppm—all falls, the first two being olivine-bronzite chondrites and the last two olivine-hypersthene chondrites. Assuming that all the gold is in the metal phase, the gold content of this phase averages 1.4 ppm, in agreement with the results of Goldberg and his co-workers.

Assuming 20% metal phase in average meteoritic matter, the gold content will be 0.3 ppm.

Mercury (80): Mercury has been determined in five olivine-bronzite and olivine-hypersthene chondrites—Beardsley, Forest City, Holbrook, Modoc, and Plainview—by Ehmann and Huizenga (1959), using neutron activation analysis. The individual figures show considerable variation, but the average content of Hg^{202} was found to be 0.03 ppm; since Hg^{202} makes up 30% of ordinary mercury, the overall mercury content should be 0.1 ppm. Reed, Kigoshi, and Turkevich (1960) have determined mercury in the Orgueil carbonaceous chondrite, and found much higher values, 11 ppm and 6.26 ppm in two samples. They also found an average of 0.007 ppm mercury in two samples of troilite from the Canyon Diablo iron. The high mercury content of Orgueil is consistent with its having been at a low temperature throughout its history; this content is also consistent with the probable cosmic abundance of mercury as estimated by Suess and Urey (1956).

Thallium (81): Thallium has been determined in meteorites by Ehmann and Huizenga (1959) and by Reed, Kigoshi, and Turkevich (1960), using neutron activation analysis. Reed and his co-workers analyzed a larger number of samples, and their results are in general agreement with those of Ehmann and Huizenga. The thallium contents show a tendency to scatter from sample to sample of the same meteorite; the thallium probably resides in the metal and sulfide phases, and variability of sampling may account for this scatter. The mean thallium content of the common (olivine-bronzite and olivine-hypersthene) chondrites is about 0.0004 ppm. Enstatite chondrites and carbonaceous chondrites contain much more thallium: Abee, 0.084 ppm; Indarch, 0.125 ppm; Mighei, 0.097 ppm; Orgueil, 0.141 ppm (the first two are enstatite chondrites, the last two carbonaceous chondrites). The much higher thallium contents cannot be explained by higher troilite or higher nickel-iron contents of these meteorites, but must be inherent in the material.

Troilite from the Canyon Diablo iron averages 0.01 ppm Tl; troilite from the Toluca iron had 0.198 ppm Tl.

Lead (82): Since lead is the heaviest stable element, its concentration is especially significant for studies relating to the abundances of the elements. In addition, it is possible to calculate an age for a meteorite from the isotopic composition of the lead it contains. As a result many studies have been made on the lead content of meteorites.

Hess and Marshall (1960) and Reed, Kigoshi, and Turkevich (1960) have determined lead in a number of meteorites, and have summarized the results of previous investigators. Their figures for the ordinary (olivine-hypersthene and olivine-bronzite) chondrites are as follows (in ppm): Richardton, 0.055 (HM); Holbrook, 0.28 (HM), 0.40 (RKT); Forest City, 0.09 (HM), 0.15 (RKT); Beardsley, 0.13 (HM), 0.15 (RKT); Plainview, 0.46 (HM); Modoc, 0.06 (RKT). These are all falls, except for Plainview; since the latter may have acquired lead during weathering, it should be excluded from further consideration. The above figures show a considerable range, even in different samples of the same meteorite. A lead content of 0.15 ppm appears to be a median value with a range of a factor of 3 each way.

Reed and co-workers found that the enstatite chondrites Abee and

Indarch, and the carbonaceous chondrites Mighei and Orgueil have an order of magnitude more lead, varying between 1 and 5 ppm, than the ordinary chondrites. This has been confirmed by Marshall (1962). These values are consistent with estimates of the absolute abundance of lead from nucleogenic theories, and indicate that ordinary chondrites have undergone some process causing depletion of this element.

Starik et al. (1960) have made an extensive study of the lead content of iron meteorites, both the metal phase and the troilite. For the metal phase they found a range of 0.02–0.40 ppm, whereas the range for troilite is 1–8 ppm. They also determined the isotopic composition of the lead from these meteorites, and found two clearly differentiated groups, one with lead of primordial isotopic composition, similar to Canyon Diablo (Patterson, 1956), the other with lead of recent terrestrial isotopic composition. They point out that most stone meteorites contain lead of recent isotopic composition, whereas in the enstatite and carbonaceous chondrites the lead has primordial isotopic composition.

Bismuth (*83*): The abundance of bismuth in meteoritic matter has been extensively studied by Reed, Kigoshi, and Turkevich (1960), using neutron activation analysis. Their results indicate low abundance of this element in chondrites, and sometimes varying amounts in different samples of the same meteorite. Since bismuth is markedly chalcophile, and is perhaps also siderophile in meteorites, these varying amounts may perhaps be due to varying amounts of nickel-iron and troilite in the different samples. They find a median value of 0.003 ppm for the common chondrites (olivine-bronzite and olivine-hypersthene chondrites). This figure is in agreement with the data of Ehmann and Huizenga (1959). However, Reed and his co-workers found much higher values, 0.08–0.18 ppm, in enstatite chondrites (Abee and Indarch) and carbonaceous chondrites (Mighei and Orgueil). These higher values cannot be accounted for by the higher total sulfur in these meteorites, which is approximately twice that of the common chondrites.

Samples of troilite from the Canyon Diablo iron gave an average of 0.04 ppm, and one sample of troilite from the Toluca iron gave 0.18 ppm.

Thorium (*90*): The amount of thorium in meteorites has long been of interest, partly because of the possibility of determining their ages by the Th^{232}-Pb^{208} method. Most of the analyses for thorium, however, have given too high figures, due to errors. Bate et al. (1959)

have determined thorium in seven stony meteorites by neutron activation analysis, with the following results (in ppm): Modoc, 0.0392; Richardton, 0.0380; Forest City, 0.0387; Holbrook, 0.0380; Beardsley, 0.0477; Nuevo Laredo, 0.476; Johnstown, 0.00587. These meteorites are all falls; the first five are chondrites, Nuevo Laredo a calcium-rich achondrite, Johnstown a calcium-poor achondrite. The thorium content shows a positive correlation with the calcium content of the meteorite.

The average for the five chondrites is 0.04 ppm, which can be taken as a good figure for the thorium content of meteoritic matter as a whole.

Uranium (92): The uranium content of meteorites has long been of interest, because of the possibility of making an age calculation on these enigmatic bodies from this information. Unfortunately, much of the information in the literature is unreliable, due to the inadequacy of the methods used. Reed et al. (1960) have made careful measurements of uranium contents of stony meteorites, with the following results (in ppm): Forest City, 0.015; Modoc, 0.014; Holbrook, 0.016; Beardsley, 0.012; Abee, 0.011; Indarch, 0.016; Mighei, 0.016; Orgueil, 0.008; Nuevo Laredo, 0.15. These meteorites are all falls; the first four are olivine-bronzite or olivine-hypersthene chondrites; Abee and Indarch, enstatite chondrites; Mighei and Orgueil, carbonaceous chondrites; Nuevo Laredo, a calcium-rich achondrite. The uranium content of the chondrites averages 0.014 ppm, which is probably a reasonable figure for meteoritic matter as a whole; this figure has been confirmed by Goles and Anders (1962). The high uranium content of Nuevo Laredo may be correlated with its high calcium content.

Reed and his co-workers found 0.004 ppm in troilite from the Canyon Diablo troilite, and 10^{-6}–10^{-4} ppm in irons and stony-irons; it is clear from these figures that almost all the uranium in meteorites is associated with the silicate phases.

11

Meteorite Ages

Introduction

Numerous determinations have been made of the ages of meteorites, using a variety of methods based on different nuclear reactions. However, it is meaningless to talk about the age of a meteorite in a general sense. Different methods, involving different elements and different assumptions, usually give different ages. Actually, each method gives a point on the time scale to a specific event in the history of the matter making up the meteorite sample. This event is defined by the particular age equation of the method and by the chemical and physical properties of the parent and daughter elements on which the method is based. Thus events such as nucleosynthesis, general chemical separation processes, the formation of the minerals in the sample, subsequent heating, the breakup of a possible parent body, and the time of fall of the meteorite, may each be recorded by specific nuclear processes. An exhaustive review of meteoritic ages is provided by Anders (1962).

The earliest work on the ages of meteorites as determined by radiogenic elements is that of Paneth and his co-workers (Paneth, 1928; Arrol, Jacobi, and Paneth, 1942). They determined the helium content of a number of iron meteorites, and, on the assumption that this helium was produced by the radioactive disintegration of uranium and thorium, obtained ages ranging from 1 to 7000×10^6 years.

Since the latter figure greatly exceeded the age of the solar system as conceived at that time, the interpretation of these results was the subject of much controversy. In 1947 Bauer suggested that much of the helium in meteorites has been produced by cosmic-ray spallation, and this suggestion was later confirmed.

Since 1950 the different dating methods based on radioactivity— the lead isotope method, the rubidium-strontium method, the potassium-argon method, and the uranium-helium method—have been extensively applied to meteorites.

The Lead Isotope Method

Patterson (1956) showed that, with the following assumptions: (1) meteorites were formed at the same time; (2) they existed as closed and isolated systems; (3) they originally contained lead of the same isotopic composition; (4) they contain uranium which has the same isotopic composition as that in the Earth, it was possible to calculate the time of formation from measurements of the isotopic composition of the lead from two or more meteorites. His calculations gave a figure of 4.55 ± 0.07 aeons (1 aeon = 10^9 years). Additional determinations on a number of stony meteorites by Hess and Marshall (1960) have given results consistent with this figure. However, if the uranium-lead ages of the stony meteorites are calculated, serious discrepancies arise—in particular, there does not seem to be enough uranium to account for the amounts of radiogenic lead present.

Iron meteorites contain so little uranium and thorium that their lead has not significantly changed in isotopic composition since these meteorites were formed; stony meteorites, on the other hand, contain appreciable amounts of uranium and thorium, and the isotopic composition of their lead has been modified by the steady addition of Pb^{206}, Pb^{207}, and Pb^{208} from the decay of these elements. The above data are interpreted to mean that 4.55 aeons ago the iron meteorites were separated from uranium and thorium, presumably by a melting process, and that this figure also measures the interval during which radiogenic lead has accumulated within the stony meteorites.

Starik et al. (1960) have shown that the lead in some iron meteorites, for example Sikhote-Alin, has isotopic composition similar to that of modern terrestrial lead. They suggest that there are two groups of meteorites—one formed a closed uranium-lead system 4.5 aeons ago with the initial lead having an isotopic composition similar to that of Canyon Diablo and the other meteorites examined by Patterson; the other group formed a closed uranium-lead system much more recently with the initial lead having an isotopic composition similar to common terrestrial lead. Fireman and Fisher (1961) have found that there is insufficient U^{235} in the Sikhote-Alin meteorite to account for the present content of Pb^{207} and that the uranium and lead contents of this meteorite are inconsistent with the assumptions made in determining lead isotope ages for meteorites.

The Rubidium-Strontium Method

Both rubidium and strontium are strongly lithophile elements, and hence are present in the stony meteorites and are practically absent in the irons. As a result rubidium-strontium age determinations are only feasible on the stones. Herzog and Pinson (1956) discuss the application of this method to meteorites, and point out that the following quantities must be known: (1) the Rb and Sr content of the sample; (2) the fraction of Sr which is radiogenic; (3) the present fraction of Rb^{87} in total sample Rb, and the variation of this fraction in past time. They were able to determine these quantities for the Homestead chondrite, and arrived at an age of 4.7 aeons. Similar ages have been determined for Pasamonte (a pigeonite-plagioclase achondrite), Bustee (an enstatite achondrite), and Forest City (an olivine-bronzite chondrite) by Schumacher (1956).

Gast (1960b) has shown that the Sr^{87}/Sr^{86} ratio in chondrites is variable, ranging from 0.739 to 0.811, whereas this ratio is practically constant in the calcium-rich achondrites, ranging from 0.700 to 0.703. He interprets these figures as indicating that the chondrites 4.5 aeons ago had Sr^{87}/Sr^{86} ratios similar to that now seen in the achondrites. This ratio has increased in the chondrites through the addition of radiogenic Sr^{87}, whereas in the achondrites, which have very low rubidium contents, this ratio has remained practically unchanged. Evidently the achondrites, if they differentiated from a source material of chondritic composition, did so some 4.5 aeons ago.

The Rhenium-Osmium Method

This method has recently been applied by Herr et al. (1961) to the determination of meteorite ages. In principle it is similar to the rubidium-strontium method, being based on the beta-decay of Re^{187} to Os^{187}. However, it is more difficult in its application, because of the very low abundance of rhenium and the present uncertainty as to its half-life. However, Herr and his co-workers conclude, on the basis of rhenium and osmium determinations on some thirty meteorites, that the results are consistent with the belief that the stone and the iron meteorites were formed between 4 and 5 aeons ago.

The Potassium-Argon Method

Probably more ages of meteorites have been determined by the potassium-argon method than by any other. This method involves a gaseous product, and the meaning of the ages so derived may differ from those obtained from the preceding methods. In principle these methods date chemical separation processes and give no information on the subsequent physical or mineralogical history, whereas a method involving a radiogenic gas in principle gives the time of crystallization or last heating. In discussing such ages, therefore, it must be remembered that these gases have significant diffusion co- efficients in solids at relatively low temperatures. Very often the cal- culated age will not represent a specific event (normally the time of crystallization) but will merely reflect the rate of diffusion of the gas. The two extremes—time of crystallization or rate of diffusion— cannot be separated from each other when interpreting a radiogenic gas age.

Potassium-argon ages for stony meteorites have been determined by Gerling and co-workers (1951, 1955), Wasserburg and Hayden (1955), and Geiss and Hess (1958). These ages range from 0.5 to 4.5 aeons, with a noticeable concentration of values between 4.0 and 4.5 aeons. It is likely that all these meteorites crystallized at least 4.5 aeons ago, and that lower ages reflect loss of argon; it can also be argued that the ages give the time of crystallization of the meteorites, and hence different meteorites have crystallized at different times. Goles, Fish, and Anders (1960) have discussed the potassium-argon ages and conclude that the first interpretation is the correct one.

The Uranium-Helium Method

As discussed earlier, this method was the first applied to the dating of meteorites, but gave spurious results, due to the formation of helium within the meteorite by cosmic-ray spallation. The method also suffers from the inherent defect of the potassium-argon method, that of diffusive loss of the radiogenic gas. A number of uranium-helium ages, corrected for cosmic-ray helium, have been determined, and range from 0.5 to 4.2 aeons (Reed and Turkevich, 1957). Where potassium-argon and uranium-helium ages have been determined on the same meteorite, the potassium-argon age is usually the greater, indicating that helium diffuses out of a meteorite more readily than argon.

To sum up, it may be said that the different radiogenic methods of dating meteorites give reasonably consistent results about 4.5 aeons. This figure is also the age ascribed to the Earth as an individual body in the solar system. The agreement between the two figures may be interpreted as indicating that the formation of the meteorites was coeval with that of the Earth and other planets in the solar system. In other words, the maximum ages deduced for meteorites are compatible with the age of the Earth and of the solar system.

Cosmic-Ray Ages

Cosmic radiation in outer space causes nuclear transformations in meteorites. The general effect of such radiation on an atomic nucleus is called spallation. Spallation products cannot be heavier than the original nucleus, and therefore the detectable products in meteorites are practically limited to nuclides equal to or lower in mass than iron and nickel.

The first suggestion that cosmic-ray-produced nuclei may be detectable in meteorites was made by Bauer (1947), who proposed that much of the helium detected in iron meteorites had been produced by cosmic-ray spallation. It was later shown (Paneth and co-workers, 1952) that up to one-third of this helium is He^3, which is one product of cosmic-ray spallation.

In the following years many more spallation products, stable and radioactive nuclides of the lighter elements (up to nickel), have been detected in meteorites. Since the radioactive nuclides range in half-life from a few days to millions of years, their measurement provides evidence concerning the intensity and distribution of cosmic radiation in space, its possible variation with time, and events in the history of the meteorites—their pre-atmospheric size, the so-called "radiation ages," and the time of their fall.

Studies of the concentrations of different radioactive spallation products with different half-lives have demonstrated that within the limits of error all these radioactive isotopes have reached a steady state, indicating that the cosmic-ray flux must have been roughly constant during the last several million years.

The concentration of spallation products within a meteorite will vary with depth from the original surface, since the cosmic radiation will have the greatest effect at the surface and will be attenuated with depth. Fireman (1958) first applied this method to determining the original (i.e., pre-terrestrial) shape and size of the Carbo meteorite. Hoffman and Nier (1958, 1959) have mapped the concentrations of He^3 and He^4 in cross sections of some iron meteorites. By contouring equal He^3 contents on these cross sections they have deduced the pre-atmospheric shape of these meteorites and hence the amount of the meteorite which has been ablated during its passage through the atmosphere. This work has been extended by Signer and Nier (1960) to the absolute and relative depth dependence of all the isotopes of argon, neon, and helium, giving a more accurate basis for calculations of original size. They estimate that the Grant meteorite, which weighs 480 kg, had a mass of approximately 2000 kg when it entered the Earth's atmosphere.

The total amount of radiation received by a particular meteorite sample can be calculated from the accumulated amount of a stable isotope. If a constant cosmic-ray intensity is assumed (a reasonable assumption, according to the preceding discussion), then the duration of the irradiation can be calculated; this is called the "radiation age" or the "cosmic-ray age."

Cosmic-ray ages have been determined for a considerable number of meteorites, and a summary of the results is provided by Anders (1962). Stones give ages ranging from 3×10^6 to 500×10^6 years, most ages, however, being of the order of 20×10^6 years; irons give ages of 100×10^6 years to 1500×10^6 years.

It is immediately apparent that the cosmic-ray ages, especially for the stone meteorites, are systematically smaller by several orders of magnitude than the ages determined by the Pb-Pb, Rb-Sr, and K-Ar methods. Evidently the cosmic-ray ages date completely different events in the history of the meteorites. The K-Ar ages give the time of the last severe heating of the meteorite material. The cosmic-ray age, on the other hand, records the integrated effect of cosmic radiation upon the meteorite. The "switching on" of the cosmic radiation may record the time at which the meteorite surface was first exposed to the radiation.

Several different models have been proposed for this exposure. One view of the cosmic-ray age is that it records the time at which a parent meteorite body broke up into the small pieces which fall on the Earth. This leads to the concept of different parent bodies for iron and stone meteorites, since the irons give far higher cosmic-ray ages than the stones. An alternative view is that the cosmic-ray age does not measure a specific event but reflects a variable loss of surface material from different meteorites, this loss being due to erosion in outer space caused by cosmic dust, interplanetary gas and low energy particles, or by a continued breakup by impact between individual meteorites. This model provides a plausible explanation for the systematic difference in cosmic-ray ages between the irons and the stones—the stones, being mechanically weaker than the irons, have lost a much greater amount of their mass by space erosion. Probably both mechanisms, breakup and space erosion, are important factors in determining cosmic-ray ages.

Terrestrial Age of Meteorites

The period which has elapsed since the fall of a meteorite on the Earth may be called its terrestrial age, and can be estimated from its present content of cosmogenic nuclides. After the fall of a meteorite it is shielded from cosmic rays by the Earth's atmosphere, and the radioactivity of each spallation nuclide will decay with its characteristic half-life. Some nuclides with comparatively short half-lives will be undetectable after a comparatively short interval; others with longer half-lives may persist for millions of years. Ehmann and Kohman (1958) estimated that the Odessa siderite fell less than about one million years ago, from its content of Be^{10} and Al^{26}. Fireman and DeFelice (1960) reported that a number of irons fell more than 1500 years ago, from the absence of Ar^{39} and H^3; one iron, Washington County, gave a small trace of Ar^{39}, indicating that it fell about 1000 years ago. The data of Honda et al. (1961) indicate that the Williamstown and Grant siderites may have fallen about 500,000 years ago. These results show that meteoritic irons weather comparatively slowly. Measurements of this kind can be useful in deciding whether a meteorite is a recent fall, or indeed whether it is a meteorite at all; one iron, reportedly seen to fall, showed no trace of cosmic-ray activity, and was subsequently proved to be a piece of manufactured iron.

For comparatively recent falls measurements of H^3 and C^{14} may give significant data as to the time of fall. Bainbridge et al. (1962) have measured tritium in Bruderheim (fell 1960), Harleton (fell 1961), and Walters (found before 1947). The tritium age of Walters compared with that of Bruderheim indicates a terrestrial age of about 15 years, and suggests very strongly that its time of fall was identical with that of an observed fireball in that region. Suess and Wänke (1962) have measured C^{14} in twelve stony meteorites and one iron; for the finds they obtained terrestrial ages of up to 20,000 years and older. Comparable results have been obtained on six chondrites by Goel and Kohman (1962).

Extinct Radioactive Nuclides

Radioactive isotopes with short half-lives, of the order of 100 million years or less, presumably were formed in the general processes of nucleosynthesis, but have long since decayed and are now extinct. However, it is conceivable that their previous existence may be manifested by the presence of their stable daughter isotopes. Meteorites, being much older than any terrestrial rocks, are particularly suitable objects for detecting such isotopes formed at an early stage in cosmic history. This possibility was first suggested by Harrison Brown in 1947, and was confirmed experimentally by Reynolds in 1960, when he detected, in the Richardton chondrite, an excess of Xe^{129} over its terrestrial abundance; the excess Xe^{129} was presumably formed from I^{129}, which has a half-life of 17 million years. Reynolds calculated that the time interval between the formation of the elements (assuming a relatively short duration of nucleosynthesis) and the formation of the meteorite was 350 million years.

The evidence of abnormal abundances of Xe^{129} in meteorites is accumulating rapidly. Because of our limited general concepts of the initial stages of development of the solar system (including the meteorites) the actual meaning of the time interval which is measured by the Xe^{129} method is still a subject of controversy. Also, if the so-called "steady state" cosmologists are correct, and the formation of the elements has been a continuous process instead of occurring in a short period, the interpretation of the Xe^{129} age must be revised. Nevertheless, this discovery is highly significant, since for the first time the decay product of an extinct radioactive nucleus has been detected and the yardstick of radioactive dating has been extended back to reach the time of formation of the elements.

Another extinct radioactive isotope which theoretically may be detectable by its daughter is Pb^{205}, which decays to Tl^{205} with a half-life of 24 million years. Anders and Stevens (1960) have extracted thallium from a variety of meteorites and measured its isotopic composition. However, no anomalies in the Tl^{205}/Tl^{203} ratio were detected. They therefore put a lower limit of 240 million years for the time interval between a short nucleosynthesis period and the formation of the meteorites.

Murthy (1961) has observed an anomaly in the isotopic composition of silver from some iron meteorites, finding a consistently higher Ag^{107}/Ag^{109} ratio (1.095) than terrestrial silver (1.064). He ascribes this to the decay of the extinct radioactive nuclide Pd^{207}; the magnitude of the anomaly, however, does not appear to be consistent with the magnitude of the Xe^{129} anomaly.

12

The Origin of Meteorites

Introduction

The origin of meteorites has been a problem ever since it was established that they are extra-terrestrial. Already in 1794 Chladni explained meteorites as solid debris reaching the Earth from outer space, and theorized that they are fragments produced by the breakup of large heavenly bodies by external impact or an internal explosion. In spite of all the meteorite investigations since that time, it cannot be said that a completely satisfying and generally accepted theory has yet been developed, although our factual knowledge bearing on the origin of meteorites has greatly increased, especially in recent years. It may be useful at this point to recapitulate some of the facts about meteorites that have a clear bearing on their origin.

Pertinent Facts

Any selection of such facts is to some degree arbitrary, and is undoubtedly conditioned by personal experience. Nevertheless, the following seem to be well-established and highly significant:

1. The chemical and mineralogical relationships between the different classes of meteorites strongly suggest they were all derived from a common parent material.

2. The available data are consistent with a common origin within the solar system.

3. Chondrites are by far the most abundant meteorites, making up over 80% of all observed falls.

4. Apart from the volatile elements O, C, S, and H, chondrites are very uniform in chemical composition as regards the major elements, except that one group has about 5% less nickel-iron than the others.

5. Most chondrites closely approach a state of internal chemical equilibrium.

6. The genesis of other classes of meteorites can be readily explained in most instances by melting and subsequent differentiation of material of chondritic composition.

7. Iron meteorites have crystallized and cooled very slowly, probably from a considerable body or bodies of iron-nickel melt.

8. The metal in iron and stony-iron meteorites commonly shows Widmanstatten structure; the metal in stones does not.

9. Age measurements indicate that the material of the different classes of meteorites crystallized about 4.5 aeons ago.

The Nature of the Problem

Unless we assume that meteorites have always existed in their present form, in which case no theory of origin save that of special creation would be required, the problem of their origin can be broken down into a number of separate but related problems. These are: (1) the nature of the original material; (2) the time of its formation; (3) the chemical differentiation that gave rise to the different meteorite types; (4) the time and place of this chemical differentiation. Since meteorites are part of the solar system, it has been generally accepted that their original material was similar to that from which the rest of the solar system was formed. Up to about 1945 this original material was usually considered as a high-temperature gas of approximately solar composition (e.g., Daly, 1943). However, since that time, the assumption that the solar system was formed by the condensation of a cold cosmic cloud of dust and gas has been widely accepted as offering a more satisfactory explanation of its origin and development. The exact composition of such material cannot be accurately known, but Latimer (1950) suggested that it would consist of H_2, H_2O, CH_4, NH_3, inert gases, oxides or their compounds of Fe and all elements more electropositive than iron, metallic

Fe and all less electropositive elements, with possibly nitrides, carbides, halides, and sulfides. [The relative abundances of the nonvolatile elements in this cosmic dust were probably similar to those in chondritic meteorites, since (*a*) chondrites are the most abundant meteorites; (*b*) chondrites show a remarkable uniformity in elemental composition (except for some variation in iron and a few trace elements); (*c*) it is possible to derive the other meteorite types by chemical differentiation from the chondrites. The low temperature and oxidized state of the major metallic elements (Fe, Mg, Si) in the cosmic dust cloud suggest that the initial material might resemble in composition that of the Type I carbonaceous chondrites.

B [The origin and time of formation of this cosmic dust cloud is an astrophysical problem. In one view of cosmogony, that of the formation of the chemical elements in a single event or series of events some 5 aeons ago, the cosmic dust cloud is part of the material formed at that time. In the continuous-creation view of cosmogony, the cosmic dust cloud would be the debris produced from giant red stars or supernovae. On the basis of the first view, Reynolds (1960*a*) interpreted the Xe^{129} content of meteorites as indicating a time interval of 350 million years between the formation of the elements and the formation of parent bodies of meteorites. On the basis of the continuous-creation theory, the cosmic dust cloud predates the meteorite parent bodies by about 200 million years (Wasserburg, Fowler, and Hoyle, 1960).

C [The aggregation and chemical differentiation of the material of the original dust cloud to give the diversity of meteorite types is the crux of current theories of meteorite origin. Briefly, the theories differ essentially in the dimensions proposed for the immediate parent body or bodies of the meteorites. These are postulated to have been (1) of planetary size; (2) two successive generations, one of lunar size and one of asteroidal size; (3) of asteroidal size only. The time of this D → chemical differentiation has been fairly well established by the dating of meteorites by the lead isotope method, the potassium-argon method, and the rubidium-strontium method. Measurements by these three methods have given concordant results indicating that the crystallization of the different meteorite types took place within a relatively short period of time about 4.5 aeons ago.

Theories of Origin

Ever since the original suggestion of Chladni in 1794, theories of the origin of meteorites by the disruption of a planetary body have been current. Since the first asteroids were discovered, and Olbers (1803) formulated the hypothesis that they are fragments of a disrupted planet which at one time existed between Mars and Jupiter, meteorites have been considered as asteroids or fragments of asteroids whose orbits have brought them within the gravitational field of the Earth. Since that time many investigators have endeavored to reconstruct a planet whose disintegration would give rise to the different types of meteorites. Many planetary models have been suggested; recent ones include those of Daly (1943), Brown and Patterson (1948), Zavaritsky (1950), Lovering (1957a, b), and Ringwood (1961a). Ringwood's hypothesis is comprehensive and cogently argued, and will be summarized here.

Ringwood assumes that the parent body formed by accretion from a cold dust cloud of solar composition. The accretion process was part of the series of events which led to the formation of the solar system about 4.5 aeons ago. After the accretion stage, it is assumed that the meteoritic planet possessed a composition similar to that of carbonaceous chondrites, but perhaps containing a higher concentration of volatiles. Such a composition would be expected for a low temperature accumulation of dust of solar composition. The planet was then subjected to internal heating, which caused melting to occur in the deep interior. When the molten region became sufficiently extensive, convection set in. The molten chondritic material, containing water and carbon under confining pressure, rose to the surface of the planet, where the confining pressure was released. Under these conditions, volatiles rapidly escaped, and the surface of the planet was subjected to volcanism on a grand scale. The rapid loss of volatiles caused rapid crystallization and resulted in the formation of the tuffaceous and chondritic structure of chondrites. During the same heating process, the carbon (and hydrogen) reacted with the oxidized iron and nickel to produce a metallic phase, while the resultant carbon dioxide was lost with the volatiles. It is suggested that nearly all the material in the meteoritic planet passed through this melting-convection-volcanism stage, thus producing the parent material of the chondritic meteorites.

The temperature at which melting occurred was around 900° C, but after the convection-reduction-volcanism stage it fell to 300° C. However, in a relatively small region in the deep interior, temperatures substantially higher than 900° C were reached, which caused complete melting and differentiation of the chondritic material. As a result the metal phase sank to the center to form a small core, separated from the relatively cool chondritic mantle by a zone of mixed iron and silicates—the pallasites and mesosiderites. The complementary eucritic and howarditic silicate differentiates possessed a lower density than the surrounding stony-irons and chondritic material, and hence rose to the surface of the planet in much the same manner as basalts on the Earth. Because of their relatively high temperature and the presence of volatiles, they lost much of their rubidium and potassium by volatilization and gas streaming.

The molten inner zone of irons and stony-irons cooled to a temperature below 500° C by heat transfer with the surrounding cool chondritic mantle. At the same time a certain amount of metamorphism and recrystallization occurred in the mantle.

Subsequently the meteorite planet was disrupted into fragments, which have since been colliding among themselves, thus further reducing their sizes. The remnants of these collisions are the asteroids and meteorites. The genetic relationships between the different groups of meteorites are illustrated in Fig. 60.

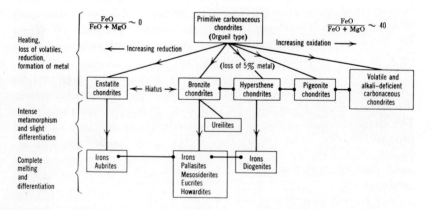
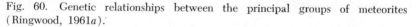

Fig. 60. Genetic relationships between the principal groups of meteorites (Ringwood, 1961a).

However, there are serious objections to the derivation of meteorites by the breakup of a planet. Breaking up a body of planetary size is extremely difficult and no truly satisfactory solution of this problem has been proposed. The mass of material in the asteroidal belt (estimated as 0.03 of a lunar mass) is clearly insufficient to form even a single body the size of the moon. The cooling history of such a body also presents apparently insuperable difficulties. The core of such a body must have been molten at one time to permit the segregation of metal and silicate, but Urey (1957) has shown that a body of lunar size, if melted by any process whatever, could not cool to the temperature indicated by the Widmanstatten structure within the entire age of the solar system.

The apparently insuperable objections to an origin of meteorites by the disintegration of a single planet led Urey (1956, 1958a, 1959) to formulate their origin from two successive generations of bodies, his primary and secondary objects. The primary objects were of lunar size or greater, and accumulated about 4.5 aeons ago at low temperatures, incorporating a substantial content of thermodynamically unstable compounds and possibly free radicals. Exothermic chemical reactions in this material produced localized reduction, melting, and segregation of metal and silicate phases, resulting in the formation of pools of perhaps meter or tens of meters dimensions. The silicate pools would differentiate upon cooling into more or less pure minerals, the precursors of the achondrites, whereas the metal pools would provide the material for the iron meteorites. Continued growth of the primary objects would cause some of these segregated portions to be buried at great enough depths to permit formation of diamonds from graphite. These primary objects cooled to about 500° C for 10^7–10^8 years, during which time the Widmanstatten structure developed in the nickel-iron segregations.

The primary objects were subsequently broken into fragments by collision between themselves; the secondary objects accumulated from this debris about 4.3 aeons ago, and were at least of asteroidal size. The irons, the stony-irons, and the achondrites are survivals from the primary objects. The chondrites, on the other hand, represent accumulations of the fine particles from the breakup of the primary objects, the chondrules themselves being formed by the crystallization of liquid silicate drops. Since the time of the accumulation of the secondary objects they have been broken up, either continuously or at specific times, and their fragments are the meteorites.

The complex nature of Urey's theory has been criticized by Anders and Goles (1961) as demanding a number of happenings of low statistical probability. Some of the difficulties of the planetary theory, particularly the problem of breaking up the primary objects, also apply to this theory. In addition, the limited composition range of the chondrites as a group and the phase equilibria within individual chondrites, as exemplified by Prior's rules and the data of Ringwood (1961a), are incompatible with these meteorites being chance aggregates of debris from the breakup of pre-existing bodies. Anders and Goles (1961) point out that the Cumberland Falls achondrite, which contains fragments of a chondrite, is inconsistent with Urey's theory, in which achondrites are made in primary objects, before the formation of the chondrites.

Theories proposing the formation of meteorites in asteroidal bodies have been developed in recent years. A number of Russian scientists have rejected theories ascribing the formation of meteorites to the breakup of a single large planet. They generally accept Schmidt's cosmogenic theory, according to which meteorites are fragments of many celestial bodies of the asteroid type. Levin (1958) argues that meteoritic matter has passed through the stage of intermediate asteroidal bodies and has undergone repeated breakup and agglomeration. Yavnel (1958) divides meteorites into five groups on chemical composition and concludes that each of these groups was formed from a single layered asteroid. Lovering (1962) has also presented a theory of the evolution of the different meteorite types in parent bodies of asteroidal or lunar dimensions.

The theory of the development of meteorites in asteroidal bodies has been carefully considered by Fish, Goles, and Anders (1960), and they develop a closely reasoned account of such a mode of formation. According to their account the asteroids, or planetesimals, as they also refer to them, accumulated some $4\frac{1}{2}$ aeons ago and were heated to melting temperatures by some transient internal energy source, such as extinct radioactivity. They show that segregation of metal and silicate phases and mineral differentiation by crystal settling will take place comparatively rapidly even in small bodies. Evidence concerning the occurrence of diamonds in meteorites is critically examined and is found to be inconsistent with an origin in large bodies; instead, they consider that diamonds were formed as a metastable phase by the decomposition of cohenite under localized stresses, or else upon impact with the Earth.

After the onset of melting the equilibrium configuration of the asteroid will comprise an inner core of metal, an outer core of molten silicates, a sintered mantle, and an unconsolidated surface layer. This stratification could account for the composition and texture of the known classes of meteorites: the materials of the highly differentiated irons, pallasites, and achondrites would come from the core; the compact, well-sintered mesosiderites and crystalline chondrites from the deeper regions of the sintered mantle; the more friable types of chondrites from the intermediate and upper layers; and the carbonaceous chondrites from the cold surface layer.

Further temperature rise in the asteroid would result in quasi-volcanic eruptions due to evolution of gases and vapors (e.g., elemental sulfur, carbon monoxide, silicon monosulfide) from the interior. This quasi-volcanic activity would cause extensive recycling of material and can explain many detailed features of the meteorites. New evidence is presented to show that the capillary veins in stone meteorites were produced by momentary action of hot sulfur-containing gases, in accord with the proposed model. Another consequence of the model is the operation of a cyclic process that would deplete the chondritic mantle in some chalcophile elements, such as In, Tl, Pb, and Bi, and might account for the discrepancies between the observed and expected abundances of these elements in chondrites.

We have now considered in brief outline the three principal theories of meteorite origin. They are not mutually exclusive, and indeed have many points in common, especially the theories of Ringwood and of Fish, Goles, and Anders, which differ essentially in the postulated size of the parent body or bodies. Variants of these theories have also been formulated. For example, Mason (1960a, b) has argued against the origin of chondritic meteorites as fragments of a large body, and has suggested their parent bodies existed as independent objects. He points out that their friable and porous nature, the intimate admixture of nickel-iron and silicate, and the chondritic structure suggest recrystallization in the solid state from material similar to that of Type I carbonaceous chondrites. He explains the other types of meteorites—achondrites, stony-irons, and irons—as fragments of a differentiated planetoid or planetoids formed by the aggregation and melting of chondritic material. His views have been severely criticized by Urey (1961), particularly the view that the initial material from which meteorites have evolved was similar in composition to carbonaceous chondrites.

It is apparent that current ideas on the origin of meteorites are in a state of flux. A great deal of research work which will throw new light on the history of these complex and enigmatic bodies is at present in progress in many parts of the world. Our concepts of the origin of meteorites will probably undergo considerable changes in the next few years. Eventually it should be possible to reconstruct the detailed history of their origin and evolution.

13

Tektites

Introduction

Tektites consist of a silica-rich (70–80% SiO_2) glass superficially resembling obsidian, yet distinct from any terrestrial obsidian. They have an unusual chemical composition, which consists in the conjunction of high silica and high alumina, potash, and lime with low magnesia, iron oxides, and soda; this composition resembles a few granites and rhyolites, and some quartz-rich sedimentary rocks. Tektites are found, generally as small (up to 200–300 grams) rounded to elongated forms in areas that preclude a volcanic origin. Unlike the other meteorite types, tektites have not been seen to fall, and their identification as meteorites is still disputed.

The term tektite was introduced by F. E. Suess (1900, p. 194) in the following words: "*Als gemeinschaftlichen Namen für die ganze Gruppe habe ich nach der Eigenschaft der Korper, welche in Gegensatze zu den übrigen Meteoriten ganzlich durchgeschmolzene Massen sind, die Bezeichnung Tektite gewählt.*" By "*die ganze Gruppe*" Suess means moldavites (from Czechoslovakia), billitonites (from the island of Billiton in the Java Sea), and australites (from Australia), which were the specimens he investigated.

Unfortunately the above quotation is a statement rather than a definition, and includes the genetic implication that tektites are meteorites, an implication unacceptable to many investigators of these enigmatic bodies. There is no satisfactory definition in the literature, and as a result there is considerable confusion as to what objects should or should not be included. The literature on tektites is extensive and widely scattered throughout many journals and books. The most comprehensive account is the monograph of Baker (1959), from which much of the information in this chapter has been extracted.

Geographical Distribution

Tektites are found (Fig. 61) in limited areas in a few regions on the Earth's surface (in contrast to meteorites, which show a random distribution over the whole Earth). The tektites from a specific region are usually given a distinctive name derived from the geography.

The first tektites to be described were found in the western part of Czechoslovakia, in the valley of the Moldau River, hence the name moldavites (not from Moldavia, which is a province of Romania). They have been known since 1787. Recently the name vlatavites, from the Czechoslovakian name for this river, has been applied to them.

Tektites are widely distributed over the southern half of the Australian continent, and on Tasmania and other islands off the south coast; they are known as australites.

There are numerous occurrences throughout the Indomalaysian region, tektites having been found in Borneo, Java (javaites), the islands of Banka and Billiton (billitonites) in the Java Sea, Malaya (malaysianites), Thailand, Indochina (indochinites), southern China, and the Philippine Islands (philippinites or rizalites).

In Africa tektites have been reported and described from the Ivory Coast region.

In North America tektites have been found in Texas (bediasites) and Georgia, and a single one in Massachusetts. There is some doubt as to the natural origin of the Georgia and Massachusetts tektites (Clarke and Carron, 1961).

The above enumeration includes all those types which by chemical composition, physical properties, and mode of occurrence are universally accepted as tektites. Besides these there are a number of occurrences of enigmatic natural glasses which are distinct from the above tektites and are probably of different origin. These include

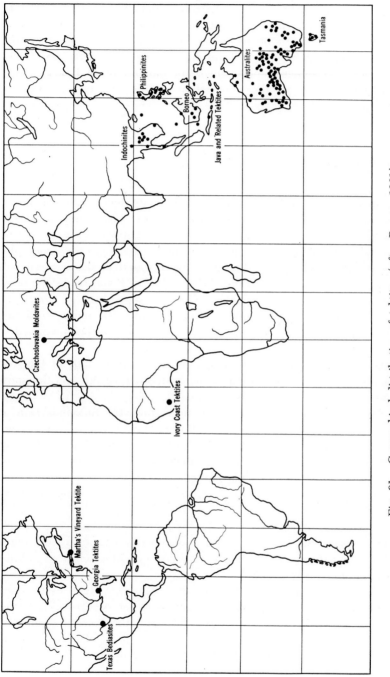

Fig. 61. Geographical distribution of tektites (after Barnes, 1961).

glasses from Columbia and Peru (amerikanites), which are probably terrestrial obsidians; Darwin glass (queenstownites) from Tasmania, which Baker (1959) believes to be fused ash from prehistoric peat bog fires; and Libyan Desert glass, an almost pure (>97% SiO_2) silica glass found as numerous fragments up to 7 kg weight in a limited area of the Libyan Desert.

Thus the recognized true tektites are:

Australites	Ivory Coast tektites
Bediasites	Javaites
Billitonites	Moldavites
Indochinites	Philippinites (or rizalites)

It has been estimated that approximately 650,000 tektite specimens have so far been recovered from the different tektite regions of the Earth, as follows: australites, 40,000; bediasites, 2000; billitonites and malaysianites, 7500; indochinites, 40,000; Ivory Coast tektites, 200; javaites, 7000; moldavites, 55,000; philippinites, 500,000.

Chemical Composition

The mean chemical composition of different groups of tektites, based on averages of a number of analyses for each group, is given in Table 20. This table shows the rather restricted variation in the

TABLE 20. MEAN COMPOSITIONS OF DIFFERENT GROUPS OF TEKTITES, CALCULATED FROM ANALYSES LISTED BY BARNES (1940)

(N = number of analyses averaged)

	N	SiO_2	Al_2O_3	FeO*	MgO	CaO	Na_2O	K_2O	TiO_2	MnO
Moldavites	10	79.60	11.02	2.45	1.30	1.92	0.51	2.90	0.80	0.11
Bediasites	2	75.64	14.59	4.37	1.29	0.05	1.36	1.85	0.81	0.01
Australites	9	73.33	12.75	4.70	1.98	3.01	1.25	2.05	0.67	0.16
Indochinites	24	73.14	12.48	5.02	2.00	2.51	1.45	2.40	0.94	0.13
Javaites	3	71.83	11.89	5.24	2.79	2.77	1.76	2.22	0.77	0.17
Philippinites	4	71.21	12.57	5.18	2.90	3.19	1.52	1.93	0.89	0.11
Ivory Coast tektites	3	71.05	14.60	5.62	3.29	1.67	1.71	1.53	0.73	0.08
Billitonites	7	70.50	12.53	5.84	3.07	3.14	1.75	2.28	0.84	0.16

* All Fe as FeO.

composition of different groups of tektites, despite their wide geographic distribution. Moldavites are notably higher in SiO_2 and lower in Al_2O_3 than other groups of tektites, between which there are no marked chemical differences. Extreme ranges, based on individual analyses listed by Barnes (1940), are: SiO_2, 68.00–82.68; Al_2O_3, 9.56–16.46; Fe_2O_3, 0.06–2.25; FeO, 1.13–6.81; MgO, 1.15–4.05; CaO, 0.04–3.92; Na_2O, 0.37–2.45; K_2O, 0.82–3.60; TiO_2, 0.08–1.03; MnO, 0.01–0.32. An inverse relationship exists between SiO_2 and Al_2O_3, high alumina occurring with low silica, and vice versa. Other noteworthy relationships shown by Table 20 are: $K_2O > Na_2O$ (except for the Ivory Coast tektites), and $CaO > MgO$ (except for the Ivory Coast tektites, the javaites, and the bediasites –the extremely low CaO in the two analyses of bediasites is probably erroneous). These relationships, and the high silica and alumina contents, are at variance with the probable cosmic abundances of these elements, and indicate that if tektites have an extra-terrestrial origin, their material has been subject to chemical differentiation.

Tektites have remarkably low water contents. Published analyses show up to 1% H_2O, but Friedman (1958) has shown that this is entirely or almost entirely adsorbed water; the true water content is usually $<0.05\%$, and averages 0.005%. Friedman points out that the low water content makes it highly probable that tektites were either melted in an environment where water vapor pressure was several orders of magnitude lower than that usually experienced in terrestrial environments, or were heated to a very high temperature, of the order of 2000° C or above.

The evidence of chemical analyses has been frequently called upon in theories of tektite origin. Three schools of thought have existed on this matter: one compares the analyses of tektites with those of igneous rocks, another with those of sedimentary rocks, whereas the third maintains that tektites are so unlike terrestrial rocks in composition as to warrant their classification as extra-terrestrial glasses. Many positive statements have been made regarding the identity or near-identity of tektite composition with sedimentary rocks; for example Urey (1958b) wrote, "Tektites have chemical compositions remarkably similar to those of more acid sedimentary rocks. . . . Such a chemical composition is not produced by any other naturally occurring chemical processes that we know of except perhaps in very rare and special circumstances." However, Mason (1959) showed that analyses of the different types of tektites could in fact be paralleled closely by analyses of igneous rocks, and remarked that the chemical composition of tektites could not be used as an argument for their origin by the fusion of sedimentary rocks. (This has been cited as proposing the theory that tektites are fused igneous rocks, which was not the intention of the paper; it was merely to show that the composition of tektites could be explained by more than one naturally occurring chemical process.) Cherry and Taylor (1961) show that the average composition of all tektites is closely duplicated by a mixture of one part of SiO_2 and three parts of average shale; however, other mixtures of feasible materials could be selected to give similar agreement. It seems doubtful whether considerations of bulk chemical composition can provide unequivocal evidence for the origin of tektites.

Until recently, comparatively little work had been done on the content of minor and trace elements in tektites. Preuss (1935) made spectrographic analyses of tektites and reported the following figures (in weight per cent): Li_2O, 0.003; BeO, 0.0005–0.001; B_2O_3, 0.004; SrO, 0.02; BaO, 0.05; TiO_2, 0.7–1.0; ZrO, 0.02; V_2O_3, 0.01; Cr_2O_3, 0.006–0.06; MnO, 0.12; NiO, 0.002–0.04; CuO, 0.0003; Ga_2O_3, 0.001–0.002; GeO_2, 0.0005; SnO_2, 0.0003; PbO, 0.0001–0.0003. These figures show that concentrations of Ti, V, Cr, Mn, Sr, and Zr are similar for tektites and for crustal rocks; Ni, Cu, Ga, Ge, Sn, and Pb show lower percentages in tektites. Heide (1936) concluded that, since the amounts of the less common elements in tektites are of the same order of abundance as in the lithosphere, some support is given to theories of a terrestrial origin; however, as Baker (1959) points out, this deduction overlooks the possibility of similar materials occurring on an extra-terrestrial body.

Cohen (1959) has recorded a remarkable uniformity of minor and trace elements in moldavites, a Georgia tektite, a bediasite, and an australite. His determinations, by spectrographic analysis, are as follows (in ppm): Ag, <1; Co, 8–10; Cr, 30–40, except the australite, 165; Li, 650 in moldavites and the australite, 65 in the Georgia tektite, 100 in the bediasite; Mn, 650; Ni, 10–30; Rb, 500–1000; Sr, 550; Ti, >1000; V, 20–50; Zr, 550. Other determinations (Taylor, 1960) give much lower values for rubidium and lithium and these figures of Cohen need confirmation.

In a further paper, Cohen (1960) has reported germanium contents in tektites (in ppm): australite, 0.06; bediasite, 0.13; Georgia tektite, 0.23; indochinites, 0.19, 0.09, 0.09; Ivory Coast tektite, 0.42; javaite, 0.61, 0.64; moldavites, 0.15, 0.16, 0.16; philippinites, 0.40, 0.41, 0.40. The germanium content increases with the ferrous iron content. Cohen claimed that the germanium contents are too low for the tektites to be of terrestrial origin. In a later paper (1961), he evidently abandoned this claim, and ascribes the tektites to the fusion of terrestrial material by the impact of asteroids.

Taylor and Sachs (1960) have made a comprehensive study of trace elements in 14 australites, using spectrographic analysis. The averages are as follows (in ppm): Ag, <0.5; As, <100; Au, <10; B, <10; Ba, 655; Be, <30; Bi, <10; Cd, <10; Ce, <100; Co, 16; Cr, 52; Cs, 2.7; Cu, 7.0; Ga, 8.6; Ge, <5; Hg, <100; In, <1; La, <50; Li, 42; Mn, 800; Mo, <10; Nb, <30; Nd, <10; Ni, 30; Pb, <20; Pd, <10; Pt, <50; Rb, 84; Sb, <20; Sc, 12; Sn, <20; Sr, 195; Th, <100; Ti, 4280; Tl, <1; U, <100; V, 75; W, <20; Y, <20; Yb, <10; Zn, <100; Zr, 470. They compare these figures with those for igneous rocks, for shales, and for chondritic meteorites, and point out general similarity between the abundances of trace elements in australites and the average abundance of these elements in crustal rocks.

Adams (1956) has reported on the thorium and uranium contents of tektites. Most tektites have between 1 and 2 ppm uranium and have thorium-uranium ratios of about 7:1.

Schnetzler and Pinson (1962) have analyzed tektites for rubidium and strontium by isotope dilution and X-ray fluorescence methods and have determined the isotopic composition of the strontium, with the following results (in ppm, number of samples in parentheses):

	Rb	Sr	Sr^{87}/Sr^{86}
Philippinites (7)	117	173	0.7181
Indochinites (8)	118	132	0.7198
Javaite (1)	98	153	0.7194
Australites (4)	120	194	0.7174
North American tektites (4)	72	163	0.7166
Moldavites (2)	146	136	0.7246

Physical Properties

With the exception of the moldavites, which are dark green, tektites are normally jet black in reflected light, but thin flakes and sections are transparent or translucent in shades of brown in transmitted light. Moldavites are bottle green or brownish green in transmitted light; they are sometimes facetted and mounted in rings as ornamental stones. Tektite glass is isotropic except for weak strain birefringence along lines of union or in areas of contorted flow. Flow streaks, frequently highly contorted, are common in many tektites. Bubbles of varying size have been observed in some, and particles identified as lechatelierite (silica glass) have been noted in bediasites, australites, moldavites, indochinites, javaites, Ivory Coast tektites, and philippinites (Barnes, 1960).

Tektites are brittle and break with a conchoidal fracture having rippled surfaces, but sometimes they crack along flow directions. They generally have a dull luster on natural surfaces, due to abrasion and weathering, but freshly fractured surfaces reveal a brilliant vitreous luster.

Refractive index and density measurements for different groups of tektites are given in Table 21. This shows a range of refractive index from 1.480 to 1.520 and a range of density from 2.30 to 2.52. As the density increases so does the refractive index (Fig. 62). When Tables 20 and 21 are compared it will be seen that the mean density of each group increases as the silica content decreases. Similarly the refractive index increases as the silica content decreases, as is illustrated in Fig. 63. Since the decrease in silica content is paralleled by the increase in iron content, the refractive index is directly related to the iron content.

Baker (1961a) has shown that both density and refractive index may vary from place to place within an individual tektite. He recorded a refractive index range from 1.495 to 1.500 within one australite, indicating a range of SiO_2 content from 78% to 74%.

The specific refractivity, k, which is calculated from the relation-

TABLE 21. REFRACTIVE INDEX AND DENSITY OF TEKTITES

	Refractive Index	Density	Mean Density (Baker, 1959)
Moldavites	1.480–1.496	2.30–2.39	2.337
Bediasites	1.488–1.512	2.33–2.43	2.374
Australites	1.498–1.520	2.31–2.51	2.410
Indochinites	1.506	2.40–2.45	2.427
Javaites	1.509	2.43–2.45	2.442
Philippinites	1.511–1.513	2.43–2.45	2.442
Ivory Coast tektites	1.499–1.518	2.40–2.52	2.451
Billitonites	1.513	2.42–2.50	2.456

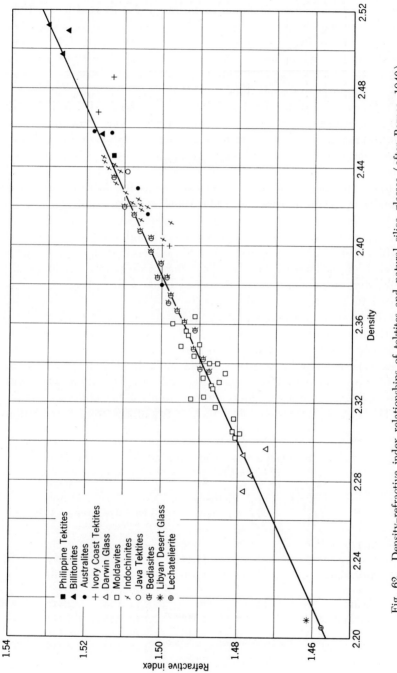

Fig. 62. Density–refractive index relationships of tektites and natural silica glasses (after Barnes, 1940).

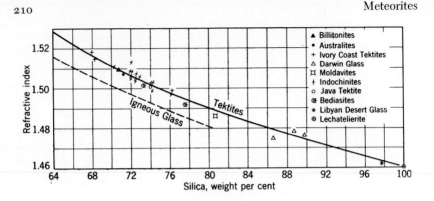

Fig. 63. Refractive index–silica relationships for tektites and silica glass, compared with that for igneous glass (after Barnes, 1940).

ship $k = (n - 1)/d$, where n is refractive index and d is density, is useful for characterizing the different groups of tektites and distinguishing them from obsidians. Figure 64, in which specific refractivity is plotted against density, shows that the different groups of tektites fall in a number of overlapping fields; points representing ob-

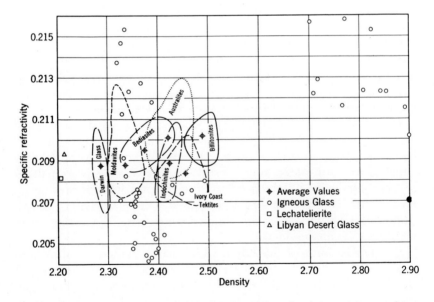

Fig. 64. Specific refractivity–density relationships of tektites, igneous glasses (obsidians), and silica glasses (after Barnes, 1940).

sidians mostly fall outside the fields of the tektites. While specific refractivity may not serve to positively distinguish a tektite from an obsidian, most obsidians can be clearly differentiated from tektite glass in this way.

Tektites are usually comparatively small. The largest recorded is an indochinite weighing 3200 grams. The largest philippinite is an almost perfect sphere 10 cm in diameter weighing 1070 grams. More than 100 philippinites weigh individually between 200 and 700 grams. Most tektites are much smaller, however. The average individual weight for many australites of all shape, excluding badly fragmented forms and pieces, is approximately 1.5 grams (Baker and Forster, 1943). The largest australite known weighs 260 grams; the smallest complete australite weighs only 0.06 gram. The largest Ivory Coast tektite is 79 grams; the largest bediasite 91 grams; the largest moldavite 500 grams; the largest javaite 750 grams.

External Form and Internal Structure

The shapes of tektites are variable (Fig. 65) and many terms have been used to describe them. Spheroidal forms are not uncommon, sometimes with a tail-like protrusion giving pear-shaped or teardrop varieties. Perhaps the commonest shape is lensoid or discoid. The australites are the group with the greatest array of different shapes, and Fenner (1934) has classified them into the following eight major categories: button, lens, core, oval, boat, dumbbell, teardrop, and canoe, which he relates to their history of development.

The surfaces of most tektites have been strongly modified by etching and abrasion, and only the australites, and few of these, still retain their original surface with little modification. Most tektites either have a dull pitted abraded surface or have a sculpture pattern of worm-like grooves, which reflects the complex internal flow structure. This sculpture pattern is evidently a natural etching; Baker (1961a) has produced it on abraded australites by treating them with dilute hydrofluoric acid.

The button form of australite, which has a central lens-like core and an outer circumferential flange, occasionally shows the original surface quite unmodified (Fig. 66). On such tektites anterior and posterior surfaces can be clearly distinguished. The anterior surface usually has concentrically or spirally arranged flow ridges. The pos-

Fig. 65. Photographs of various types of tektites: 1–5, indochinites; 6–17, australites; 18, billitonite; 19, moldavite; 20–28, philippinites; larger diameter of moldavite is 6 cm (courtesy The American Museum of Natural History).

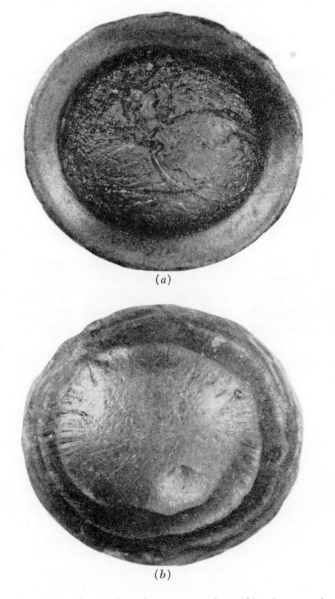

(a)

(b)

Fig. 66. Posterior surface (a) and anterior surface (b) of a complete oval australite from Port Campbell, Victoria; longer diameter is 24 mm (Baker, 1961b).

terior surface shows numerous small bubble pits, circular or elongated
in outline, which are often so abundant as to give a finely honey-
combed appearance. The equatorial region of these australites has an
annular band of glass known as the flange. Flanges are most common on button forms but have also been observed on other australite
forms. The only record of a flange on a non-Australian tektite is an
imperfect example from Java. The occurrence of flanges shows that
these tektites were subjected to two periods of melting, the flange
having been formed later than the main part of the tektite. Two
periods of melting are most readily explained if a glass body were
plunged into the Earth's atmosphere at high velocity. It would melt
on the anterior side, the area of greatest pressure and friction. The
melted glass would be dragged over the anterior surface by the friction of the air and would collect around the equatorial zone forming
the flange. This is very persuasive evidence of an extra-terrestrial
origin for tektites.

The morphology of the australites has been thoroughly investigated
by Baker (1959), who has shown that all the structures, sculpture
patterns, and present shapes of australites can be adequately explained in terms of a few primary forms developed in an extra-terrestrial environment, subsequent modification by aerodynamical phe-
nomena during high-speed flight through the Earth's atmosphere,
and further modification by fragmentation, abrasion, and solution
etching of the shapes so developed. Chapman (1960) has interpreted
the morphology of the australites from theoretical and experimental
(wind tunnel) studies of their ablation patterns. He has shown that
the australites must have entered the upper atmosphere with velocities between 12 and 13 km/sec. This significant information indicates that they are extra-terrestrial in origin and were traveling in
an orbit round the Sun similar to the Earth's orbit.

Internally tektites show a contorted flow structure due to the presence of schlieren with slightly different chemical compositions and
hence differences in refractive index and sometimes in color (Fig. 67).
The flow structure is usually unrelated to external surfaces and is
often sharply truncated by them, suggesting that it originated in the
initial formation of a larger mass from which the individual tektites
were derived. Some flow lines open out on the external surfaces
into furrows, referred to as flow grooves, channels, gutters, or
bubble tracks, which are frequently over-deepened by natural etching.

Tektite glass commonly contains inclusions which may be either

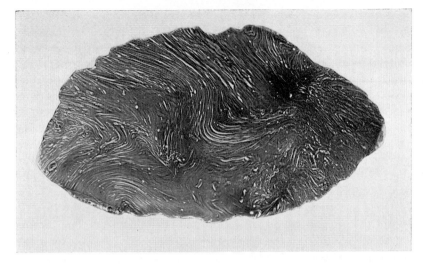

Fig. 67.   Thin section of a bediasite in transmitted light, showing flow structure (courtesy V. E. Barnes).

gas bubbles, or isotropic particles which have been identified as lechatelierite (Barnes, 1940; Baker, 1944).   These lechatelierite particles are minute in size, being normally visible only under the highest power of the petrographical microscope.   In bediasites they have been observed to vary in size from 0.015 mm to 0.48 mm.   This lechatelierite has been interpreted as fused quartz grains.   The presence of these particles in tektite glass indicates limited liquid miscibility (Cassidy and Segnit, 1955).   The original material is presumed to have melted rapidly, and high viscosity has prevented the fused quartz from thoroughly mixing with the rest of the glass.   The presence of these lechatelierite particles is significant in theories of the origin of tektites.   They could be remnants of incompletely resorbed quartz-bearing material from which the tektites were formed. Whether they had an extra-terrestrial or terrestrial origin is a controversial question.   Barnes considered that their presence probably excludes an extra-terrestrial origin for tektites, but there is nothing to disprove that they could have developed in an extra-terrestrial environment.

Chao et al. (1962a) have detected tiny nickel-iron spherules in some philippinites.

Most tektites contain small bubbles and a few have large internal cavities; one Ivory Coast tektite had an internal cavity 1 cm in diameter, and fragments of hollow forms have been recorded from the australites and moldavites indicating internal cavities as much as 5 cm in diameter. These bubbles are, however, no proof of the presence of considerable amounts of gas in tektites. In fact, as Suess (1951) has shown, there is no measureable amount of gas in them, and the bubbles must represent a fairly good vacuum. This is understandable if they were formed under conditions of high temperature and low gas pressure.

Ages of Tektites

The age of tektites involves two quite different concepts: (a) the time at which they arrived at their present geographical location—this we may call their geological age, or age on Earth, since it is measured by the age of the geological formations in which or on which they are found; (b) the time of formation of the tektite glass itself—this we may call their physical age, since it is measured by physical methods such as K-Ar, U-Pb, etc.

The geological ages are different for different groups. The Ivory Coast tektites may be derived from formations possibly late Mesozoic in age. Bediasites are usually found resting on rocks of the Jackson group of formations of late Eocene age, from which they are believed to be weathering. The Georgia tektites are found on the surface of the Hawthorn formation of Middle or Lower Miocene age. The moldavites occur in beds of soft sandstone of Middle Miocene age. Indochinites are said to occur in Middle Pliocene formations, javaites in Middle Pleistocene formations (associated with fossil man), philippinites in early Late Pleistocene formations. The australites are probably the most recent tektites geologically, occurring on the surface or embedded in surface soils; Baker believes that they fell about 5000 years ago.

Most physical dating of tektites has been done by the potassium-argon method, for which they are well suited, since they contain about 2% K. The first work (Suess, 1951) established that the time of fusion of tektite glass was comparatively recent, since the material contains very little argon. The results were not very precise but placed upper limits of 10 million years (m.y.) and 32 m.y. on the age of a philippinite and an australite, respectively. Reynolds (1960b), using more refined techniques, has reported the following K-Ar ages: philippinite, 0.3 m.y.; australites, 0.44, 0.80 m.y.; tektite, Sumatra, 0.50 m.y.; indochinite, 0.79 m.y.; moldavite, 13.5 m.y.; bediasite, 29.0 m.y.; Georgia tektite, 32.0 m.y. Similar results have been obtained by Gentner and Zähringer (1960). It can be seen that these ages are reasonably consistent with the geological ages—somewhat younger indeed for the geologically older groups, which may well be due to some degree of argon leakage. These ages are quite different from the K-Ar ages of meteorites, which are of the order of 4000 m.y.

Other dating methods are less precise than the K-Ar method, and have failed to give consistent results. Pinson et al. (1958) applied the Rb-Sr method, but were unable to detect any radiogenic strontium in tektites; they concluded that tektites are very young, too young to be dated by this method (the precision of the measurements would permit Rb-Sr ages up to about 75 m.y.). However, Schnetzler and Pinson (1962) report that these results were erroneous; they found that the average Sr^{87}/Sr^{86} ratio in 18 tektites was 0.7190, and that tektites exhibit a direct correlation of Sr^{87}/Sr^{86} and Rb/Sr ratios, suggesting that they differentiated from a common source material 175 million years ago. Tilton (1958) studied the isotopic composition of lead in tektites and found it to be similar to that of modern terrestrial lead. This, however, is inconsistent with the results of Starik, Sobotovich, and Shats (1959), who found the isotopic composition of lead from an indochinite quite different from that of modern terrestrial lead. They obtained the following figures for the absolute age: $Pb^{206}/U^{238} = 4700$ m.y.; $Pb^{207}/U^{235} = 4200$ m.y.; $Pb^{207}/Pb^{206} = 3700$ m.y.

Ehmann and Kohman (1958) have estimated the time of fall of tektites from the presence of cosmic-ray-induced radioactivities in them. On the basis of a half-life of 1 m.y. for Al^{26} they calculated from the specific activity of australites that they fell less than 500,000 years ago, whereas the lack of Al^{26} activity in bediasites and moldavites indicated that they fell more than 4 m.y. ago. However, Anders (1960) has criticized these results and claims there is no evidence for Al^{26} activity in australites.

Origin of Tektites

As mentioned at the beginning of this chapter, the origin of tektites is still a matter of controversy. Before discussing the theories that have been proposed, it may be helpful to enumerate some of the significant facts about these enigmatic bodies:

1. They are comparatively uniform in chemical composition, despite wide geographical distribution and differences in age.
2. The chemical composition shows the following specific characters: high SiO_2 (70–80%); moderate Al_2O_3 (11–15%), in inverse relationship to SiO_2; $K_2O > Na_2O$ (except for some Ivory Coast tektites); very low H_2O content.
3. The chemical composition is quite different from that of any known meteorite.
4. The chemical composition is independent of the formations with which they are associated.
5. The presence of particles identified as lechatelierite. If these are fused quartz grains, then the temperature of fusion must have exceeded 1710° C.
6. Specimens which have not been subjected to abrasion or significant natural etching show evidence of two periods of melting, consistent with their being glass objects which entered the Earth's atmosphere at high speed.
7. The contorted flow structure of tektite glass probably developed in small masses which cooled quickly.
8. The potassium-argon ages are compatible with the geological ages of the formations with which they are associated.
9. Tektites occur in limited areas in a few regions on the Earth's surface.

The theories of origin of tektites can be divided into two groups, depending upon whether a terrestrial or extra-terrestrial source is postulated for the tektite material.

A. Tektites have been formed from terrestrial materials by:
   1. Impact (*a*) of meteorites; (*b*) of comets.
   2. Lightning (*a*) fusing soil; (*b*) fusing dust particles in the atmosphere.
   3. Natural fires: burning straw, forest fires, coal seams, etc.

4. Volcanic activity.

5. Human activity: furnace slags, artificial glasses, etc.

B. Tektites are of extra-terrestrial origin; they came from:

1. The Moon, from (*a*) lunar volcanoes; (*b*) splashes from meteorite impact.

2. Comets.

3. A disrupted planetary body having a glassy surface layer.

4. Meteorites consisting of free Si, Al, Mg, etc.

5. Stony meteorites, by fusion in the Earth's atmosphere.

It is clear from the facts already presented that many of these theories are untenable; others are so speculative that they are exceedingly difficult to prove or disprove.

The theory of formation of tektites by the fusion of terrestrial material by the impact of giant meteorites was expounded by Spencer (1933*b*), and has been favored by several investigators, including Krinov (1958) and Barnes (1961). This theory would explain certain features of tektites, such as their occurrence in limited strewn-fields. However, impactite glasses are markedly different from tektites, being slaggy and porous and having abundant inclusions of partly fused material.

The cometary impact theory has been propounded by Urey (1957*b*). He postulates a comet colliding with the Earth's atmosphere and the resulting shock wave striking the ground, forming a large shallow crater and melting large amounts of surface rock; these melted rocks being thrown into the outer atmosphere, chilled, and partly remelted upon their fall back to the Earth's surface. This theory does not satisfactorily account for the rather uniform and peculiar composition of tektites, since the wide variation in the composition of surface rocks should produce a similar variation in tektite composition. Baker (1960) has discussed Urey's theory in detail and concludes that cometary collisions are incapable of satisfactorily explaining tektite origin and distribution.

The remaining theories of terrestrial origin for tektites all appear to have insuperable objections. Lightning will fuse surface soil, but produces small tubes and rods quite different from tektites; nevertheless, Hawkins (1960) argues for such an origin. There is no evidence that lightning will cause atmospheric dust to aggregate and fuse; as Nininger (1952) has pointed out, thunderstorms accompanied by dust clouds are common in the Great Plains area of the U.S.A., yet no tektites have ever been found there. Neither natural fires nor human activities can reasonably account for the composition and distribution of tektites. Volcanic activity seems to be eliminated by the absence of volcanoes from most areas of tektite occurrence, and by the differences in composition between most volcanic glasses and tektites.

The theories of extra-terrestrial origin are difficult to prove or disprove, because of our lack of knowledge of conditions in outer space. We can perhaps dispose of the theories 4 and 5 most readily. The postulate of meteorites consisting of free Si, Al, Mg, etc., which will oxidize and fuse in the Earth's atmosphere to give tektites is an assumption for which there is no plausible evidence—indeed, from the cosmic abundances of the elements we would not expect such material to exist in outer space. That tektites are ablation products of stony meteorites is controverted by their composition, which is quite unlike the composition of the fusion products of meteorites, and by their distribution, which is far more limited than that of meteorites. If tektites represent the glassy surface layer of a disrupted planetary body, then this body must have had an unusual chemical composition, judging by the peculiarities of tektite composition. However, this theory has been carefully discussed by Cassidy (1958), who suggests the possibility of the separation of a glassy surface layer by a process of liquid immiscibility. Insufficient is known about the composition of comets or the composition of the surface layers of the Moon to decide whether these are feasible sources of tektite material. Varsavsky (1958) has shown that the mechanical processes required to carry the material from the Moon to the Earth and distribute it in the tektite strewn-fields are reasonable. The origin of tektites as secondary bodies from the infall of meteorites on the Moon has been favorably discussed by O'Keefe (1959).

All in all, it appears that the problems of the genesis of tektites cannot be satisfactorily resolved on the evidence at present available. They may well be of extra-terrestrial origin, i.e., meteorites, but absolute proof is still lacking.

Chemical Analyses of Meteorites
and Their Interpretation

CHEMICAL analysis of meteorites presents difficult problems—problems of sampling, problems of the methods to be used, problems of the interpretation of the results. Analyses of iron meteorites may be compared with analyses of artificial alloys, analyses of stone meteorites with those of rocks, but in each case additional difficulties arise from the inhomogeneity of the meteorites and the presence of unusual compounds.

The iron meteorites are the simplest in this respect. As far as sampling is concerned, a suitably sized piece as free of non-metallic inclusions as possible is normally selected. Yet this sampling immediately introduces a bias into the results. Iron meteorites usually contain inclusions of troilite, variable in size and irregularly distributed. Normally these inclusions are avoided in sampling. Hence the analyses of iron meteorites show a low sulfur and therefore a low troilite content. Henderson and Perry (1958) have discussed this problem and compare the sulfur shown by chemical analyses of some iron meteorites with that estimated from the direct measurement of the amount of troilite in cross sections of these meteorites. Their results are given in Table 22.

This table shows clearly that the sulfur content shown by the chemical analysis of an iron meteorite is not an accurate measure of the average amount of combined sulfur in the meteorite. This can best

TABLE 22. COMPARISON OF SULFUR PERCENTAGES DETERMINED CHEMI-
CALLY BY ANALYSES OF COARSE OCTAHEDRITES WITH SULFUR PERCENT-
AGES DETERMINED STATISTICALLY BY MEASURING SECTIONS FROM THE
SAME METEORITES

(The sulfur chemically determined is a weight percentage and is not equivalent to sulfur
reported in the last column, which was obtained after estimating the percentage of troilite
in the total area of a slice)

		Chemical Determination		Statistical Determination	
Meteor	Reference	% Sulfur	% Troilite in Section	% Sulfur in Section
Coolac, Australia	Hodge-Smith, 1937	1.27	4.76	1.73
	Henderson, 1951	none		
Canyon Diablo, Arizona	Moissan, 1904	trace	5.95	2.17
	Barringer, 1905	0.004		
	Merrill and Tassin, 1907	0.005		
	Merrill, 1913	0.01		
	Buddhue, 1950	0.13		
Odessa, Texas	Merrill, 1922	0.03	3.43	1.15
	Beck and LaPaz, 1951	0.02		
Osseo, Canada	Marble, 1938	none	3.42	1.25
Wichita County, Texas			2.72	1.00

be obtained by careful measurement of the amount of troilite shown
by several slices of the meteorite in question.

Henderson, in his description of the Aggie Creek meteorite (1949),
recommends the following procedure for the analysis of an iron meteorite:

A slice was cut from this meteorite and after polishing and etching, an
area, with typical average structure for this iron, was selected for the
chemical analysis. This was treated as follows: The selected sample for
analysis was divided into two portions and a specific gravity determination
was made on each portion. The two pieces were then dissolved in 1–3
HCl and the gas liberated was passed through a series of wash bottles containing lead acetate solution to collect any H_2S that would be given off
from the troilite. After 36 hours of this acid treatment, and many inter-
mittent boilings, the acid soluble portion was decanted and separately
analysed. The weights of the recovered elements are given in Table 1
(A). The insoluble residue from the 1–3 HCl was then dissolved in aqua

regia and analysed separately (B). The results of B indicate that the insoluble residue is schreibersite.

Moss, Hey, and Bothwell (1961) have discussed in detail the problems involved in the sampling and analysis of iron meteorites, and have described simple chemical procedures (colorimetric and gravimetric) for the determination of Co, Cr, Cu, Ga, Ni, P, and S; Fe is normally obtained by difference, but may be determined directly if desired.

For the commonest type of meteorites, the chondrites, the problems of sampling, analysis, and interpretation are far more difficult than for the iron meteorites. The chondrites contain distinct phases of very different chemical and physical properties—nickel-iron, troilite, silicates, and minor constituents such as chromite. The size of an adequate sample must be determined by consideration of the particular meteorite, and will largely depend upon the degree of uniformity of distribution of the nickel-iron. Probably at least 10 grams is necessary to provide an adequate sample of the usual chondrite. Having obtained this sample, either as a sawn piece or as fragments, the problem then arises of preparing it for analysis. Here we are faced with the almost insoluble problem of crushing material which includes malleable metal usually in all sizes from slugs a millimeter or more in diameter downwards.

This brings up the next problem—what procedure to follow in order to analyze such material? The analysis of a silicate rock follows a well-established procedure leading to the determination of SiO_2, TiO_2, Al_2O_3, Fe_2O_3, FeO, MnO, MgO, CaO, Na_2O, and K_2O, with the underlying assumption that all the elements are present as oxidic compounds unless there is mineralogical evidence to the contrary. However, this procedure cannot be applied directly to chondritic meteorites, because the underlying assumption is no longer valid. Iron is present as free metal, as sulfide, and in oxidic compounds. It is comparatively straightforward to determine total iron in a meteorite sample, but it is important to know how this total iron is distributed between the above forms, and this is an extremely difficult problem. The normal procedure is to determine total sulfur and report this as FeS, deducting sufficient iron for this purpose; to determine metallic iron [either by using a solvent such as mercuric ammonium chloride (Fletcher, 1894) or by analyzing a magnetically separated sample (Prior, 1913)]; and then report the remaining iron as FeO.* This procedure involves a number of as-

* Moss, Hey, and Bothwell (1961) recommend heating the meteorite in a stream of dry chlorine, which removes iron and troilite, leaving a residue of the silicates for separate analysis.

sumptions: (a) all S is present as FeS (this is generally true, but in the carbonaceous chondrites S is present largely as free sulfur and other non-sulfide compounds, pentlandite is present in a few chondrites, and the enstatite chondrites usually contain CaS and other sulfides); (b) the amount of metallic iron can be accurately determined by analysis (very difficult, since solvents may attack iron-bearing compounds as well as metal, and fail to dissolve small grains enclosed in silicates; magnetic fractions are never pure metal, but contain inclusions of other iron-bearing compounds, which must be allowed for); (c) the remaining iron is all present as FeO (certainly not true if the meteorite has been weathered, as are all finds). All the errors in this procedure will be cumulative in the figure given for FeO. As a result this figure is frequently erroneous: comparison even of the "superior" analyses selected by Urey and Craig (1953) for FeO by chemical analysis and FeO as inferred from the composition of the ferromagnesian silicates (determined by refractive index measurements) reveals many discrepancies. These discrepancies are particularly serious where the true FeO content is comparatively low, as in the olivine-bronzite chondrites. Possibly direct determination of total oxygen could provide a useful check on the FeO determination, but no procedure for the direct and accurate determination of total oxygen has been suggested for these meteorites. Phosphorus is also a problem; it is usually reported as P_2O_5 in the stones, but schreibersite inclusions have been described in the metal phase of these meteorites, and the actual state of the phosphorus shown by analysis is uncertain.

Different types of chondrites present specific problems of chemical analysis. The highly reduced enstatite chondrites may contain Ca as CaS, Mn as MnS, Cr as $FeCr_2S_4$, and silicon as Si alloyed with nickel-iron [Prior (1916) noted the presence of "SiO_2" in excess in the magnetic fraction of enstatite chondrites, but the presence of free Si was first established by Ringwood (1961b)]. The carbonaceous chondrites, besides containing sulfur in several forms, contain ferric iron in the form of magnetite or trevorite, and organic compounds—as a result the H_2O reported by analyses represents H_2O (absorbed), H_2O (water of crystallization), OH groups, and H (hydrocarbons), and the elucidation of this figure is an almost insoluble problem.

Normally the analysis of a chondritic meteorite is reported in the following form: Fe, Ni, Co (total is free nickel-iron), FeS, SiO_2, TiO_2, Al_2O_3, FeO, MnO, MgO, CaO, Na_2O, K_2O, P_2O_5. Besides the assumptions already mentioned, this form of reporting involves others. Nickel and cobalt are assumed to be in the free state, alloyed with iron; this is a reasonable assumption, in view of the "nobler" character of Ni and Co with respect to Fe. However, in the carbonaceous chondrites, which contain no free metal, the Ni and Co are presumably present as oxidic compounds, and in some olivine-pigeonite chondrites Ni is present in part as pentlandite.

The interpretation of the chemical analysis of an iron meteorite is comparatively simple. The bulk of the meteorite is clearly an alloy of iron and nickel, with a little cobalt. Any sulfur in the analysis is calculated as FeS; phosphorus is calculated as schreibersite; chromium is usually reported as daubreelite, $FeCr_2S_4$, although it may be present as chromite; carbon is interpreted as graphite, unless it is clearly present as cohenite (the identification of graphite should, however, be checked by mineralogical examination).

The interpretation of analyses of stony meteorites is usually given in terms of the norm calculation. The application of this calculation to meteorite analyses has been discussed by Wahl (1951). The norm is in effect a calculated mineral composition based on the following assumptions:

(a) The FeO/MgO ratio is the same in coexisting olivine and pyroxene.

(b) All Al_2O_3 is present as feldspar.

(c) All S is present as FeS.

(d) All Cr_2O_3 is present as $FeCr_2O_4$.

(e) All TiO_2 is present as $FeTiO_3$.

(f) All P is present as apatite.

Wiik (1956) has criticized the norm calculation of meteorite analyses because of these assumptions, none of which are necessarily true and some of which are demonstrably false. For example, the FeO/MgO ratio is usually not the same in coexisting olivine and pyroxene (however, it is normally not very different); some Al_2O_3 is always present in pyroxene; and so on. Nevertheless the norm calculation is a valuable indication of the actual mineral composition of the stony meteorites (except the carbonaceous chondrites), and if there are serious discrepancies between the normative mineral composition and the actual mineral composition the reasons for the discrepancy must be elucidated.

For good analyses of most stony meteorites the norm calculation reflects quite accurately the mineralogical composition of the meteorite. Normative plagioclase is somewhat greater than actual plagioclase, since some Al_2O_3 is combined in the pyroxene; some, if not all, TiO_2 may be present in pyroxene, so ilmenite may be in small amount or absent; and some Cr_2O_3 is present in pyroxene, whereby the actual amount of chromite may be considerably less than normative $FeCr_2O_4$.

Meteorites of the United States

Group symbols:

C = chondrite
Ce = enstatite chondrite
Cb = olivine-bronzite chondrite
Ch = olivine-hypersthene chondrite
Cp = olivine-pigeonite chondrite
Cc = carbonaceous chondrite
Ae = enstatite achondrite
Ah = hypersthene achondrite
Ap = pyroxene-plagioclase achondrite
Ad = diopside-olivine achondrite
M = mesosiderite
P = pallasite
H = hexahedrite
O = octahedrite
D = nickel-rich ataxite

An asterisk indicates an observed fall

Alabama

Name	County	Coordinates	Date of Fall or Find	Weight (kg)	Group
*Athens	Limestone	34°45'; 87°06'	7/11/1933	0.26	Ch
Auburn	Lee	32°38'; 85°30'	1867	3.5	H
Boaz	Marshall	34°15'; 86°12'	1955	6.8	O
Chulafinnee	Cleburne	33°30'; 85°35'	1873	16.2	O
*Danville	Morgan	34°24'; 87°04'	11/27/1868	2	Ch
*Felix	Perry	32°30'; 87°09'	5/15/1900	3	Cp
*Frankfort	Franklin	34°30'; 87°50'	12/5/1868	0.65	Ap
Ider	De Kalb	34°41'; 85°39'	1957	140	O
*Leighton	Colbert	34°35'; 87°30'	1/12/1907	0.88	C
Lime Creek	Monroe	31°33'; 87°31'	1834	0.6	D
Selma	Dallas	32°24'; 87°01'	1906	140	Cb
Summit	Blount	34°15'; 86°25'	1890	1	H
*Sylacauga	Talladega	33°11'; 86°10'	11/30/1954	5.5	Cb
Tombigbee River	Choctaw	32°13'; 88°10'	1859	46	H
Walker Co.	Walker	33°50'; 87°15'	1832	75	H

Alaska

Aggie Creek [a]		64°53'; 163°10'	1942	43	O
Chilkoot Inlet		59°20'; 136°00'	1881	43	O
Cold Bay		55°11'; 162°33'	1921	0.32	P

[a] The so-called Fairbanks meteorite is a piece of Aggie Creek (E. P. Henderson, pers. comm.).

Arizona

Ashfork	Yavapai	34°56'; 112°36'	1901	27.2	O
Bagdad	Yavapai	34°30'; 113°15'	1961	2.2	O
Camp Verde	Yavapai	34°34'; 111°51'	1915	61.5	O
Canyon Diablo	Coconino	35°03'; 111°02'	1891	30,000	O
Clover Springs	Coconino	34°27'; 111°22'	1956	7.7	M
Coon Butte	Coconino	35°03'; 111°03'	1905	2.7	Ch
Cottonwood	Yavapai	34°50'; 112°01'	1955	0.8	Cb
Ehrenberg	Yuma	33°31'; 114°32'	1862	4.5	O
Gun Creek	Gila	34°00'; 111°00'	1909	22.2	O
*Holbrook	Navajo	34°57'; 110°02'	7/19/1912	220	Ch
Houck	Apache	35°16'; 109°16'	1927	66	O
Kofa	Yuma	33½° ; 114°	1893	0.49	O
Navajo	Apache	35°20'; 109°30'	1921	2188	H
Pima County	Pima	32°12'; 111°00'	Before 1947	0.21	H
San Francisco Mts.	Coconino	35°21'; 111°43'	About 1920	1.7	O
Seligman	Coconino	35°17'; 112°52'	1949	2.2	O

Arizona

Name	County	Coordinates	Date of Fall or Find	Weight (kg)	Group
Silver Bell	Pima	32°44'; 111°30'	Before 1947	5.09	O
Tucson	Pima	31°51'; 110°58'	Before 1850	975	D
Wallapai	Mohave	35°48'; 113°42'	1927	430	O
Weaver Mts.	Maricopa	33°58'; 112°35'	1898	38.8	D
Wickenburg (iron)	Maricopa	33°58'; 112°45'	1940	0.25	O
Wickenburg (stone)	Maricopa	33°58'; 112°40'	1940	9.2	Ch
Winona	Coconino	35°12'; 111°24'	Prehistoric	24	M

Arkansas

Name	County	Coordinates	Date of Fall or Find	Weight (kg)	Group
*Cabin Creek	Johnson	35°24'; 93°22'	3/27/1886	47.4	O
*Fayetteville	Washington	36°03'; 94°10'	12/26/1934	2.4	Cb
Hatfield	Polk	34°29'; 94°27'	1941	0.02	O
Joe Wright Mt.	Independence	35°49'; 91°37'	1884	42.5	O
*Miller	Cleburne	35°24'; 92°03'	7/13/1930	16.7	Cb
Newport	Jackson	35°36'; 91°16'	1923	5.6	P
*Norfork	Baxter	36°13'; 92°16'	10/1918	1.05	O
*Paragould	Greene	36°04'; 90°30'	2/17/1930	409	Ch
*Success	Clay	36°29'; 90°40'	4/18/1924	3.5	C
Western Arkansas		35° ; 94°	Before 1890	1.8	H

California

Name	County	Coordinates	Date of Fall or Find	Weight (kg)	Group
Canyon City	Trinity	40°55'; 123°05'	1875	8.6	O
Dale Dry Lake	San Bernardino	34°02'; 115°54'	1957	0.3	Ch
Death Valley	Inyo	36°21'; 116°49'	1956	?	Cb
Goose Lake	Modoc	41°59'; 120°33'	1938	1170	O
Imperial	Imperial	32°52'; 115°35'	1908	0.004	Cb
Ivanpah	San Bernardino	35°28'; 115°31'	1880	58.3	O
Muroc	Kern	34°55'; 117°50'	1936	0.02	C
Muroc Dry Lake	Kern	34°55'; 117°50'	1936	0.22	C
Neenach	Los Angeles	34°48'; 118°30'	1948	13.8	Ch
Oroville	Butte	39°27'; 121°30'	1893	24	O
Owens Valley	Inyo	37°28'; 118°04'	1913	193	O
Pinto Mts.	Riverside	33°42'; 116°06'	1954	17.8	C
Rosamond Dry Lake	Kern	34°50'; 118°04'	1940	0.85	C
San Emigdio	Kern	35°15'; 118°15'	1887	36	Cb
Shingle Springs	El Dorado	38°38'; 120°59'	1869–70	38.5	D
Surprise Springs	San Bernardino	34°33'; 115°48'	1899	1.52	O
Twentynine Palms	San Bernardino	36°04'; 115°57'	1955	19.6	Ch
Valley Wells	San Bernardino	35°28'; 115°40'	1929	0.13	Ch

Colorado

Name	County	Coordinates	Date of Fall or Find	Weight (kg)	Group
Adams Co.	Adams	39°58′; 103°46′	1928	5.7	Cb
Akron	Washington	40°09′; 103°10′	1940	4	Cb
Akron No. 2	Washington	40°09′; 103°10′	1954	0.64	Cb
Alamosa	Alamosa	37°28′; 105°52′	1937	1.8	Ch
Arapahoe	Cheyenne	38°51′; 102°10′	1940	19	Ch
Arriba	Lincoln	39°18′; 103°15′	1936	31	Ch
Bear Creek	Jefferson	39°48′; 105°05′	1866	230	O
Bethune	Kit Carson	39°18′; 102°25′	1941	0.07	C
Bishop Canyon	San Miguel	38°05′; 109°00′	1912	9	O
Briggsdale	Weld	40°40′; 104°19′	1949	2.2	O
Cope	Washington	39°40′; 102°50′	1934	12	Cb
Cortez	Montezuma	37°21′; 108°41′	1940	0.7	Cb
De Nova	Washington	39°51′; 102°57′	1940	12.7	Ch
Doyleville	Gunnison	38°25′; 106°35′	1887	0.11	Cb
Fleming	Logan	40°41′; 102°49′	1940	1.7	Cb
Franceville	El Paso	38°49′; 104°37′	1890	18.3	O
Guffey	Fremont	38°46′; 105°31′	1907	310	D
Holly	Prowers	38°04′; 102°06′	1937	0.3	Cb
Holyoke	Phillips	40°34′; 102°18′	About 1933	5.5	Cb
Horse Creek	Baca	37°35′; 102°46′	1937	0.57	H?
Hugo	Lincoln	39°08′; 103°29′	1936	0.08	Cb
*Johnstown	Weld	40°21′; 104°54′	7/6/1924	40	Ah
Karval	Lincoln	38°43′; 103°31′	1936	1.1	Cb
Kelly	Logan	40°28′; 103°02′	1937	44.3	Ch
Lincoln Co.	Lincoln	39°22′; 103°10′	1937	0.5	Ch
Lost Lake	Alamosa	37°39′; 105°44′	About 1931	0.01	C
Mesa Verde Park	Montezuma	37°10′; 108°30′	1922	3.5	O
Mount Ouray	Chaffee	38°25′; 106°13′	1898	0.91	O
Newsom	Alamosa	37°36′; 105°50′	1939	0.89	Ch
Ovid	Sedgwick	40°58′; 102°24′	1939	6.2	Cb
Peetz	Logan	40°57′; 103°05′	1937	11.5	Ch
Phillips Co.	Phillips	40°27′; 102°23′	1935	1.5	P
Rifle	Garfield	39°03′; 107°45′	1948	102	O
Rush Creek	Kiowa	38°37′; 102°43′	1938	9.3	Ch
Russel Gulch	Gilpin	39°45′; 105°40′	1863	13	O
Seibert	Kit Carson	39°18′; 102°50′	1941	3.6	Cb
Shaw	Lincoln	39°32′; 103°20′	1937	3.7	Ch
Springfield	Baca	37°23′; 102°38′	1937	0.28	Ch
Sterling	Logan	40°36′; 103°11′	About 1900	0.68	P
Stonington	Baca	37°17′; 102°12′	Before 1942	2.7	Cb
Ute Pass	Summit	39°48′; 106°10′	1894	0.12	O
Washington Co.	Washington	39°42′; 103°10′	1927	5.75	D
Weldona	Morgan	40°21′; 103°57′	1934	27.7	Cb
Wiley	Prowers	38°09′; 102°40′	1938	3.5	D
Wray	Yuma	40°03′; 102°12′	1936	0.28	Cb

Connecticut

Name	County	Coordinates	Date of Fall or Find	Weight (kg)	Group
*Weston	Fairfield	41°15′; 73°23′	12/14/1807	150	Cb

Florida

Name	County	Coordinates	Date of Fall or Find	Weight (kg)	Group
Bonita Springs	Lee	26°16′; 81°45′	1938	41.2	Cb
Eustis	Lake	28°50′; 81°41′	1918	0.5	Cb
Okechobee	Palm Beach	26°41′; 80°48′	Before 1916	1.1	Ch

Georgia

Name	County	Coordinates	Date of Fall or Find	Weight (kg)	Group
Aragon	Polk	34°01′; 85°03′	1898	0.005	H
Canton	Cherokee	34°12′; 84°30′	1894	7	O
Cedartown	Polk	34°06′; 85°16′	Before 1898	11	H
Dalton	Whitfield	34°57′; 84°52′	1877	59	O
*Forsyth	Monroe	33°00′; 83°55′	5/8/1829	16	Ch
Holland's Store	Chattooga	34°21′; 85°23′	1887	12	H
Locust Grove	Henry	33°20′; 84°08′	1857	11	H
Losttown	Cherokee	34°10′; 84°30′	1868	3	O
*Lumpkin	Stewart	32°03′; 84°59′	10/6/1869	0.357	Ch
Paulding Co.	Paulding	34°00′; 84°50′	1901	0.725	O
Pickens Co.	Pickens	34°30′; 84°30′	1908	0.400	C
*Pitts	Wilcox	31°55′; 83°36′	4/20/1921	3.7	O
Pulaski	Pulaski	32°15′; 83°30′	1955	0.116	O
Putnam County	Putnam	33°20′; 83°20′	1839	32.5	O
Sardis	Jenkins	32°57′; 81°52′	1940	800	O
Smithonia	Oglethorpe	34°00′; 83°11′	1940	70	H
Social Circle	Walton	33°40′; 83°44′	Before 1926	99	O
*Thomson	McDuffie	33°25′; 82°29′	10/15/1888	0.234	Ch
Twin City	Emanuel	32°25′; 82°01′	1955	5	D
Union County	Union	34°52′; 83°55′	1854	7	O

Hawaii

Name	County	Coordinates	Date of Fall or Find	Weight (kg)	Group
*Honolulu		21°18′; 157°52′	9/27/1825	3	Ch

Idaho

Name	County	Coordinates	Date of Fall or Find	Weight (kg)	Group
Hayden Creek	Lemhi	44°56′; 113°40′	1895	0.27	O
Jerome	Jerome	42°38′; 114°50′	1954	6.8	Ch
Oakley	Cassia	42°22′; 113°46′	1926	112.7	O
Parma Canyon	Ada	43°48′; 116°55′	1940	2.15	O?

Illinois

Name	County	Coordinates	Date of Fall or Find	Weight (kg)	Group
*Benld	Macoupin	39°05′; 89°49′	9/29/1938	1.77	Cb
Havana	Mason	40°20′; 90°03′	Prehistoric	—	O
South Dixon	Lee	41°50′; 89°29′	1947	3.5	C
*Tilden	Randolph	38°12′; 89°41′	7/13/1927	75	Ch
Woodbine	Jo Daviess	42°21′; 90°10′	1953	48.2	O

Indiana

Name	County	Coordinates	Date of Fall or Find	Weight (kg)	Group
*Hamlet	Starke	41°20′; 86°35′	10/13/1959	2.05	Ch
*Harrison County	Harrison	38°03′; 85°59′	3/4/1859	0.7	Ch
*Helt Township	Vermillion	39°46′; 87°30′	About 1883–4	0.22	O
Kokomo	Howard	40°30′; 86°05′	1862	2	D
Lafayette	Tippecanoe	40°25′; 86°53′	Before 1931	0.99	Ad
La Porte	La Porte	41°36′; 86°43′	1900	14.5	O
Plymouth	Marshall	41°21′; 86°17′	1893	6	O
*Rochester	Fulton	41°05′; 86°15′	12/21/1876	0.34	Cb
Rush County	Rush	39°55′; 85°26′	1948	4.3	Cb
Rushville	Franklin	39°22′; 85°03′	1866	0.05	Ch
South Bend	St. Joseph	41°39′; 86°13′	1893	2.37	P

Iowa

Name	County	Coordinates	Date of Fall or Find	Weight (kg)	Group
*Estherville	Emmet	43°25′; 94°50′	5/10/1879	337	M
*Forest City	Winnebago	43°15′; 93°45′	5/2/1890	122	Cb
*Homestead	Iowa	41°45′; 91°53′	2/12/1875	220	Ch
Mapleton	Monona	42°11′; 95°43′	1939	49	O
*Marion	Linn	42°02′; 91°35′	2/25/1847	28.3	Ch

Kansas

Name	County	Coordinates	Date of Fall or Find	Weight (kg)	Group
Achilles	Rawlins	39°46′; 100°48′	1924	16	Cb
Admire	Lyon	38°30′; 96°25′	1881	95	P
Anthony	Harper	37°05′; 98°03′	1919	20	Cb
Argonia	Sumner	37°16′; 97°46′	Before 1940	34	P
*Beardsley	Rawlins	39°49′; 101°14′	10/15/1929	12.5	Cb
Belle Plaine	Sumner	37°19′; 97°15′	1955	24	Ch
Brenham	Kiowa	37°38′; 99°05′	1882	1000	P
Brewster	Thomas	39°15′; 101°20′	1940	17	Ch
Cedar	Smith	39°42′; 98°59′	1937	4.9	Cb
Colby	Thomas	39°25′; 101°03′	1940	2.4	Cb
Coldwater (iron)	Comanche	37°16′; 99°20′	1923	18.4	O

Kansas (*Continued*)

Name	County	Coordinates	Date of Fall or Find	Weight (kg)	Group
Coldwater (stone)	Comanche	37°16'; 99°20'	1924	11	Cb
Coolidge	Hamilton	37°50'; 101°59'	1937	4.5	Cb
Covert	Osborne	39°12'; 98°47'	Before 1896	37	Cb
Cullison	Pratt	37°37'; 98°55'	1911	10	Cb
Densmore	Norton	39°39'; 99°41'	1879	37.2	Ch
Dispatch	Smith	39°30'; 98°32'	1956	0.22	Cb
Dwight	Geary	38°51'; 96°35'	1940	4.1	Ch
Elkhart	Morton	37°01'; 101°53'	1936	0.57	Cb
Elm Creek	Lyon	38°30'; 96°12'	1906	7	Cb
*Farmington	Washington	39°58'; 97°15'	6/25/1890	90	Ch
Garnett	Anderson	38°16'; 95°15'	1938	4.8	Cb
Goodland	Sherman	39°21'; 101°40'	1923	3.6	Ch
Grant Co.	Grant	37°28'; 101°26'	1936	2.3	Ch
Gretna	Phillips	39°56'; 99°13'	1912	59	Ch
Haven	Reno	37°58'; 97°45'	1950	2.95	Cb
Haviland	Kiowa	37°37'; 99°06'	1937	1	Cb
Hesston	Harvey	38°12'; 97°30'	1951	12.9	Ch
Hill City	Graham	39°22'; 99°51'	1947	11.7	O
Horace	Greeley	38°28'; 101°48'	1940	9.2	C
Hugoton	Stevens	37°12'; 101°21'	1927	355	Cb
Ingalls	Gray	37°50'; 100°27'	1937	0.23	Cb
Jerome	Gove	38°46'; 100°14'	1894	30	Cb
Johnson City	Stanton	37°33'; 101°41'	1937	10.4	Ch
Ladder Creek	Greeley	38°37'; 101°38'	1937	35	Ch
Lawrence	Douglas	38°58'; 95°10'	1928	0.5	Ch
Long Island	Phillips	39°56'; 99°36'	1891	600	Ch
Marion	Marion	38°15'; 97°10'	1955	2.89	Ch
Mayday	Riley	39°28'; 96°55'	1955	6.9	Cb
Miller	Lyon	38°38'; 96°01'	1950	0.97	Cb
*Modoc (1905)	Scott	38°30'; 101°06'	9/2/1905	32.8	Ch
Modoc (1948)	Scott	38°30'; 101°06'	1948	1.8	Cb
Morland	Graham	39°20'; 100°04'	About 1890	280	Cb
Nashville [a]	Kingman	37°27'; 98°25'	Before 1939	23	Cb
Ness Co. (1894)	Ness	38°30'; 99°36'	1894	17	Ch
Ness Co. (1938)	Ness	38°29'; 99°55'	1938	0.65	Cb
New Almelo	Norton	39°40'; 100°08'	About 1917	4.1	Ch
Norcateur	Decatur	39°49'; 100°12'	1940	3.2	Ch
*Norton Co.	Norton	39°41'; 99°52'	2/18/1948	1079	Ae
Oakley	Logan	38°57'; 101°01'	1895	27	Cb
Oberlin	Decatur	39°48'; 100°31'	About 1911	2.8	Ch
Otis	Rush	38°32'; 99°03'	1940	2.6	Ch
*Ottawa	Franklin	38°36'; 95°13'	4/9/1896	0.84	Ch
Penokee	Graham	39°21'; 99°55'	Before 1947	3.6	Cb

[a] The Barber Co. meteorite is a synonym for Nashville (E. P. Henderson, pers. comm.).

Kansas (*Continued*)

Name	County	Coordinates	Date of Fall or Find	Weight (kg)	Group
Pierceville (iron)	Finney	37°52′; 100°40′	1917	100	O?
Pierceville (stone)	Finney	37°52′; 100°40′	1939	2.1	Ch
Pleasanton	Linn	38°11′; 94°43′	1935	2.3	Cb
Prairie Dog Creek	Decatur	39°38′; 100°30′	1893	2.9	Cb
Ransom	Ness	38°37′; 99°56′	1938	15	Cb
Reager	Norton	39°47′; 100°00′	1948	0.23	C
Rolla b	Morton	37°07′; 101°36′	1936	1	Cb
St. Peter	Graham	39°24′; 100°02′	—	—	Ch
Saline	Sheridan	39°22′; 100°29′	1901	30	Cb
Scott City	Scott	38°28′; 100°56′	1905	2.1	Cb
Seneca	Nemaha	39°50′; 96°04′	1936	1.9	Cb
Smith Center	Smith	39°50′; 99°01′	1937	1.6	Ch
Sublette	Haskell	37°30′; 100°50′	1952	1.3	C
Tonganoxie	Leavenworth	39°06′; 97°10′	1886	11.5	O
Ulysses	Grant	37°36′; 101°15′	About 1927	3.9	Cb
Waconda	Mitchell	39°28′; 98°30′	1874	45	Ch
Waldo	Russell	39°06′; 98°50′	1937	1.3	Ch
Wathena	Doniphan	39°49′; 94°55′	1939	0.57	H
Wilburton	Morton	37°05′; 101°46′	1940	0.21	Ch
Willowdale	Kingman	37°32′; 98°22′	1951	3	C
Wilmot	Cowley	37°23′; 96°52′	1944	2	Cb

b H. H. Nininger has recognized five different Rolla meteorites, but they are all olivine-bronzite chondrites of similar composition, and are listed here as a single find.

Kentucky

Name	County	Coordinates	Date of Fall or Find	Weight (kg)	Group
*Bath Furnace	Bath	38°05′; 83°45′	11/15/1902	93.2	Ch
Campbellsville	Taylor	37°22′; 85°22′	1929	15.4	O
Casey Co.	Casey	37°15′; 85°	1877	0.73	O
Clark Co.	Clark	38°00′; 84°10′	Before 1937	11.8	O
*Cumberland Falls	Whitley	36°46′; 84°15′	4/9/1919	24.1	Ae
*Cynthiana	Harrison	38°23′; 84°17′	1/23/1877	6	Ch
Eagle Station	Carroll	38°37′; 84°58′	1880	36.5	P
Edmonton	Metcalfe	37°02′; 85°38′	1942	10.2	O
Frankfort	Franklin	38°08′; 84°50′	1866	11	O
Franklin	Simpson	36°43′; 86°34′	1921	9.06	C
Glasgow	Barren	37°01′; 85°55′	1922	20.3	O
Kenton County	Kenton	38°49′; 84°36′	1889	163	O
La Grange	Oldham	38°25′; 85°30′	1860	51	O
Marshall County	Marshall	36°50′; 88°20′	1860	6.8	O
Mount Vernon	Christian	36°56′; 87°24′	1868	159	P
*Murray	Calloway	36°36′; 88°06′	9/20/1950	12.6	Cc

Kentucky (*Continued*)

Name	County	Coordinates	Date of Fall or Find	Weight (kg)	Group
Nelson County	Nelson	37°50'; 85°25'	1856	73	O
Providence	Trimble	38°38'; 85°20'	1903	6.8	O
Salt River	Bullitt	37°58'; 85°38'	About 1850	4	O
Scottsville	Allen	36°43'; 86°06'	1867	10	H
Smithland	Livingston	37°10'; 88°25'	1839–40	5	D
Williamstown	Grant	38°38'; 84°32'	1892	31	O

Louisiana

Name	County	Coordinates	Date of Fall or Find	Weight (kg)	Group
Atlanta	Winn	31°48'; 92°45'	1938	5.5	Ce

Maine

Name	County	Coordinates	Date of Fall or Find	Weight (kg)	Group
*Andover	Oxford	44°36'; 70°42'	8/5/1898	3.17	Ch
*Castine	Hancock	44°24'; 68°46'	5/20/1848	0.09	Ch
*Nobleborough	Lincoln	44°03'; 69°28'	8/7/1823	2	Ap
*Searsmont	Waldo	44°20'; 69°10'	5/21/1871	5	Cb

Maryland

Name	County	Coordinates	Date of Fall or Find	Weight (kg)	Group
Emmitsburg	Frederick	39°42'; 77°19'	1854	0.5	O
Lonaconing	Alleghany	39°35'; 78°38'	1882	1.26	O
*Nanjemoy	Charles	38°25'; 77°10'	2/10/1825	7.4	Ch
*St. Mary's Co.	St. Mary's	38°10'; 76°23'	6/20/1919	0.02	C

Michigan

Name	County	Coordinates	Date of Fall or Find	Weight (kg)	Group
*Allegan	Allegan	42°32'; 85°53'	7/10/1899	30.5	Cb
Grand Rapids	Kent	42°58'; 85°41'	1883	51.5	O
Reed City	Osceola	43°52'; 85°32'	1895	19.8	O
*Rose City	Ogemaw	44°26'; 83°57'	10/17/1921	10	Cb
Seneca Township	Lenawee	41°47'; 84°11'	1923	11.5	O

Minnesota

Name	County	Coordinates	Date of Fall or Find	Weight (kg)	Group
Arlington	Sibley	44°36'; 94°06'	1894	9	O
*Fisher	Polk	47°49'; 96°51'	4/9/1894	10	Ch
Hardwick	Rock	43°48'; 96°10'	1937	7.8	Ch

Mississippi

Name	County	Coordinates	Date of Fall or Find	Weight (kg)	Group
*Baldwyn	Lee	34°30'; 88°40'	2/2/1922	0.35	Ch
Oktibbeha Co.	Oktibbeha	33°18'; 88°47'	1854	0.15	D
*Palahatchie	Rankin	32°19'; 89°43'	10/17/1910	—	C

Missouri

Name	County	Coordinates	Date of Fall or Find	Weight (kg)	Group
*Archie	Cass	38°29'; 94°22'	8/10/1932	5	Cb
*Baxter	Stone	36°38'; 93°30'	1/18/1916	0.61	Ch
Billings	Christian	37°10'; 93°30'	1903	24.5	O
Butler	Bates	38°15'; 94°18'	1874	36	O
*Cape Girardeau	Cape Girardeau	37°14'; 89°31'	8/14/1846	2	Cb
Central Missouri		37° ; 93°	1855	25	O
Harrisonville	Cass	38°39'; 94°20'	1933	30	Ch
Kansas City	Jackson	39°06'; 94°38'	1903	36	Cb
Lanton	Howell	36°32'; 91°48'	1932	13.8	O
*Little Piney	Pulaski	37°55'; 92°05'	2/13/1839	22.7	Ch
Mincy	Taney	36°35'; 93°12'	1857	90	M
Perryville	Perry	37°44'; 89°51'	1906	17.5	D
St. Francois Co.	St. Francois	37°49'; 89°55'	1863	2.4	O
St. Genevieve Co.	St. Genevieve	37°47'; 90°22'	1888	244	O
*Warrenton	Warren	38°50'; 91°10'	1/3/1877	45	Cp

Montana

Name	County	Coordinates	Date of Fall or Find	Weight (kg)	Group
Illinois Gulch	Deer Lodge	46° ; 113°	1899	2.5	D
Livingston	Park	45°40'; 110°24'	1936	1.6	O
Lombard	Broadwater	46°06'; 111°24'	1953	7	H

Nebraska

Name	County	Coordinates	Date of Fall or Find	Weight (kg)	Group
Ainsworth	Brown	42°33'; 99°48'	1907	10.7	O
Amherst	Buffalo	40°42'; 99°10'	1947	8.5	Cb
Arcadia	Valley	41°25'; 99°06'	1937	19.4	Ch
Boelus	Howard	41°06'; 98°36'	1941	0.73	Ch
Broken Bow	Custer	41°26'; 99°42'	1937	6.8	Cb
Bushnell	Kimball	41°14'; 103°54'	1939	1.2	Cb
Cotesfield	Howard	41°22'; 98°38'	1928	1.16	Ch
Culbertson	Hitchcock	40°14'; 100°50'	1913	6.3	Cb
Dix	Kimball	41°14'; 103°29'	1927	44	Ch
Farnum	Lincoln	40°45'; 100°14'	1937	4.2	Ch
Hayes Center	Hayes	40°31'; 101°02'	1941	4.5	Ch
Hildreth	Franklin	40°20'; 99°02'	1894	3.1	Ch

Nebraska (*Continued*)

Name	County	Coordinates	Date of Fall or Find	Weight (kg)	Group
Indianola	Red Willow	40°14'; 100°25'	1939	4	Ch
Kearney	Buffalo	40°52'; 98°48'	1934	10	Cb
Lancaster Co.	Lancaster	40°40'; 96°45'	1903	13	O?
Linwood	Butler	41°26'; 96°58'	1940	46	O
Loomis	Phelps	40°28'; 99°30'	1933	3	Ch
*Mariaville	Rock	42°43'; 99°23'	10/16/1898	0.34	O?
Marsland	Dawes	42°27'; 103°18'	1933	4.6	Cb
Morrill	Sioux	42°11'; 103°56'	1920	1.4	O
Ogallala	Keith	41°10'; 101°40'	1918	3.3	O
Ponca Creek	Holt	42°52'; 98°30'	1863	45	O
Potter	Cheyenne	41°14'; 103°18'	1941	261	Ch
Red Willow Co.	Red Willow	40°22'; 100°30'	About 1899	2.77	O
St. Ann	Frontier	40°27'; 100°45'	1938	0.37	Cb
Sidney	Cheyenne	41°03'; 102°54'	1941	6	Ch
*Sioux Co.	Sioux	42°35'; 103°40'	8/8/1933	4.1	Ap
Tryon	McPherson	41°33'; 100°58'	1934	15	Ch
Whitman	Grant	42°02'; 101°30'	1937	0.22	Cb
York (iron)	York	40°45'; 97°30'	1878	0.83	O
York (stone)	York	40°52'; 97°36'	1928	1.4	Ch

Nevada

Name	County	Coordinates	Date of Fall or Find	Weight (kg)	Group
Las Vegas	Clark	36°34'; 114°58'	1930	3	O
Quartz Mt.	Nye	37°12'; 116°42'	1935	4.8	O
Quinn Canyon	Nye	38°05'; 115°32'	1908	1450	O
Tonopah	Nye	38°09'; 117°11'	Before 1947	0.03	O

New Jersey

Name	County	Coordinates	Date of Fall or Find	Weight (kg)	Group
*Deal	Monmouth	40°15'; 74°00'	8/15/1829	0.03	Ch

New Mexico

Name	County	Coordinates	Date of Fall or Find	Weight (kg)	Group
Acme	Chaves	33°38'; 104°16'	1947	75	Cb
Alamogordo	Otero	32°54'; 105°56'	1938	13.6	Cb
Albuquerque	Bernalillo	35°00'; 106°48'	Before 1943	0.16	O
Aurora	Colfax	36°20'; 105°03'	1938	1	Cb
*Aztec	San Juan	36°49'; 107°58'	2/1/1938	2.83	Ch
Beenham	Union	36°10'; 103°54'	1937	44.4	Ch
Breece	McKinley	35°18'; 108°18'	1921	50	O
Chico	Colfax	36°30'; 104°12'	1954	105	C

New Mexico (*Continued*)

Name	County	Coordinates	Date of Fall or Find	Weight (kg)	Group
Clovis	Curry	34°18'; 103°08'	1961	283	Cb
Costilla Peak	Taos	36°55'; 105°30'	1881	35	O
El Capitan	Lincoln	33°40'; 105°17'	1893	27.5	O
Farley	Colfax	36°23'; 104°14'	1936	19.4	Cb
Four Corners	San Juan	36°52'; 108°53'	About 1924	25	O
Gladstone	Union	36°18'; 103°37'	1936	57.3	Cb
Glorieta Mt. [a]	Santa Fe	35°34'; 105°45'	1884	146	O
Grady (1933)	Curry	34°48'; 103°19'	1933	4.2	Ch
Grady (1937)	Curry	34°48'; 103°19'	1937	9.3	Cb
Grant	Valencia	34°33'; 108°19'	About 1929	482	O
Hobbs	Lea	32°34'; 103°17'	1933	2.3	Cb
Kingston	Sierra	32°54'; 107°44'	1891	12.9	O
La Lande	De Baca	34°27'; 104°08'	1933	30	Ch
Luis Lopez	Socorro	34°00'; 106°58'	1896	6.9	O
*Malaga	Eddy	32°13'; 104°00'	11/1933	0.15	C
Melrose	Curry	34°23'; 103°37'	Before 1933	36.4	Ch
New Mexico	Valencia	34½°; 107°	1935	0.13	H
Oscuro Mts.	Socorro	33°50'; 106°35'	1895	3.4	O
*Pasamonte	Union	36°10'; 103°24'	3/24/1933	4	Ap
Picacho	Lincoln	33°12'; 105°00'	1952	22	O
Pinon	Chaves	32°40'; 105°06'	1928	17.8	D
Pojoaque	Santa Fe	35°43'; 105°54'	Before 1931	0.08	P
Puente-Ladron	Socorro	34°24'; 106°51'	1944	0.01	Ch
Roy (1933)	Harding	35°57'; 104°12'	1933	47.2	Ch
Roy (1934)	Harding	35°57'; 104°12'	1934	0.35	Ch
Sacramento Mts.	Eddy	32°55'; 104°40'	1896	237	O
Sandia Mts.	Sandoval	35°06'; 106°29'	1925	45	H
Taiban	De Baca	34°27'; 104°01'	1934	14	Ch
Tatum	Lea	33°14'; 103°17'	1938	1.8	C?
Tequezyuito Creek	Harding	35°58'; 104°	1934	5.4	C?
Ute Creek	Union	36°09'; 103°37'	1936	2	Cb

[a] The so-called Santa Fe meteorite is a piece of Glorieta Mt. (E. P. Henderson, pers. comm.)

New York

*Bethlehem	Albany	42°37'; 73°45'	8/11/1859	0.01	Cb
Burlington	Otsego	42°45'; 75°11'	1819	68	O
Cambria	Niagara	43°13'; 78°50'	1818	16.3	O
Mount Morris	Livingston	42°42'; 77°53'	1897	0.01	Cb
Seneca Falls	Seneca	42°55'; 76°47'	1850	4	O
South Byron	Genesee	43°02'; 78°02'	1915	6	D
Tomhannock Creek	Rensselaer	42°53'; 73°36'	1863	1.5	Cb
*Yorktown	Westchester	41°17'; 73°49'	9/1869	0.2	Ch

North Carolina

Name	County	Coordinates	Date of Fall or Find	Weight (kg)	Group
Alexander Co.	Alexander	35°57'; 81°13'	1875	0.25	O
Asheville	Buncombe	35°35'; 82°32'	1839	0.5	O
*Bald Mt.	Yancey	35°58'; 82°29'	7/9/1929	3.7	Ch
Black Mt.	Buncombe	35°44'; 82°20'	About 1839	0.6	O
Bridgewater	Burke	35°43'; 81°52'	1890	13.2	O
*Castalia	Nash	36°11'; 77°50'	5/14/1874	7.3	Cb
*Caswell Co.	Caswell	36½° ; 79¼°	1/30/1810	1.3	C?
Colfax	Rutherford	35°18'; 81°44'	1880	2.2	O
*Cross Roads	Wilson	35°38'; 78°08'	5/24/1892	0.16	Cb
Deep Springs	Rockingham	36°20'; 79°35'	1846	11.5	D
Duel Hill (1854)	Madison	35°51'; 82°42'	1854	21.7	O
Duel Hill (1873)	Madison	35°51'; 82°42'	1873	11	O
*Farmville	Pitt	35°33'; 77°32'	12/4/1934	56	Cb
*Ferguson	Wilkes	36°06'; 81°25'	7/18/1889	0.2	C
Forsyth Co.	Forsyth	36°05'; 80°15'	1891	23	H
Guilford Co.	Guilford	36°04'; 79°48'	Before 1822	13	O
Hendersonville	Henderson	35°19'; 82°28'	1901	6	Ch
Lick Creek	Davidson	35°40'; 80°15'	1879	1.2	H
Linville	Burke	35°48'; 81°55'	1882	0.44	D
Mayodan	Rockingham	36°23'; 79°58'	1920	15	H
McDowell Co.	McDowell	35°45'; 82°11'	About 1923	0.85	O
*Monroe	Cabarrus	35°15'; 80°30'	10/31/1849	8.8	Cb
*Moore Co.	Moore	35°25'; 79°23'	4/21/1913	1.8	Ap
Murphy	Cherokee	35°06'; 84°02'	1899	7.7	H
Nashville	Nash	35°58'; 77°58'	Before 1934	11.3	O
Persimmon Creek	Cherokee	35°06'; 84°07'	1903?	5	O
*Rich Mountain	Jackson	35°17'; 83°02'	6/30/1903	0.67	Ch
Smith's Mt.	Rockingham	36°30'; 79°45'	About 1863	5	O
Uwharrie	Randolph	35°42'; 79°45'	1930	72.7	O?
Wood's Mt.	McDowell	35°41'; 82°11'	1918	3.02	O

North Dakota

Name	County	Coordinates	Date of Fall or Find	Weight (kg)	Group
Freda	Grant	46°23'; 101°14'	1919	0.27	D
Jamestown	Stutsman	46°37'; 98°39'	1885	4	O
New Leipzig	Grant	46°23'; 101°56'	1936	20	O
Niagara	Grand Forks	47°56'; 97°50'	1879	0.12	O
*Richardton	Stark	46°53'; 102°19'	6/30/1918	100	Cb

Ohio

Name	County	Coordinates	Date of Fall or Find	Weight (kg)	Group
Anderson	Hamilton	39°10'; 84°18'	Prehistoric	0.85	P
Cincinnati	Hamilton	30°07'; 84°30'	1870	0.20	H
Dayton	Montgomery	39°48'; 84°12'	1892 or 1893	26.3	D

Ohio (*Continued*)

Name	County	Coordinates	Date of Fall or Find	Weight (kg)	Group
Enon	Clark	39°52'; 83°57'	About 1883	0.76	M
Hopewell Mounds	Ross	39°23'; 83°02'	Prehistoric	0.13	O
*New Concord	Muskingum	40°02'; 81°46'	5/1/1860	227	Ch
New Westville	Preble	39°48'; 84°49'	1941	4.8	O
*Pricetown	Highland	39°11'; 83°44'	2/13/1893	0.9	Ch
Wooster	Wayne	40°50'; 81°58'	1858	22.5	O

Oklahoma

Name	County	Coordinates	Date of Fall or Find	Weight (kg)	Group
Amber	Grady	35°06'; 97°54'	1934	4.5	C
*Atoka	Atoka	34°19'; 96°09'	9/17/1945	3	Ch
*Blackwell	Kay	36°50'; 97°20'	5/1906	2.4	C?
Cashion	Kingfisher	35°51'; 97°42'	1936	5.9	Cb
Crescent	Logan	35°57'; 97°35'	1936	0.08	Cc
Cushing	Payne	35°58'; 96°46'	1932	0.57	Cb
Keyes	Cimarron	36°43'; 102°30'	1939	142	Ch
Kingfisher	Kingfisher	35°50'; 97°56'	1950	1?	Ch
Knowles	Beaver	36°54'; 100°13'	1903	160	O
Lake Murray	Carter	34°06'; 97°00'	1933	540	H
*Leedey	Dewey	35°53'; 99°20'	11/25/1943	50	Ch
Logan	Beaver	36°35'; 100°12'	1918	1.3	Cb
Marlow	Stephens	34°36'; 97°55'	1936	0.34	C
Soper	Choctaw	34°02'; 95°35'	1938	3.7	H
Walters	Cotton	34°20'; 98°18'	Before 1947	28	Ch
Weatherford	Custer	35°30'; 98°42'	1926	2	M
Woodward Co.	Woodward	36°29'; 99°16'	1933	45	Cb
Zaffra	Le Flore	34°30'; 94°30'	1919	3	O

Oregon

Name	County	Coordinates	Date of Fall or Find	Weight (kg)	Group
Klamath Falls	Klamath	44°10'; 121°51'	1952	13.6	O
Port Orford	Curry	42°45'; 124°30'	1859	10,000?	P
Sams Valley	Jackson	42°32'; 122°52'	1894	6.9	O
Willamette	Clackamas	45°21'; 122°37'	1952	13.6	O

Pennsylvania

Name	County	Coordinates	Date of Fall or Find	Weight (kg)	Group
Bald Eagle	Lycoming	41°10'; 77°03'	1891	3.3	O
*Black Moshannan Park	Center	40°55'; 78°05'	7/10/1941	0.52	Ch
*Bradford Woods	Allegheny	40°30'; 80°05'	1886	0.76	C
*Chicora	Butler	40°56'; 79°44'	6/24/1938	0.30	Ch

Pennsylvania (*Continued*)

Name	County	Coordinates	Date of Fall or Find	Weight (kg)	Group
Mount Joy	Adams	39°47'; 77°13'	1887	384	H
New Baltimore	Somerset	40°00'; 78°51'	1922	18	O
Pittsburg	Allegheny	40°26'; 80°00'	About 1850	132	O
Shrewsbury	York	39°46'; 76°40'	1907	12.2	O

South Carolina

Name	County	Coordinates	Date of Fall or Find	Weight (kg)	Group
*Bishopville	Lee	34°10'; 80°17'	3/25/1843	6	Ae
*Cherokee Springs	Spartenburg	35°02'; 81°53'	7/1/1933	8.4	Ch
Chesterville	Chester	34°43'; 81°13'	Before 1849	16.5	H
Laurens Co.	Laurens	34°30'; 82°02'	1857	2.2	O
Lexington Co.	Lexington	33°58'; 81°07'	1880	4.8	O
Ruff's Mt.	Lexington	34°18'; 81°24'	1844	53	O

South Dakota

Name	County	Coordinates	Date of Fall or Find	Weight (kg)	Group
*Bath	Brown	45°28'; 98°21'	8/29/1892	21.2	Cb
Bennett Co.	Bennett	43°28'; 101°09'	1934	89	H
Cavour	Beadle	44°20'; 98°02'	Before 1943	23.9	Cb
Fort Pierre	Stanley	44°21'; 100°23'	1856	16	O
Harding Co.	Harding	45½° ; 103½°	1941	3.1	Ch
Mission	Todd	43°19'; 100°46'	1949	12	Ch

Tennessee

Name	County	Coordinates	Date of Fall or Find	Weight (kg)	Group
Babb's Mill	Greene	36°18'; 82°52'	1842	142	D
Bristol	Sullivan	36°34'; 82°11'	1937	20	O
Carthage	Smith	36°16'; 85°59'	1840	127	O
*Charlotte	Dickson	36°10'; 87°20'	7/31/1835	4.5	O
Cleveland	Bradley	35°10'; 84°53'	1860	115	O
Clinton	Anderson	36°05'; 84°12'	Before 1950	7.7	O?
Cookeville	Putnam	36°10'; 85°31'	About 1913	2.1	O
Coopertown	Robertson	36°26'; 87°02'	1860	17	O
Cosby's Creek	Cocke	35°47'; 83°15'	1837	960	O
Crab Orchard	Cumberland	35°50'; 84°55'	1887	48.6	M
*Drake Creek	Sumner	36°24'; 86°30'	5/9/1827	5.2	Ch
Harriman	Roane	35°57'; 84°34'	Before 1947	13	O
Jackson Co.	Jackson	36°25'; 85°30'	1846	0.43	O
Jonesboro	Washington	36°18'; 82°28'	1891	0.03	O
Livingston	Overton	36°25'; 85°15'	1937	0.12	O
Morristown	Hamblen	36°12'; 83°23'	1887	16	M
Murfreesboro	Rutherford	35°50'; 86°25'	1847	8.5	O

Tennessee (*Continued*)

Name	County	Coordinates	Date of Fall or Find	Weight (kg)	Group
*Petersburg	Lincoln	35°18'; 86°38'	8/5/1855	1.7	Ap
Savannah	Hardin	35°10'; 88°11'	About 1923	60	O
Smithville	De Kalb	35°59'; 85°51'	1840	60	O
Tazewell	Claiborne	36°26'; 83°34'	1853	27	O
Waldron Ridge	Claiborne	36°38'; 83°50'	1887	14	O

Texas

Name	County	Coordinates	Date of Fall or Find	Weight (kg)	Group
Abernathy	Lubbock	33°51'; 101°48'	1941	2.9	Ch
Adrian	Deaf Smith	35°09'; 102°43'	1936	22.6	Cb
Aiken	Floyd	34°08'; 101°30'	1936	0.96	C?
Allen	Collin	33°07'; 96°39'	About 1923	1.4	Ch
Ballinger	Runnels	31°46'; 99°59'	1927	1.2	H
Bartlett	Bell	30°50'; 97°30'	1938	4	O
*Bells	Grayson	33°36'; 96°28'	9/9/1961	0.3	Cc
*Blanket	Brown	31°50'; 98°50'	5/30/1909	3.1	Ch
Bluff	Fayette	29°55'; 96°50'	About 1878	150	Cb
Boerne	Kendall	29°46'; 98°46'	1932	1.1	Cb
Brady	McCulloch	31°03'; 99°27'	1937	0.93	Ch
Briscoe	Briscoe	34°21'; 101°24'	1940	1.8	Ch
Brownfield	Terry	33°13'; 102°11'	1937	0.32	Cb
Burkett	Coleman	32°02'; 99°15'	1913	8.4	O
Calliham	McMullen	28°25'; 98°15'	1958	40	Ch
Carlton	Hamilton	31°55'; 98°02'	1887	81.4	O
Cedar	Fayette	29°52'; 96°56'	1900	14	Cb
Chamberlin	Dallam	36°12'; 102°27'	1941	2.4	Cb
Channing	Hartley	35°43'; 102°17'	1936	15.3	Cb
Chico Mts.	Brewster	29°14'; 103°15'	1915	2000	H
Cleburne	Johnson	32°19'; 97°25'	1907	6.8	O
Comanche	Comanche	31°54'; 98°30'	1940	19.7	O
Concho	Glasscock	31°55'; 101°18'	1939	93.5	Ch
Cuero	De Witt	29°01'; 97°17'	1936	46.5	Cb
Davis Mts.	Jeff Davis	30°33'; 104°02'	1903	690	O
Davy	De Witt	29°05'; 97°32'	1940	45	Ch
Denton County	Denton	33°12'; 97°10'	1856	5	O
Deport	Red River	33°31'; 95°18'	1926	15	O
Dexter	Cooke	33°50'; 96°58'	1889	1.7	O
Dimmitt	Castro	34°35'; 102°10'	Before 1947	13.5	Cb
Dumas	Moore	35°54'; 101°54'	1956	46	Cb
Duncanville	Dallas	32°38'; 96°52'	1961	17.8	C
Elton	Dickens	33°41'; 100°45'	1936	1.9	O
Estacado	Hale	33°54'; 101°45'	1883	412	Cb
Ferguson Switch	Hale	34° ; 101½°	1937	1.3	Cb
*Florence	Williamson	30°50'; 97°46'	1/21/1922	3.6	Cb

Texas *(Continued)*

Name	County	Coordinates	Date of Fall or Find	Weight (kg)	Group
Floydada	Floyd	33°59'; 101°17'	Before 1912	12.5	O
Forestburg	Montague	33°30'; 97°39'	1957	26.6	C
Gail	Borden	32°42'; 101°36'	1948	4.7	C
Glen Rose	Somervell	32°15'; 97°43'	1934	11	O?
Gruver	Hansford	36°20'; 101°24'	1934	11.1	Cb
Hale Center No. 1	Hale	34°03'; 101°45'	1936	0.61	Ch
Hale Center No. 2	Hale	34°03'; 101°45'	1936	0.69	Cb
*Harleton	Harrison	32°41'; 94°31'	5/30/1961	8	Ch
Haskell	Haskell	33°09'; 99°45'	1909	36.3	Ch
Holliday	Archer	33°45'; 98°50'	1950	0.01	O
Howe	Grayson	33°30'; 96°36'	1938	8.6	Cb
Iredell	Bosque	31°58'; 97°52'	1898	1.5	H
Junction	Kimble	30°30'; 99°50'	1932	0.24	C
Kaufman	Kaufman	32°35'; 96°25'	1893	23	Cb
Kendall County	Kendall	29°24'; 98°30'	1887	21	H
*Kendleton	Ft. Bend	29°26'; 96°02'	5/2/1939	6.9	Ch
Kimble County	Kimble	30°25'; 99°24'	1918	154	Cb
*Kirbyville	Jasper	30°45'; 95°57'	11/12/1906	0.1	Ap
Laketon	Gray	35°34'; 100°40'	1937	3.6	Ch
La Villa	Hidalgo	26°16'; 97°54'	1956	19.8	C
Leander	Williamson	30°36'; 97°54'	1940	0.76	Ch
Lockney	Hale	34°09'; 101°18'	1944	0.82	Ch
Lubbock	Lubbock	33°36'; 101°44'	1938	1.4	Ch
Mart	McLennan	31°30'; 96°53'	1898	7.1	O
McAdoo	Dickens	33°45'; 100°56'	1935	1.1	Ch
McKinney	Collin	33°11'; 96°43'	1870	152	Ch
McLean	Gray	35°14'; 100°36'	1939	4.3	Cb
Mertzon	Irion	31°16'; 100°50'	Before 1947	3.8	O
Miami	Roberts	35°40'; 100°36'	1930	57.7	Cb
Monahans	Ward	31°28'; 102°50'	1938	27.9	D
Naruna	Burnet	30°58'; 98°19'	1935	0.67	C
Nazareth	Castro	34°36'; 102°02'	1938	0.04	C
Nordheim	De Witt	28°52'; 97°37'	1932	15.2	D
Odessa	Ector	31°43'; 102°24'	Before 1922	225	O
Ozona	Crockett	30°44'; 101°18'	1929	127.5	Cb
Palisades Park	Randall	35°06'; 101°52'	1935	0.12	O
Paloduro	Armstrong	34°47'; 101°11'	1935	3	O
Peck's Spring	Midland	31°57'; 101°46'	1926	1.6	Ch
*Pena Blanca Spring	Marathon	30°07'; 103°07'	8/2/1946	70	Ae
Pipe Creek	Bandera	29°41'; 98°55'	1887	13.6	Cb
Plainview (1917)	Hale	34°07'; 101°47'	1917	520	Cb
Plainview (1950)	Hale	34°07'; 101°47'	1950	2.2	Cb
*Plantersville	Grimes	30°20'; 95°52'	9/4/1930	2.1	Cb
Red River	Johnson	32°20'; 97°10'	1808	743	O
Richland	Navarro	31°54'; 96°24'	1951	13.6	H

Texas (Continued)

Name	County	Coordinates	Date of Fall or Find	Weight (kg)	Group
Romero	Hartley	35°46′; 102°57′	1938	17.2	Cb
Rosebud	Falls	30°59′; 97°00′	Before 1915	55	Cb
Round Top	Fayette	30°02′; 96°44′	1934	7.7	C
San Angelo	Tom Green	31°25′; 100°21′	1897	88	O
Sanderson	Terrell	30°09′; 102°24′	1936	6.8	O
San Pedro Springs	Bexar	29°30′; 98°30′	1887	0.07	Ch
Scurry	Scurry	32½°; 101°	1937	115	Cb
Shafter Lake	Andrews	32°24′; 102°35′	About 1933	2.8	C
Shallowater	Lubbock	33°42′; 101°56′	1936	4.7	Ae
Silverton	Briscoe	34°32′; 101°11′	1938	1.4	C
Somervell Co.	Somervell	32°11′; 97°48′	About 1919	11.8	P
Spearman	Hansford	36°15′; 101°13′	1934	10.4	O
Temple	Bell	31°07′; 97°18′		0.2	Ch
Texline	Dallam	36°24′; 103°01′	1937	26	Cb
Travis Co.	Travis	30°20′; 97°43′	1889	150	Cb
*Troup	Smith	32°10′; 95°06′	4/26/1917	1.1	Ch
Tulia	Swisher	34°32′; 101°42′	1917	24	Cb
Uvalde	Uvalde	29°12′; 99°46′	About 1915	7.5	C
Vigo Park	Swisher	34°41′; 101°23′	1934	0.04	C
Wellman	Terry	33°02′; 102°20′	1940	50	Cb
Wichita Co.	Wichita	34°04′; 98°55′	Before 1836	150	O
Ysleta	El Paso	31°39′; 106°11′		140	O
Zapata Co.	Zapata	27°; 99°	1930	?	O

Utah

Name	County	Coordinates	Date of Fall or Find	Weight (kg)	Group
Drum Mts.	Millard	39°30′; 112°54′	1944	529	O
Duchesne	Duchesne	40°10′; 110°24′	1906	22.8	O
*Garland	Box Elder	41°41′; 112°08′	1950	0.10	Ah
Ioka	Duchesne	40°15′; 110°05′	1931	31	C
Moab	Garfield	38°03′; 110°19′		19.5	O
Salina	Sevier	38°59′; 111°51′	About 1908	0.24	O
Salt Lake City	Salt Lake	40°55′; 111°40′	1869	0.87	Cb

Virginia

Name	County	Coordinates	Date of Fall or Find	Weight (kg)	Group
Botetourt Co.	Botetourt	37½°; 79¾°	1850	—	D
Cranberry Plains	Giles	37°14′; 80°44′	1852	0.09	O
Dungannon	Scott	36°51′; 82°27′	1922–23	13	O
*Forksville	Mecklenburg	36°47′; 78°05′	7/16/1924	6.06	Ch
Hopper	Henry	36°33′; 79°46′	1889	1.92	O
Indian Valley	Floyd	36°56′; 80°30′	1887	14.2	H
Keen Mt.	Buchanan	37°13′; 82°00′	1950	6.7	H

Virginia (*Continued*)

Name	County	Coordinates	Date of Fall or Find	Weight (kg)	Group
Norfolk	Norfolk	36°56′; 76°08′	1907	23	O
*Richmond	Chesterfield	37°28′; 77°30′	6/4/1828	2	Ch
*Sharps	Richmond	37°50′; 76°42′	4/1/1921	1.27	Ch
Staunton	Augusta	38°09′; 79°04′	1858–59	120	O

Washington

Name	County	Coordinates	Date of Fall or Find	Weight (kg)	Group
*Washougal	Clark	45°35′; 122°21′	7/2/1939	0.22	Ap
Waterville	Douglas	47°44′; 120°19′	1927	33	O

West Virginia

Name	County	Coordinates	Date of Fall or Find	Weight (kg)	Group
Greenbrier Co.	Greenbrier	37°49′; 80°26′	1880	5	O
Jenny's Creek	Wayne	38°20′; 82°22′	1883	10	O

Wisconsin

Name	County	Coordinates	Date of Fall or Find	Weight (kg)	Group
Algoma	Kewaunee	44°35′; 87°25′	1887	4	O
Angelica	Shawano	44°15′; 88°15′	1916	14.8	O
*Colby	Clark	44°54′; 90°17′	7/4/1917	104.5	Ch
Hammond	St. Croix	44°58′; 92°38′	1884	24	O
*Kilbourn	Columbia	43°35′; 89°36′	6/16/1911	0.77	Cb
Mount Morris	Waushara	44°08′; 89°10′	Before 1937	0.68	C
Pine River	Waushara	44°13′; 89°06′	1931	3.6	O
Trenton	Washington	43°22′; 88°08′	1858	65	O
*Vernon Co.	Vernon	43°30′; 91°10′	3/25/1865	1.5	Cb

Wyoming

Name	County	Coordinates	Date of Fall or Find	Weight (kg)	Group
Albin (pallasite)	Laramie	41°30′; 104°06′	1915	38	P
Albin (stone)	Laramie	41°25′; 104°06′	1949	15.4	Ch
Bear Lodge	Crook	44°34′; 104°17′	1931	48.7	O
Clareton	Weston	43°42′; 104°42′	Before 1937	1.05	Ch
Hat Creek	Niobrara	42°55′; 104°25′	1939	8.9	Cb
Hawk Springs	Goshen	41°47′; 104°17′	1935	0.37	Cb
Lusk	Niobrara	42°46′; 104°21′	1940	0.05	O
Pine Bluffs	Laramie	41°11′; 104°04′	1935	2.7	C?
Silver Crown	Laramie	41°10′; 105°20′	1887	11.6	O
*Torrington	Goshen	42°04′; 104°10′	9/23/1944	0.26	Cb
Willow Creek	Natrona	43°28′; 106°46′	About 1914	51.2	O

Bibliography

Adams, J. A. S., 1956: "Uranium contents and alpha particle activities of tektites." *XX Intern. Geol. Congr., Resumenes,* 207.

Ahrens, L. H., R. A. Edge, and S. R. Taylor, 1960: "The uniformity of concentration of lithophile elements in chondrites—with particular reference to Cs." *Geochim. et Cosmochim. Acta,* **20,** 260–272.

Alderman, A. R., 1932: "The meteorite craters at Henbury, Central Australia." *Mineral. Mag.,* **23,** 19–32.

Amiruddin, A., and W. D. Ehmann, 1962: "Tungsten abundances in meteoritic and terrestrial materials." *Geochim. et Cosmochim. Acta,* in press.

Anders, E., 1960: "The record in the meteorites. II. On the presence of aluminum-26 in meteorites and tektites." *Geochim. et Cosmochim. Acta,* **19,** 53–62.

Anders, E., 1962: "Meteorite ages." *Rev. Mod. Phys.,* in press.

Anders, E., and G. G. Goles, 1961: "Theories on the origin of meteorites." *J. Chem. Educ.,* **38,** 58–66.

Anders, E., and C. M. Stevens, 1960: "Search for extinct lead 205 in meteorites." *J. Geophys. Research,* **65,** 3043–3048.

Andersen, O., 1915: "The system anorthite-forsterite-silica." *Am. J. Sci.,* **39,** 407–454.

Arrol, W. J., R. B. Jacobi, and F. A. Paneth, 1942: "Meteorites and the age of the solar system." *Nature,* **149,** 235–238.

Atkins, D. H. F., and A. A. Smales, 1960: "The determination of tantalum and tungsten in rocks and meteorites by neutron activation analysis." *Anal. Chim. Acta,* **22,** 462–478.

Bacharev, A. M., 1956: "Second Murgab expedition." *Meteoritika,* **14,** 110–112.

Bainbridge, A. E., H. E. Suess, and H. Wänke, 1962: "The tritium content of three stony meteorites and one iron meteorite." *Geochim. et Cosmochim. Acta,* **26,** 471–474.

Baker, G., 1944: "The flanges of australites." *Mem. Natl. Museum Victoria,* **14,** 7–22.

Baker, G., 1959: "Tektites." *Mem. Natl. Museum Victoria*, **23**, 313 pp.

Baker, G., 1960: "Origin of tektites." *Nature*, **185**, 291–294.

Baker, G., 1961*a*: "Einige Erscheinungen des Ätzverhaltens der Australite." *Chem. Erde*, **21**, 101–117.

Baker, G., 1961*b*: "A complete oval australite." *Proc. Roy. Soc. Victoria*, **74**, 47–54.

Baker, G., and H. C. Forster, 1943: "The specific gravity relationships of australites." *Am. J. Sci.*, **241**, 377–406.

Bannister, F. A., 1941: "Osbornite, meteoritic titanium nitride." *Mineral. Mag.*, **26**, 36–44.

Barnes, V. E., 1940: "North American tektites." *Univ. Texas Publ.*, **3945**, 477–582.

Barnes, V. E., 1960: "Significance of inhomogeneity in tektites." *Rept. XXI Intern. Geol. Congr.*, Part XIII, 328–338.

Barnes, V. E., 1961: "Tektites." *Sci. American*, **205**, no. 5, 58–65.

Bate, G. L., J. R. Huizenga, and H. A. Potratz, 1959: "Thorium in stone meteorites by neutron activation analysis." *Geochim. et Cosmochim. Acta*, **16**, 88–100.

Bate, G. L., H. A. Potratz, and J. R. Huizenga, 1960: "Scandium, chromium and europium in stone meteorites by simultaneous neutron activation analysis." *Geochim. et Cosmochim. Acta*, **18**, 101–107.

Bauer, C. A., 1947: "The production of helium in meteorites by cosmic radiation." *Phys. Rev.*, **72**, 354–355; **74**, 225–226, 501–502.

Beals, C. S., 1958: "Fossil meteorite craters." *Sci. American*, **199**, no. 1, 32–39.

Behne, W., 1953: "Untersuchungen zur Geochemie des Chlor und Brom." *Geochim. et Cosmochim. Acta*, **3**, 186–214.

Bernal, J. D., 1961: "Significance of carbonaceous chondrites in theories on the origin of life." *Nature*, **190**, 129–131.

Berwerth, F., 1912: "Quarz und Tridymit als Gemengteile der meteorischen Eukrite." *Sitzber. Akad. Wiss. Wien*, **121**, 763–783.

Berzelius, J. J., 1834: "Om meteorstenar." *Handl. Svenska Vetenskaps-Akad.*, 115–183.

Boato, G., 1954: "The isotopic composition of hydrogen and carbon in the carbonaceous chondrites." *Geochim. et Cosmochim. Acta*, **6**, 209–220.

Bowen, N. L., and J. F. Schairer, 1935: "The system MgO-FeO-SiO_2." *Am. J. Sci.*, **29**, 151–217.

Bowen, N. L., and O. F. Tuttle, 1949: "The system MgO-SiO_2-H_2O." *Bull. Geol. Soc. Am.*, **60**, 439–460.

Boyd, F. R., and J. L. England, 1961: "Melting of silicates at high pressures." *Carnegie Inst. Wash. Yearbook*, **60**, 113–125.

Brezina, A., 1885: "Die Meteoritensammlung des k.k. mineralogischen Hofkabinettes in Wien." *Jahrb. k.k. Geol. Reichsanstalt*, **35**, 151–276.

Brezina, A., 1904: "The arrangement of collections of meteorites." *Proc. Am. Phil. Soc.*, **43**, 211–247.

Briggs, M. H., 1961: "Organic constituents of meteorites." *Nature*, **191**, 1137–1140.

Brown, H., 1947: "An experimental method for the estimation of the age of the elements." *Phys. Rev.*, **72**, 348–349.

Brown, H., 1961: "The density and mass distribution of meteoritic bodies in the neighborhood of the Earth's orbit." *J. Geophys. Research*, **66**, 1316–1317.

Brown, H., and E. O. Goldberg, 1950: "Radiometric determination of gold and rhenium." *Anal. Chem.*, **22**, 308–310.

Brown, H., and C. Patterson, 1947: "The composition of meteoritic matter. II. The composition of iron meteorites and of the metal phase of stony meteorites." *J. Geol.*, **55**, 508–510.

Brown, H., and C. Patterson, 1948: "The composition of meteoritic matter. III. Phase equilibria, genetic relations, and planet structure." *J. Geol.*, **56**, 85–111.

Brunn, A. F., E. Langer, and H. Pauly, 1955: "Magnetic particles found by raking the deep-sea bottom." *Deep-Sea Research*, **2**, 230–246.

Buddhue, J. D., 1950: "Meteoritic dust." *Univ. New Mexico Publ. in Meteoritics*, no. 2, 102 pp.

Buddhue, J. D., 1957: "The oxidation and weathering of meteorites." *Univ. New Mexico Publ. in Meteoritics*, no. 3, 161 pp.

Calvin, M., 1961: "The chemistry of life. 3. How life originated on Earth and in the world beyond." *Chem. Eng. News*, **39**, 96–104.

Cassidy, W. A., 1958: "Achondrite investigations and their bearing on the origin of tektites." *Geochim. et Cosmochim. Acta*, **14**, 304–315.

Cassidy, W. A., and E. R. Segnit, 1955: "Liquid immiscibility in a silicate melt." *Nature*, **176**, 305.

Ceplecha, Z., 1961: "Multiple fall of Pribram meteorites photographed." *Bull. Astron. Inst. Czechoslovakia*, **12**, 21–47.

Chackett, K. F., P. Reasbeck, and E. J. Wilson, 1953: "Recent studies on iron meteorites. II. Determination of the helium content." *Geochim. et Cosmochim. Acta*, **3**, 261–271.

Chao, E. C. T., I. Adler, E. J. Dwornick, and J. Littler, 1962a: "Metallic spherules in tektites from Isabela, the Philippine Islands." *Science*, **135**, 97–98.

Chao, E. C. T., J. J. Fahey, J. L. Littler, and D. J. Milton, 1962b: "Stishovite, SiO_2, a very high pressure new mineral from Meteor Crater, Arizona." *J. Geophys. Research*, **67**, 419–421.

Chao, E. C. T., E. M. Shoemaker, and B. M. Madsen, 1960: "First natural occurrence of coesite." *Science*, **132**, 220–222.

Chapman, D. R., 1960: "Recent re-entry research and the cosmic origin of tektites." *Nature*, **188**, 353–355.

Cherry, R. D., and S. R. Taylor, 1961: "Studies of tektite composition. II. Derivation from a quartz-shale mixture." *Geochim. et Cosmochim. Acta*, **22**, 164–168.

Clarke, R. S., and M. K. Carron, 1961: "Comparison of tektite specimens from Empire, Georgia, and Martha's Vineyard, Massachusetts." *Smithsonian Misc. Collections*, **143**, no. 4, 18 pp.

Claus, G., and B. Nagy, 1961: "A microbiological examination of some carbonaceous chondrites." *Nature*, **192**, 594–596.

Cloez, S., 1864: "Analyse chimique de la pierre météoritique d'Orgueil." *Compt. rend.*, **59**, 37–38.

Cohen, A. J., 1959: "Moldavites and similar tektites from Georgia, U.S.A." *Geochim. et Cosmochim. Acta*, **17**, 150–153.

Cohen, A. J., 1960: "Germanium content of tektites and other natural glasses: implications concerning the origin of tektites." *Rept. XXI Session Intern. Geol. Congr.*, Part 1, 30–39.

Cohen, A. J., 1961: "A semi-quantitative hypothesis of tektite origin by meteorite impact." *J. Geophys. Research*, **66**, 2521.

Cohen, A. J., T. E. Bunch, and A. M. Reed, 1961: "Coesite discoveries establish cryptovolcanics as fossil meteorite craters." *Science*, **134**, 1624–1625.

Cohen, E., 1894: *Meteoritenkunde, Heft 1: Untersuchungsmethoden und Charakteristik der Gemengtheile.*

Schweizerbart'sche Verlagshandlung, Stuttgart, 340 pp.

Cohen, E., 1900: "Meteoreisen-Studien XI." *Ann. k.k. naturhist. Hofmus. Wien*, **15**, 385–386.

Cohen, E., 1906: "On the meteoric stone which fell at the mission station of St. Mark's, Transkei, on January 3, 1903." *Ann. South African Museum*, **5**, 1–16.

Curvello, W., 1958: "Sulfetos meteoriticos." *Bol. museu nacl. Brasil, Geol.*, no. 27, 51 pp.

Daly, R. A., 1943: "Meteorites and an Earth-model." *Bull. Geol. Soc. Am.*, **54**, 401–456.

Daubree, A., 1864: "Note sur les meteorites tombees le 14 Mai aux environs d'Orgueil (Tarn-et-Garonne)." *Compt. rend.*, **58**, 985–990.

Dawson, K. R., J. A. Maxwell, and D. E. Parsons, 1960: "A description of the meteorite which fell near Abee, Alberta, Canada." *Geochim. et Cosmochim. Acta*, **21**, 127–144.

Dietz, R. S., 1961: "Astroblemes." *Sci. American*, **205**, no. 2, 50–58.

DuFresne, A., 1960: "Selenium and tellurium in meteorites." *Geochim. et Cosmochim. Acta*, **20**, 141–148.

DuFresne, E. R., and E. Anders, 1961: "The record in the meteorites. V. A thermometer mineral in the Mighei carbonaceous chondrite." *Geochim. et Cosmochim. Acta*, **23**, 200–208.

DuFresne, E. R., and E. Anders, 1962: "On the chemical evolution of the carbonaceous chondrites." *Geochim. et Cosmochim. Acta*, in press.

DuFresne, E. R., and S. K. Roy, 1961: "A new phosphate mineral from the Springwater pallasite." *Geochim. et Cosmochim. Acta*, **24**, 198–205.

Eberhardt, P., and A. Eberhardt, 1961: "Neon in some stone meteorites." *Z. Naturforsch.*, **16a**, 236–238.

Edwards, A. B., 1953: "The Wedderburn meteoritic iron." *Proc. Roy. Soc. Victoria*, **64**, 73–76.

Edwards, G., 1955a: "Isotopic composition of meteoritic hydrogen." *Nature*, **176**, 109–111.

Edwards, G., 1955b: "Sodium and potassium in meteorites." *Geochim. et Cosmochim. Acta*, **8**, 285–294.

Edwards, G., and H. C. Urey, 1955: "Determination of alkali metals in meteorites by a distillation process." *Geochim. et Cosmochim. Acta*, **7**, 154–168.

Eggleton, R. E., and E. M. Shoemaker, 1961: "Breccia at Sierra Madera, Texas." *Geol. Soc. Am., Annual Meeting Program*, 44–45.

Ehmann, W. D., 1961: "Recent improvement in our knowledge of cosmic abundances." *J. Chem. Educ.*, **38**, 53–57.

Ehmann, W. D., and J. R. Huizenga, 1959: "Bismuth, thallium and mercury in stone meteorites by activation analysis." *Geochim. et Cosmochim. Acta*, **17**, 125–135.

Ehmann, W. D., and T. P. Kohman, 1958: "Cosmic-ray-induced radioactivities in meteorites. II. Al^{26}, Be^{10} and Co^{60}, aerolites, siderites and tektites." *Geochim. et Cosmochim. Acta*, **14**, 364–369.

Ellitsgaard-Rasmussen, K., 1954: "Meteoric shower in north-east Greenland?" *Medd. Dansk. Geol. Foren.*, **12**, 433–435.

Farrington, O. C., 1915: *Meteorites*. Published by the author, Chicago, 233 pp.

Fenner, C., 1934: "Australites, Part I. Classification of the W. H. C. Shaw collection." *Proc. Roy. Soc. South Australia*, **58**, 62–79.

Fermor, L. L., 1938: "On khoharite, a new garnet, and on the nomenclature of garnets." *Records Geol. Survey India*, **73**, 145–156.

Fesenkov, V. G., 1961: "The nature of the Tunguska meteorite." *Meteoritika*, **20**, 27–31.

Fireman, E. L., 1958: "Distribution of helium-3 in the Carbo meteorite." *Nature*, **181**, 1725.

Fireman, E. L., 1959: "The distribution of helium-3 in the Grant meteorite and a determination of the original mass." *Planetary and Space Sci.*, **1**, 66–70.

Fireman, E. L., and J. DeFelice, 1960: "Argon 37, argon 39, and tritium in meteorites and the spatial constancy of cosmic rays." *J. Geophys. Research*, **65**, 3035–3042.

Fireman, E. L., and D. E. Fisher, 1961: "Search for uranium in the Sikhote-Alin meteorite and its relation to the lead method of age determination." *Nature*, **192**, 644–645.

Fireman, E. L., and D. Schwarzer, 1957: "Measurement of Li^6, He^3, and H^3 in meteorites and its relation to cosmic radiation." *Geochim. et Cosmochim. Acta*, **11**, 252–262.

Fish, R. A., G. G. Goles, and E. Anders, 1960: "The record in the meteorites. III. On the development of meteorites in asteroidal bodies." *Astrophys. J.*, **132**, 243–258.

Fisher, D. E., 1961: "Space erosion of the Grant meteorite." *J. Geophys. Research*, **66**, 1509–1511.

Fitch, F., H. P. Schwarcz, and E. Anders, 1962: " 'Organized elements' in carbonaceous chondrites." *Nature*, **193**, 1123–1125.

Fletcher, L., 1894: "Chemical analysis of the meteoric stone found at Makariwa, near Invercargill, New Zealand, in the year 1879." *Mineral. Mag.*, **10**, 287–325.

Folinsbee, R. E., and L. A. Bayrock, 1961: "The Bruderheim meteorite—fall and recovery." *J. Roy. Astron. Soc. Can.*, **55**, 218–228.

Foote, A. E., 1891: "A new locality for meteoric iron with a preliminary notice of the discovery of diamonds in the iron." *Proc. Am. Assoc. Adv. Sci.*, **40**, 279–283.

Foote, W. M., 1912: "Preliminary note on the shower of meteoric stones near Holbrook, Navajo County, Arizona, July 19, 1912, including a reference to the Perseid swarm of meteors visible from July 11 to August 22." *Am. J. Sci.*, **34**, 437–456.

Foshag, W. F., 1938: "Petrology of the Pasamonte, New Mexico, meteorite." *Am. J. Sci.*, **35**, 374–382.

Foshag, W. F., 1940: "The Shallowater meteorite; a new aubrite." *Am. Mineralogist*, **25**, 779–786.

Friedman, I., 1958: "The water, deuterium, gas and uranium content of tektites." *Geochim. et Cosmochim. Acta*, **14**, 316–322.

Game, P. M., 1957: "Plagioclases from Juvinas meteorite and from allivalite from the Isle of Rhum." *Mineral. Mag.*, **31**, 656–671.

Gast, P. W., 1960a: "Alkali metals in stone meteorites." *Geochim. et Cosmochim. Acta*, **19**, 1–4.

Gast, P. W., 1960b: "Limitations on the composition of the upper mantle." *J. Geophys. Research*, **65**, 1287–1297.

Geiss, J., and D. C. Hess, 1958: "Argon-potassium ages and the isotopic composition of argon from meteorites." *Astrophys. J.*, **127**, 224–236.

Gentner, W., and J. Zähringer, 1960: "Das Kalium-Argon Alter von Tektiten." *Z. Naturforsch.*, **15a**, 93–99.

Gerling, E. K., and L. K. Levskii, 1956: "On the origin of inert gases in stony meteorites." *Doklady Akad. Sci. U.S.S.R.*, **110**, 750–753.

Gerling, E. K., and T. G. Pavlova, 1951: "Determination of the geological age of two stony meteorites by the argon method." *Doklady Acad. Sci. U.S.S.R.*, **77**, 85–86.

Gerling, E. K., and K. G. Rik, 1955: "Determination of the ages of meteoritic stones by the argon method." *Doklady Acad. Sci. U.S.S.R.*, **101**, 433–435.

Geze, B., and A. Cailleux, 1950: "Existence probable de crateres meteoritiques à Cabrerolles et à Faugères (Herault)." *Compt. rend.*, **230**, 1534–1536.

Goel, P. S., and T. P. Kohman, 1962: "Cosmogenic carbon-14 in meteorites and terrestrial ages of 'finds.'" *Science*, **136**, in press.

Goldberg, E. D., 1961: "Chemical and mineralogical aspects of deep-sea sediments." *Phys. Chem. Earth*, **4**, 281–302.

Goldberg, E., A. Uchiyama, and H. Brown, 1951: "The distribution of nickel, cobalt, gallium, palladium and gold in iron meteorites." *Geochim. et Cosmochim. Acta*, **2**, 1–25.

Goldschmidt, V. M., 1937: "Geochemische Verteilungsgesetze der Elemente. XI. Die Mengenverhältnisse der Elemente und der Atom-Arten." *Norske Videnskaps-Akad. Skrifter, Math.-Naturv. Klasse*, no. 4, 148 pp.

Goldschmidt, V. M., and C. Peters, 1932: "Zur Geochemie des Bors." *Nachr. Ges. Wiss. Göttingen, Math.-physik. Kl.*, 377–401.

Goldschmidt, V. M., and C. Peters, 1933: "Zur Kenntnis der Troilit-Knollen der Meteoriten, ein Beitrag zur Geochemie von Chrom, Nickel, und Zinn." *Nachr. Ges. Wiss. Göttingen, Math.-physik. Kl.*, 278–287.

Goles, G. G., and E. Anders, 1962: "Abundances of iodine, tellurium, and uranium in meteorites." *Geochim. et Cosmochim. Acta*, in press.

Goles, G. G., R. A. Fish, and E. Anders, 1960: "The record in the meteorites. I. The former environment of stone meteorites as deduced from K^{40}–Ar^{40} ages." *Geochim. et Cosmochim. Acta*, **19**, 177–195.

Gordon, S. G., 1931: "The Grootfontein, Southwest Africa, meteoric iron." *Proc. Acad. Nat. Sci. Phila.*, **83**, 251–255.

Guppy, D. J., and R. S. Matheson, 1950: "Wolf Creek meteorite crater, Western Australia." *J. Geol.*, **58**, 30–36.

Haidinger, W., 1847: "Uber das Meteoreisen von Branau." *Ann. Physik.*, **72**, 580–582.

Hara, T., and E. B. Sandell, 1960: "Meteoritic abundance of ruthenium." *Geochim. et Cosmochim. Acta*, **21**, 145–150.

Hawkins, G. S., 1960: "Tektites and the Earth." *Nature*, **185**, 300–301.

Heide, F., 1923: "Die Meteorite von Grimma i.S." *Centralb. Min.*, 69–78.

Heide, F., 1936: "Seltene Elemente in den Tektiten." *Forsch. u. Fortschr.*, **12**, 232.

Heide, F., 1957: *Kleine Meteoritenkunde* (second edition). Springer-Verlag, Berlin, 142 pp.

Henderson, E. P., 1941: "Chilean hexahedrites and the composition of all hexahedrites." *Am. Mineralogist*, **26**, 545–550.

Henderson, E. P., 1949: "The Aggie Creek meteorite from Seward, Alaska." *Am. Mineralogist*, **34**, 229–232.

Henderson, E. P., and C. W. Cooke, 1942: "The Sardis (Georgia) meteorite." *Proc. U.S. Natl. Museum*, **92**, 141–150.

Henderson, E. P., and S. H. Perry, 1954: "A discussion of the densities of iron meteorites." *Geochim. et Cosmochim. Acta*, **6**, 221–240.

Henderson, E. P., and S. H. Perry, 1958: "Studies of seven siderites." *Proc. U.S. Natl. Museum*, **107**, 339–403.

Herr, W., W. Hoffmeister, B. Hirt, J. Geiss, and F. G. Houtermans, 1961: "Versuch zur Datierung von Eisen-

meteoriten nach der Rhenium-Os-
mium-Methode." *Z. Naturforsch.,*
16a, 1053–1058.

Herzog, L. F., and W. H. Pinson, 1956:
"Rb/Sr age, elemental and isotopic
abundance studies of stony meteorites." *Am. J. Sci.,* **254,** 555–566.

Hess, D. C., and R. R. Marshall, 1960:
"The isotopic compositions and concentrations of lead in some chondritic
meteorites." *Geochim. et Cosmochim. Acta,* **20,** 284–299.

Hess, D. C., R. R. Marshall, and H. C.
Urey, 1957: "Surface ionization of
silver; silver in meteorites." *Science,*
126, 1291–1293.

Hess, H. H., 1960: "Stillwater igneous
complex, Montana." *Mem. Geol.
Soc. Am.,* **80,** 230 pp.

Hess, H. H., and E. P. Henderson,
1949: "The Moore County meteorite:
a further study with comment on its
primordial environment." *Am. Mineralogist,* **34,** 494–507.

Hodge, P. W., and R. Wildt, 1958: "A
search for airborne particles of meteoritic origin." *Geochim. et Cosmochim. Acta,* **14,** 126–133.

Hoering, T. C., and P. L. Parker, 1961:
"The geochemistry of the stable isotopes of chlorine." *Geochim. et Cosmochim. Acta,* **23,** 186–199.

Hoffman, J. H., and A. O. Nier, 1958:
"Production of helium in iron me-
teorites by the action of cosmic rays."
Phys. Rev., **112,** 2112–2218.

Hoffman, J. H., and A. O. Nier, 1959:
"The cosmogenic He^3 and He^4 distribution in the meteorite Carbo."
Geochim. et Cosmochim. Acta, **17,**
32–36.

Honda, M., J. P. Shedlovsky, and J. R.
Arnold, 1961: "Radioactive species
produced by cosmic rays in iron meteorites." *Geochim. et Cosmochim.
Acta,* **22,** 133–154.

Hunter, W., and D. W. Parkin, 1960:
"Cosmic dust in recent deep-sea sedi-

ments." *Proc. Roy. Soc. London,*
255A, 382–397.

Hunter, W., and D. W. Parkin, 1961:
"Cosmic dust in Tertiary rock and
the lunar surface." *Geochim. et Cosmochim. Acta,* **24,** 32–39.

Jerofejeff, M., and P. Latschinoff, 1888:
"Der Meteorit von Nowo-Urei."
*Verhand. Russ.-Kais. Mineral. Ge-
sell.,* **24,** 263–294.

Karpoff, R., 1953: "The meteorite
crater of Talemzane in southern Al-
geria." *Meteoritics,* **1,** 31–38.

Kemp, D. M., and A. A. Smales, 1960a:
"The determination of vanadium in
rocks and meteorites by neutron-ac-
tivation analysis." *Anal. Chim. Acta,*
23, 397–410.

Kemp, D. M., and A. A. Smales, 1960b:
"The determination of scandium in
rocks and meteorites by neutron-
activation analysis." *Anal. Chim.
Acta,* **23,** 410–418.

Krinov, E. L., 1958: "Some considerations on tektites." *Geochim. et Cosmochim. Acta,* **14,** 259–266.

Krinov, E. L., 1959: "Über die Natur
der Mikrometeoriten." *Chem. Erde,*
20, 28–35.

Krinov, E. L., 1960: *Principles of meteoritics.* Pergamon Press, New York,
535 pp.

Krinov, E. L., 1961: "The Kaalijarv
meteorite craters on Saarema Island,
Esthonian SSR." *Am. J. Sci.,* **259,**
430–440.

Krummenacher, D., C. M. Merrihue, R.
O. Pepin, and J. H. Reynolds, 1962:
"Meteoritic krypton and barium ver-
sus the general isotopic anomalies in
meteoritic xenon." *Geochim. et Cosmochim. Acta,* **26,** 251–262.

Ksanda, C. J., and E. P. Henderson,
1939: "Identification of diamond in
the Canyon Diablo iron." *Am. Mineralogist,* **24,** 677–680.

Kuno, H., and K. Nagashima, 1952:
"Chemical compositions of hypersthene and pigeonite in equilibrium

in magma." *Am. Mineralogist,* **37,** 1000–1006.

Kuroda, P. K., and E. B. Sandell, 1954: "Geochemistry of molybdenum." *Geochim. et Cosmochim. Acta,* **6,** 35–63.

Kvasha, L. G., 1948: "Investigation of the stony meteorite Staroye Boriskino." *Meteoritika,* **4,** 83–96.

Kvasha, L. G., 1958: "Über einige Typen von Steinmeteoriten." *Chem. Erde,* **19,** 249–274.

Kvasha, L. G., 1961: "Some new data on the structure of chondrites." *Meteoritika,* **20,** 124–136.

Lacroix, A., 1926: "L'eucrite de Béréba (Haute-Volta) et les météorites feldspathiques en général." *Arch. Museum Hist. Nat. Paris,* ser. 6, **1,** 15–58.

LaPaz, L., 1947: "A possible meteorite crater in the Aleutians." *Pop. Astron.,* **55,** 156–167.

LaPaz, L., 1958: "The effects of meteorites upon the Earth (including its inhabitants, atmosphere, and satellites)." *Adv. Geophys.,* **4,** 217–350.

Latimer, W. M., 1950: "Astrochemical problems in the formation of the Earth." *Science,* **112,** 101–104.

Leonard, F. C., 1956: "A classificational catalog of the meteoritic falls of the world." *Univ. Calif. Publ. Astron.,* **2,** 1–80.

Leonard, F. C., and B. Slanin, 1941: "Statistical studies of the meteorite falls of the world: 3. Their time distribution." *Pop. Astron.,* **49,** 551–560.

Levin, B. J., 1958: "Über den Ursprung der Meteoriten." *Chem. Erde,* **19,** 286–295.

Levin, B. Y., S. V. Kozlovskaia, and A. G. Starkova, 1956: "The average chemical composition of meteorites." *Meteoritika,* **14,** 38–53.

Levin, B. Y., and G. L. Slonimsky, 1958: "Question of the origin of me-teoritic chondrules." *Meteoritika,* **16,** 30–36.

Lipman, C. B., 1932: "Discovery of combined nitrogen in stony meteorites (aerolites)." *Am. Museum Novitates,* no. 589, 2 pp.

Lipschutz, M. E., and E. Anders, 1961: "The record in the meteorites. IV. Origin of diamonds in iron meteorites." *Geochim. et Cosmochim. Acta,* **24,** 83–105.

Littler, J., J. J. Fahey, R. S. Dietz, and E. C. T. Chao, 1961: "Coesite from Lake Bosumtwi Crater, Ashanti, Ghana." *Geol. Soc. Am., Annual Meeting Program,* 94.

Lovering, J. F., 1957a: "Differentiation in the iron-nickel core of a parent meteorite body." *Geochim. et Cosmochim. Acta,* **12,** 238–252.

Lovering, J. F., 1957b: "Pressures and temperatures within a typical parent meteorite body." *Geochim. et Cosmochim. Acta,* **12,** 253–261.

Lovering, J. F., 1959: "Frequency of meteorite falls throughout the ages." *Nature,* **183,** 1664–1665.

Lovering, J. F., 1962: "The evolution of the meteorites—evidence for the co-existence of chondritic, achondritic and iron meteorites in a typical parent meteorite body." *Researches on Meteorites* (Carleton B. Moore, ed.), John Wiley and Sons, New York, pp. 179–198.

Lovering, J. F., W. Nichiporuk, A. Chodos, and H. Brown, 1957: "The distribution of gallium, germanium, cobalt, chromium, and copper in iron and stony-iron meteorites in relation to nickel content and structure." *Geochim. et Cosmochim. Acta,* **11,** 263–278.

Lovering, J. F., L. G. Parry, and J. C. Jaeger, 1960: "Temperature and mass losses in iron meteorites during ablation in the Earth's atmosphere." *Geochim. et Cosmochim. Acta,* **19,** 156–167.

Madigan, C. T., 1937: "The Boxhole crater and the Huckitta meteorite (Central Australia)." *Trans. Roy. Soc. S. Australia,* **61**, 187–190.

Marshall, R. R., 1962: "Mass spectrometric study of the lead in carbonaceous chondrites." *J. Geophys. Research,* **67**, in press.

Martin, G. R., 1953: "Recent studies on iron meteorites. IV. The origin of meteoritic helium and the ages of meteorites." *Geochim. et Cosmochim. Acta,* **3**, 288–309.

Maskelyne, N. S., 1870: "On the mineral constituents of meteorites." *Phil. Trans. Roy. Soc.,* **160**, 189–214.

Mason, B., 1959: "Chemical composition of tektites." *Nature,* **183**, 254–255.

Mason, B., 1960a: "Origin of chondrules and chondritic meteorites." *Nature,* **186**, 230–231.

Mason, B., 1960b: "The origin of meteorites." *J. Geophys. Research,* **65**, 2965–2970.

Mason, B., 1962: "The classification of the chondritic meteorites." *Am. Museum Novitates,* no. 2085, 20 pp.

Mason, B., and H. B. Wiik, 1961a: "The Kyushu, Japan, chondrite." *Geochim. et Cosmochim. Acta,* **21**, 272–275.

Mason, B., and H. B. Wiik, 1961b: "The Holbrook, Arizona, chondrite." *Geochim. et Cosmochim. Acta,* **21**, 276–283.

Massalski, T. B., 1962: "Some metallurgical aspects in the study of meteorites." *Researches on Meteorites* (Carleton B. Moore, ed.), John Wiley and Sons, New York, pp. 107–122.

Meen, V. B., 1952: "Solving the riddle of Chubb Crater." *Natl. Geog. Mag.,* **101**, 1–32.

Meen, V. B., 1957: "Merewether crater—a possible meteor crater." *Proc. Geol. Assoc. Can.,* **9**, 49–67.

Melikoff, P., and W. Krschischanowsky, 1899: "Chemische Analyse des Meteoriten von Migheja." *Zeits. Anorg. Chem.,* **19**, 11–17.

Merriam, R., and J. G. Holwerda, 1957: "Al Umchaimin, a crater of possible meteoritic origin in western Iraq." *Geog. J.,* **123**, 231–233.

Merrill, G. P., 1912: "A recent meteorite fall near Holbrook, Navajo County, Arizona." *Smithsonian Misc. Collections,* **60**, no. 9.

Merrill, G. P., 1915: "On the monticellite-like mineral in meteorites, and on oldhamite as a meteoric constituent." *Proc. Natl. Acad. Sci.,* **1**, 302–308.

Merrill, G. P., 1924: "Quartz in meteoric stones." *Am. Mineralogist,* **9**, 112–113.

Merrill, G. P., 1930: "Composition and structure of meteorites." *U.S. Natl. Museum Bull.,* **149**, 62 pp.

Merz, E., 1962: "The determination of hafnium and zirconium in meteorites by neutron activation analysis." *Geochim. et Cosmochim. Acta,* **26**, 347–349.

Meunier, S., 1909: *Guide dans la collection des météorites avec le catalogue des chutes représentees au muséum.* Museum National d'Histoire Naturelle, Paris, 55 pp.

Michel, H., 1912: "Die Feldspate der Meteoriten." *Tschermak's mineral. u. petrog. Mitt.,* **31**, 563–658.

Miller, S. L., 1957: "The formation of organic compounds on the primitive Earth." *Ann. N. Y. Acad. Sci.,* **69**, 260–275.

Moissan, H., 1904: "Nouvelles recherches sur la météorite de Cañon Diablo." *Compt. rend.,* **139**, 773–780.

Monod, T., and A. Pourquié, 1951: "Le cratère d'Aouelloul (Adrar, Sahara occidental)." *Bull. Inst. Franc. Afrique Noire,* **13**, 293–311.

Moore, C. B., 1962: "The petrochemistry of the achondrites." *Researches* on *Meteorites*, John Wiley and Sons, New York, pp. 164–178.

Moore, C. B., and H. Brown, 1962: "The distribution of manganese and titanium in stony meteorites." *Geochim. et Cosmochim. Acta*, **26**, 495–502.

Morrison, P., 1962: "Carbonaceous 'snowflakes' and the origin of life." *Science*, **135**, 663.

Moss, A. A., M. H. Hey, and D. I. Bothwell, 1961: "Methods for the chemical analysis of meteorites: I. Siderites." *Mineral. Mag.*, **32**, 802–816.

Mueller, G., 1953: "The properties and theory of genesis of the carbonaceous complex within the Cold Bokkeveld meteorite." *Geochim. et Cosmochim. Acta*, **4**, 1–10.

Murthy, V. R., 1961: "The isotopic composition of silver in iron meteorites." *J. Geophys. Research*, **66**, 2548.

Nagy, B., W. G. Meinschein, and D. J. Hennessy, 1961: "Mass spectroscopic analysis of the Orgueil meteorite: evidence for biogenic hydrocarbons." *Ann. N. Y. Acad. Sci.*, **93**, 25–35.

Nash, L. K., and G. P. Baxter, 1947: "The determination of the gases in meteoritic and terrestrial irons and steels." *J. Am. Chem. Soc.*, **69**, 2534–2544.

Nichiporuk, W., and A. A. Chodos, 1959: "The concentration of vanadium, chromium, iron, cobalt, nickel, zinc and arsenic in the meteoritic iron sulphide nodules." *J. Geophys. Research*, **64**, 2451–2463.

Nininger, H. H., 1943: "The Eaton, Colorado, meteorite: introducing a new type." *Pop. Astron.*, **51**, 273–280.

Nininger, H. H., 1952: *Out of the sky.* University of Denver Press, 336 pp. (Reprinted 1959 by Dover Publications, New York).

Nininger, H. H., and G. L. Huss, 1960: "The unique meteorite crater at Dal-garanga, Western Australia." *Mineral. Mag.*, **32**, 619–639.

Nishimura, M., and E. B. Sandell, 1962: "Zinc in meteorites." *Univ. Minnesota, Final Report NSF-G9910*, 51 pp.

Noddack, I., 1935: "Die Haufigkeiten der seltenen Erden in Meteoriten." *Z. anorg. Chem.*, **225**, 337–364.

Noddack, I., and W. Noddack, 1930: "Die Haufigkeit der chemischen Elemente." *Naturwiss.*, **18**, 757–764.

Noddack, I., and W. Noddack, 1934: "Die geochemischen Verteilungs-Koeffizientin der Elemente." *Svensk Kem. Tidskr.*, **46**, 173–201.

Nordenskiöld, A. E., 1878: "Trenne markeliga eldmeteorer, sedda i Sverige under åren 1876 och 1877." *Geol. Fören. i Stockholm Förh.*, **4**, 45–61.

O'Keefe, J. A., 1959: "Origin of tektites." *Science*, **130**, 97–98.

Olbers, W., 1803: "Uber die vom Himmel gefellenen Steine." *Ann. Physik.*, **14**, 38–45.

Onishi, H., 1956: "Notes on the geochemistry of germanium." *Bull. Chem. Soc. Japan*, **29**, 686–694.

Onishi, H., and E. B. Sandell, 1955a: "Geochemistry of arsenic." *Geochim. et Cosmochim. Acta*, **7**, 1–33.

Onishi, H., and E. B. Sandell, 1955b: "Notes on the geochemistry of antimony." *Geochim. et Cosmochim. Acta*, **8**, 213–221.

Onishi, H., and E. B. Sandell, 1956: "Gallium in chondrites." *Geochim. et Cosmochim. Acta*, **9**, 78–82.

Onishi, H., and E. B. Sandell, 1957: "Meteoritic and terrestrial abundance of tin." *Geochim. et Cosmochim. Acta*, **12**, 262–270.

Owen, E. A., and Y. H. Liu, 1949: "Further X-ray study of the equilibrium diagram of the iron and nickel system." *J. Iron Steel Inst.*, **163**, 132–137.

Paneth, F. A., 1928: "Uber den Helium-Gehalt und das Alter von Meteoriten." *Z. Elektrochem.*, **34**, 645–652.

Paneth, F. A., 1951: "A 17th century report on copper meteorites." *Geochim. et Cosmochim. Acta*, **1**, 117–118.

Paneth, F. A., 1956: "The frequency of meteorite falls throughout the ages." *Vistas in Astronomy, Volume 2, 1680–1686*, Pergamon Press, London and New York.

Paneth, F. A., P. Reasbeck, and K. I. Mayne, 1952: "Helium-3 content and age of meteorites." *Geochim. et Cosmochim. Acta*, **2**, 300–303.

Patterson, C., 1956: "Age of meteorites and the Earth." *Geochim. et Cosmochim. Acta*, **10**, 230–237.

Perry, S. H., 1944: "The metallography of meteoric iron." *Bull. U.S. Natl. Museum*, **184**, 206 pp.

Petterson, H., 1960: "The accretion of cosmic matter to the Earth." *Endeavour*, **19**, 142–146.

Pettersson, H., and K. Fredriksson, 1958: "Magnetic spherules in deep-sea deposits." *Pacific Sci.*, **12**, 71–81.

Pinson, W. H., L. H. Ahrens, and M. L. Franck, 1953: "The abundances of Li, Sc, Sr, Ba, and Zr in chondrites and some ultramafic rocks." *Geochim. et Cosmochim. Acta*, **4**, 251–260.

Pinson, W. H., L. F. Herzog, H. W. Fairbairn, and R. F. Cormier, 1958: "Rb/Sr age study of tektites." *Geochim. et Cosmochim. Acta*, **14**, 331–339.

Pisani, F., 1864: "Etude chimique et analyse de l'aerolithe d'Orgueil." *Compt. rend.*, **59**, 132–135.

Preuss, E., 1935: "Spektralanalytische Untersuchung der Tektite." *Chem. Erde*, **9**, 365–418.

Preuss, E., 1951: "Hochtemperatur-Plagioklase im Meteorit von Olden-burg." *Heidelberger Beitr. Mineral. u. Petrog.*, **2**, 538–546.

Prior, G. T., 1912: "The meteoric stones of El Nakhla El Baharia (Egypt)." *Mineral. Mag.*, **16**, 274–281.

Prior, G. T., 1913: "The meteoric stones of Baroti, Punjab, India, and Wittekrantz, South Africa." *Mineral Mag.*, **17**, 22–32.

Prior, G. T., 1916: "The meteoric stones of Launton, Warbreccan, Cronstad, Daniel's Kuil, Khairpur, and Soko-Banja." *Mineral. Mag.*, **18**, 1–25.

Prior, G. T., 1918: "On the mesosiderite-grahamite group of meteorites: with analyses of Vaca Muerta, Hainholz, Simondium, and Powder Mill Creek." *Mineral. Mag.*, **18**, 151–172.

Prior, G. T., 1920: "The classification of meteorites." *Mineral. Mag.*, **19**, 51–63.

Prior, G. T., 1953: *Catalogue of Meteorites*. British Museum, London, 432 pp. (second edition, revised by M. H. Hey).

Ramdohr, P., 1962: "The opaque minerals in stony meteorites." *Proc. U.S. Natl. Museum*, in press.

Rankama, K., 1948: "On the geochemistry of niobium." *Ann. Acad. Sci. Fennicae*, ser. AIII, no. 13, 57 pp.

Reed, G. W., K. Kigoshi, and A. Turkevich, 1960: "Determinations of concentrations of heavy elements in meteorites by activation analysis." *Geochim. et Cosmochim. Acta*, **20**, 122–140.

Reed, G. W., and A. Turkevich, 1957: "Uranium, helium and the age of meteorites." *Nature*, **180**, 594–596.

Reynolds, J. H., 1960a: "Determination of the age of the elements." *Phys. Rev. Letters*, **4**, 8–10.

Reynolds, J. H., 1960b: "Rare gases in tektites." *Geochim. et Cosmochim. Acta*, **20**, 101–114.

Reynolds, J. H., C. M. Merrihue, and R. O. Pepin, 1962: "Extinct radioactivity and primordial rare gases in iron meteorites." *Phys. Rev. Letters*, **6**, in press.

Richter, N., 1954: "Zwei neue Meteoritenkrater?" *Die Sterne*, **30**, 66.

Rinehart, J. S., and C. T. Elvey, 1951: "A possible meteorite crater near Duckwater, Nye County, Nevada." *Pop. Astron.*, **59**, 209–211.

Ringwood, A. E., 1959: "On the chemical evolution and densities of the planets." *Geochim. et Cosmochim. Acta*, **15**, 257–283.

Ringwood, A. E., 1960a: "The Novo Urei meteorite." *Geochim. et Cosmochim. Acta*, **20**, 1–4.

Ringwood, A. E., 1960b: "Cohenite as a pressure indicator in iron meteorites." *Geochim. et Cosmochim. Acta*, **20**, 155–158.

Ringwood, A. E., 1961a: "Chemical and genetic relationships among meteorites." *Geochim. et Cosmochim. Acta*, **24**, 159–197.

Ringwood, A. E., 1961b: "Silicon in the metal phase of enstatite chondrites and some geochemical implications." *Geochim. et Cosmochim. Acta*, **25**, 1–13.

Rohleder, H. P. T., 1933: "The Steinheim basin and the Pretoria salt pan. Volcanic or meteoric origin." *Geol. Mag.*, **70**, 489–498.

Rose, G., 1861: "Über das Vorkommen von krystallisierten Quarz in dem Meteoreisen von Xiquipilco in Mexico." *Monatsber. Akad. Wiss. Berlin*, 406–409.

Rose, G., 1863: "Beschreibung und Eintheilung der Meteoriten auf Grund der Sammlung im mineralogischen Museum zu Berlin." *Physik. Abhandl. Akad. Wiss. Berlin*, 23–161.

Roy, S. K., 1957: "The problems of the origin and structure of chondrules in stony meteorites." *Fieldiana, Geol.*, **10**, 383–396.

Roy, S. K., and R. K. Wyant, 1955: "The Paragould meteorite." *Fieldiana, Geol.*, **10**, 283–364.

Rushbrooke, P. R., and W. D. Ehmann, 1962: "Iridium in stone meteorites by neutron activation analysis." *Geochim. et Cosmochim. Acta*, in press.

Salpeter, E., 1952: "Spektroskopische Chlorbestimmung in Steinmeteoriten." *Ricerche spettroscop., Lab. astrofis. spècola vaticana*, **2**, no. 1.

Sandberger, F., 1889: "Ein neuer Meteorit aus Chile." *Neues Jahrb. Mineral. Geol.*, **2**, 173–180.

Sangster, R. L., 1957: "Another meteorite crater in Australia?" *Sky and Telescope*, **16**, 429.

Sarma, D. V. N., and T. Mayeda, 1961: "Meteorite analysis: the search for diamond." *Geochim. et Cosmochim. Acta*, **22**, 169–175.

Schaeffer, O. A., and J. Zähringer, 1960: "Helium, neon, and argon isotopes in some iron meteorites." *Geochim. et Cosmochim. Acta*, **19**, 94–99.

Schindewolf, U., 1960: "Selenium and tellurium content of stony meteorites by neutron activation." *Geochim. et Cosmochim. Acta*, **19**, 134–138.

Schindewolf, U., and M. Wahlgren, 1960: "The rhodium, silver and indium content of some chondritic meteorites." *Geochim. et Cosmochim. Acta*, **18**, 36–41.

Schmitt, R. A., A. W. Mosen, C. S. Suffredini, J. E. Lasch, R. A. Sharp, and D. A. Olehy, 1960: "Abundances of the rare-earth elements, lanthanum to lutetium, in chondritic meteorites." *Nature*, **186**, 863–866.

Schmitt, R. A., and R. H. Smith, 1961: "A program of research for the determination of rare-earth abundances in meteorites." Quarterly progress report for the period ending December 15, 1961, Contract NASA-75, National Aeronautics and Space Administration, 40 pp.

Schnetzler, C. C., and W. H. Pinson, 1962: "Variations of strontium isotopes in tektites." *Geochim. et Cosmochim. Acta,* in press.

Schumacher, E., 1956: "Age of meteorites by the Rb[87]-Sr[87] method." *Publ. Natl. Research Council,* **400,** 90–96.

Selivanov, L. S., 1940: "Chemical analysis of the Saratov meteorite." *Compt. rend. acad. sci. U.R.S.S.,* **26,** 388–392.

Shand, S. J., 1947: *Eruptive rocks* (third edition), John Wiley and Sons, New York, 488 pp.

Shannon, E. V., and E. S. Larsen, 1925: "Merrillite and chlorapatite from stony meteorites." *Am. J. Sci.,* **9,** 250–260.

Shoemaker, E. M., and E. C. T. Chao, 1961: "New evidence for the impact origin of the Ries Basin, Bavaria, Germany." *J. Geophys. Research,* **66,** 3371–3378.

Signer, P., and A. O. Nier, 1960: "The distribution of cosmic-ray-produced rare gases in iron meteorites." *J. Geophys. Research,* **65,** 2947–2964.

Smales, A. A., D. Mapper, J. W. Morgan, R. K. Webster, and A. J. Wood, 1958: "Some geochemical determinations using radioactive and stable isotopes." *Proc. Second U.N. Intern. Conf. on the Peaceful Uses of Atomic Energy,* **2,** 242–248.

Smales, A. A., D. Mapper, and A. J. Wood, 1957: "The determination by radioactivation of small quantities of nickel, cobalt, and copper in rocks, marine sediments and meteorites." *Analyst,* **82,** 75–88.

Smith, J. L., 1855: "A description of five new meteoric irons, with some theoretical considerations on the origin of meteorites based on their physical and chemical characters." *Am. J. Sci.,* **19,** 322–343.

Smith, J. L., 1876: "Aragonite on the surface of a meteoric iron, and a new mineral (daubreelite) in the concretions of the interior of the same." *Am. J. Sci.,* **12,** 107–110.

Smith, W. C., and M. H. Hey, 1952: "The silica-glass from the crater of Aouelloul (Adrar, western Sahara)." *Bull. Inst. Franc. Afrique Noire,* **14,** 762–776.

Sorby, H. C., 1864: "On the microscopical structure of meteorites." *Phil. Mag.,* **28,** 157–159.

Sorby, H. C., 1877: "On the structure and origin of meteorites." *Nature,* **15,** 495–498.

Spencer, L. J., 1932: "Hoba (South-West Africa), the largest known meteorite." *Mineral. Mag.,* **23,** 1–18.

Spencer, L. J., 1933a: "Meteorite craters as topographical features on the Earth's surface." *Geog. J.,* **81,** 227–248.

Spencer, L. J., 1933b: "Meteoritic iron and silica-glass from the meteoritic craters of Henbury (Central Australia) and Wabar (Arabia)." *Mineral. Mag.,* **23,** 387–404.

Stanyukovich, K. P., 1950: "Elements of the physical theory of meteors and crater-forming meteorites." *Meteoritika,* **7,** 39–62.

Starik, I. E., E. V. Sobotovich, G. P. Lovtsyus, M. M. Shats, and A. V. Lovtsyus, 1960: "Lead and its isotopic composition in iron meteorites." *Sov. Phys. (Doklady),* **5,** 926–928.

Starik, I. E., E. V. Sobotovich, and M. M. Shats, 1959: "The age of tektites." *Izvest. Akad. Sci. U.S.S.R.,* Geol. Ser., 80–81.

Stauffer, H., 1961: "Primordial argon and neon in carbonaceous chondrites and ureilites." *Geochim. et Cosmochim. Acta,* **24,** 70–82.

Stauffer, H., and M. Honda, 1961: "Cosmic-ray-produced V[50] and K[40] in the iron meteorite Aroos." *J. Geophys. Research,* **66,** 3584–3586.

Stulov, N. N., 1960: "Investigation of the X-ray powder pattern of the component substances of some meteorites." *Meteoritika*, **19**, 63–85.

Suess, F. E., 1900: "Die Herkunft der Moldavite und verwandter Gläser." *Jahrb. k.k. geol. Reichsanstalt Wien*, **50**, 193–382.

Suess, F. E., 1937: "Der Meteor-Krater von Köfels bei Umhausen im Ötztale, Tirol." *Neues Jahrb. Mineral., Beil. Band, Abt. A*, **72**, 98–155.

Suess, H. E., 1951: "Gas content and age of tektites." *Geochim. et Cosmochim. Acta*, **2**, 76–79.

Suess, H. E., and H. C. Urey, 1956: "Abundances of the elements." *Rev. Mod. Phys.*, **28**, 53–74.

Suess, H. E., and H. Wänke, 1962: "Radiocarbon content and terrestrial age of twelve stony meteorites and one iron meteorite." *Geochim. et Cosmochim. Acta*, **26**, 475–480.

Sztrokay, K. I., 1960: "Über einige Meteoritenmineralien des kohlenwasserstoffhaltingen Chondrites von Kaba, Ungarn." *Neues Jahrb. Mineral., Abhandl.*, **94**, 1284–1294.

Taylor, S. R., 1960: "Abundance and distribution of alkali elements in australites." *Geochim. et Cosmochim. Acta*, **20**, 85–100.

Taylor, S. R., and M. Sachs, 1960: "Trace elements in australites." *Nature*, **188**, 387–388.

Thiel, E., and R. A. Schmidt, 1961: "Spherules from the Antarctic Ice Cap." *J. Geophys. Research*, **66**, 307–310.

Tiller, D., 1961: "Natural variations in isotopic abundances of silicon." *J. Geophys. Research*, **66**, 3003–3013.

Tilton, G. R., 1958: "Isotopic composition of lead from tektites." *Geochim. et Cosmochim. Acta*, **14**, 323–330.

Tschermak, G., 1870: "Der Meteorit von Lodran." *Sitzber. Akad. Wiss.*

Wien, Math.-naturw. Kl., Abt. II, **61**, 465–475.

Tschermak, G., 1872a: "Die Meteoriten des k.k. mineralogischen Museum am 1 October 1872." *Mineralog. Mitt.*, 165–172.

Tschermak, G., 1872b: "Die Meteoriten von Shergotty und Gopalpur." *Sitzber. Akad. Wiss. Wien, Math.-naturw. Kl., Abt. I*, **65**, 122–146.

Tschermak, G., 1883: "Beitrag zur Classification der Meteoriten." *Sitzber. Akad. Wiss. Wien, Math.-naturw. Kl., Abt. I*, **88**, 347–371.

Tschermak, G., 1885: *Die mikroskopische Beschaffenheit der Meteoriten erläutert durch photographische Abbildungen.* Schweizerbart'sche Verlagshandlung, Stuttgart, 24 pp.

Turner, F. J., H. Heard, and D. T. Griggs, 1960: "Experimental deformation of enstatite and accompanying inversion to clinoenstatite." *Proc. Intern. Geol. Congr., XXI Session*, **18**, 399–408.

Uhlig, H. H., 1954: "Contribution of metallurgy to the study of meteorites. Part I—Structure of metallic meteorites, their composition and the effect of pressure." *Geochim. et Cosmochim. Acta*, **6**, 282–301.

Uhlig, H. H., 1955: "Contribution of metallurgy to the origin of meteorites. Part II—The significance of Neumann bands in meteorites." *Geochim. et Cosmochim. Acta*, **7**, 34–42.

Umemoto, S., 1962: "Isotopic composition of barium and cerium in stone meteorites." *J. Geophys. Research*, **67**, 375–379.

Urey, H. C., 1952: "The abundances of the elements." *Phys. Rev.*, **88**, 248–252.

Urey, H. C., 1956: "Diamonds, meteorites, and the origin of the solar system." *Astrophys. J.*, **124**, 623–637.

Urey, H. C., 1957a: "Boundary conditions for theories of the origin of the solar system—The evidence given by meteorites." *Phys. Chem. Earth,* **2,** 60–68.

Urey, H. C., 1957*b*: "Origin of tektites." *Nature,* **179,** 556–557.

Urey, H. C., 1958*a*: "The early history of the solar system as indicated by the meteorites." *Proc. Chem. Soc.* (*London*), 57–78.

Urey, H. C., 1958*b*: "Origin of tektites." *Nature,* **182,** 1078.

Urey, H. C., 1959: "Primary and secondary objects." *J. Geophys. Research,* **64,** 1721–1737.

Urey, H. C., 1961: "Criticism of Dr. B. Mason's paper on 'The origin of meteorites.'" *J. Geophys. Research,* **66,** 1988–1991.

Urey, H. C., and H. Craig, 1953: "The composition of the stone meteorites and the origin of the meteorites." *Geochim. et Cosmochim. Acta,* **4,** 36–82.

Urey, H. C.; F. Fitch, H. P. Schwarcz, and E. Anders; M. H. Briggs and G. B. Kitto; J. D. Bernal; B. Nagy, G. Claus, and D. J. Hennessy; 1962: "Life-forms in meteorites: a symposium." *Nature,* **193,** 1119–1133.

Urey, H. C., and T. Mayeda, 1959: "The metallic particles of some chondrites." *Geochim. et Cosmochim. Acta,* **17,** 113–124.

Urey, H. C., A. Mele, and T. Mayeda, 1957: "Diamonds in stone meteorites." *Geochim. et Cosmochim. Acta,* **13,** 1–4.

Varsavsky, C. M., 1958: "Dynamical limits on a lunar origin for tektites." *Geochim. et Cosmochim. Acta,* **14,** 291–303.

Vilcsek, E., 1959: "Der Meteorit von Breitscheid. II. Chemische Analyse." *Geochim. et Cosmochim. Acta,* **17,** 320–322.

Vincent, E. A., and J. H. Crocket, 1960: "Studies in the geochemistry of gold —II. The gold content of some basic and ultrabasic rocks and stone meteorites." *Geochim. et Cosmochim. Acta,* **18,** 143–148.

Vinogradov, A. P., E. I. Dontsova, and M. S. Chupakhin, 1960: "Isotopic ratios of oxygen in meteorites and igneous rocks." *Geochim. et Cosmochim. Acta,* **18,** 278–293.

Vinogradov, A. P., I. K. Zadorozhnii, and K. G. Knorre, 1960: "Argon in meteorites." *Meteoritika,* **18,** 92–99.

Vogel, R., and T. Herman, 1950: "Über Daubreelith." *Neues Jahrb. Mineral., Monatsh.,* 175–190.

Wahl, W., 1907: "Die Enstatitaugite." *Tschermak's mineral. u. petrog. Mitt.,* **26,** 1–131.

Wahl, W., 1910: "Beiträge zur Chemie der Meteoriten." *Z. anorg. u. allgem. Chem.,* **69,** 52–96.

Wahl, W., 1951: "Interpretation of meteorite analyses." *Mineral. Mag.,* **29,** 416–426.

Wahl, W., 1952: "The brecciated stony meteorites and meteorites containing foreign fragments." *Geochim. et Cosmochim. Acta,* **2,** 91–117.

Wänke, H., 1961: "Über den Kaliumgehalt der Chondrite, Achondrite, und Siderite." *Z. Naturforsch.,* **16a,** 127–130.

Wardani, S. A., 1957: "On the geochemistry of germanium." *Geochim. et Cosmochim. Acta,* **13,** 5–19.

Wasserburg, G. J., W. A. Fowler, and F. Hoyle, 1960: "Duration of nucleosynthesis." *Phys. Rev. Letters,* **4,** 112–114.

Wasserburg, G. J., and R. J. Hayden, 1955: "Age of meteorites by the A^{40}-K^{40} method." *Phys. Rev.,* **97,** 86–87.

Webster, R. K., J. W. Morgan, and A. A. Smales, 1957: "Some recent Harwell analytical work on geochronology." *Trans. Am. Geophys. Union,* **38,** 543–546.

Webster, R. K., J. W. Morgan, and

A. A. Smales, 1958: "Caesium in chondrites." *Geochim. et Cosmochim. Acta*, **15**, 150–152.

Weinschenk, E., 1889: "Uber einige Bestandtheile des Meteoreisens von Magura, Arva, Ungarn." *Ann. k.k. naturhist. Hofmus. Wien*, **4**, 94–101.

Wherry, E. T., 1917: "Merrillite, meteoritic calcium phosphate." *Am. Mineralogist*, **2**, 119.

Whipple, F. L., 1950: "The theory of micrometeorites." *Proc. Natl. Acad. Sci.*, **36**, 687–695.

Whipple, F. L., and E. L. Fireman, 1959: "Calculation of erosion in space from the cosmic-ray exposure ages of meteorites." *Nature*, **183**, 1315.

Wiik, H. B., 1956: "The chemical composition of some stony meteorites." *Geochim. et Cosmochim. Acta*, **9**, 279–289.

Winchester, J. W., and A. H. W. Aten, 1957: "The content of tin in iron meteorites." *Geochim. et Cosmochim. Acta*, **12**, 57–60.

Wöhler, F., 1860: "Neuere Untersuchungen über die Bestandtheile des Meteorsteines vom Capland." *Sitzber. Akad. Wiss. Wien, Math-naturw. Kl.*, **41**, 565–567.

Wülfing, E. A., 1897: *Die Meteoriten in Sammlungen und ihre Literatur*. Laupp'schen Buchhandlung, Tübingen, 461 pp.

Yavnel, A. A., 1950: "Spectrographic analysis of the Sikhote-Alin meteorite." *Meteoritika*, **8**, 134–148.

Yavnel, A. A., 1958: "Classification of meteorites according to their chemical composition." *Meteoritika*, **15**, 115–135; published in English translation in *Intern. Geol. Rev.*, **2**, 380–396.

Yavnel, A. A., and M. I. Dyakonova, 1958: "The chemical composition of meteorites." *Meteoritika*, **15**, 136–151; published in English in *Intern. Geol. Rev.*, **2**, 298–310.

Yoder, H. S., and T. G. Sahama, 1957: "Olivine X-ray determinative curve." *Am. Mineralogist*, **42**, 475–491.

Zavaritsky, A. N., 1950: "On some structural peculiarities of meteorites." *Meteoritika*, **8**, 100–115.

Index

Names of meteorites are in **boldface** type.